NEW DIRECTIONS IN HUMAN INFORMATION BEHAVIOR

Information Science and Knowledge Management

Volume 8

Editor-in-Chief:

J. Mackenzie Owen, *University of Amsterdam, Amsterdam*

Editorial Board:

M. Bates, *University of California, Los Angeles*
P. Bruza, *The University of Queensland, Brisbane*
R. Capurro, *Hochschule der Medien, Stuttgart University of Applied Sciences, Stuttgart*
E. Davenport, *Napier University, Edinburgh*
R. Day, *Wayne State University, Detroit*
M. Hedstorm, *University of Michigan, Ann Arbor*
A.M. Paci, *Istituto di Studi Sulla Ricerca e Documentazione Scientifica, Roma*
C. Tenopir, *University of Tennessee, Knoxville*
M. Thelwall, *University of Wolverhampton, Wolverhampton*

The titles published in this series are listed at the end of this volume.

NEW DIRECTIONS IN HUMAN INFORMATION BEHAVIOR

Edited by

AMANDA SPINK
University of Pittsburgh, Pittsburgh, U.S.A.

and

CHARLES COLE
McGill University, Montreal, Canada

 Springer

A C.I.P. Catalogue record for this book is available from the Library of Congress.

ISBN-13 978-90-481-6923-8
ISBN-10 1-4020-3670-1 (e-book)
ISBN-13 978-1-4020-3670-5 (e-book)

Published by Springer,
P.O. Box 17, 3300 AA Dordrecht, The Netherlands.

www.springer.com

Printed on acid-free paper

Table of Contents

SECTION 1
Introduction   1

Chapter 1
Introduction: New Directions in Human Information Behavior   3
Amanda Spink and Charles Cole

SECTION 2
Evolutionary and Social HIB Frameworks   11

Chapter 2
Emerging Evolutionary Approach to Human Information
Behavior   13
Amanda Spink and James Currier

Chapter 3
Information Behavior in Pre-literate Societies   33
Andrew D. Madden, Jared Bryson, and Joe Palimi

Chapter 4
Toward a Social Framework for Information Seeking   55
Eszter Hargittai and Amanda Hinnant

SECTION 3
Spatial and Collaborative HIB Frameworks   71

Chapter 5
Mapping Textually Mediated Information Practice in Clinical
Midwifery Care   73
Pamela J. McKenzie

Chapter 6
Information Grounds: Theoretical Basis and Empirical Findings
on Information Flow in Social Settings   93
Karen E. Fisher and Charles M. Naumer

Chapter 7
Information Sharing   113
Sanna Talja and Preben Hansen

SECTION 4
Multitasking, Non-linear, Organizing, and Digital Frameworks   **135**

Chapter 8
Multitasking and Co-ordinating Framework for Human Information
Behavior   **137**
Amanda Spink, Minsoo Park, and Charles Cole

Chapter 9
A Non-linear Perspective on Information Seeking   **155**
Allen Foster

Chapter 10
A Cognitive Framework for Human Information Behavior: The Place
of Metaphor in Human Information Organizing Behavior   **171**
Charles Cole and John E. Leide

Chapter 11
The Digital Information Consumer   **203**
David Nicholas, Paul Huntington, Peter Williams, and Tom Dobrowolski

SECTION 5
Integrating Framework and Further Research   **229**

Chapter 12
Integrations and Further Research   **231**
Amanda Spink and Charles Cole

Biographies of Authors   **239**

Index   **247**

SECTION 1

Introduction

Chapter 1

Introduction: New Directions in Human Information Behavior

Amanda Spink
School of Information Sciences
University of Pittsburgh

Charles Cole
Graduate School of Library and Information Studies
McGill University

1. INTRODUCTION

Humans have sought, organized, and used information for millennia as they evolved and learned patterns of human information behaviors (HIBs) to help resolve their human problems and continue to survive. The field of library and information science (LIS) has historically been a leading discipline in conducting research that seeks to understand human information-related behaviors (Spink & Cole, 2004, in press). The dominant framework within the LIS discipline for understanding HIB has been the information-seeking/problem-solving approach (Spink & Cole, 2001, in press). However, other interdisciplinary approaches have emerged, including a sense-making approach (Dervin, 1992), an everyday life information-seeking approach (Savolainen, 1995), and an information-foraging approach (Pirolli & Card, 1999).

The goal of our book is to provide an overview of new HIB research directions. This book does not provide a history of the research field of HIB. Wilson (2000) and Case (2002) are sources for historical background to the HIB research field. In this book, we confront new ways of looking at information in life, in society, and in the human condition. Information was once considered to be part of a document, and it was the role of the author of the document to transmit and the information seeker to receive that information. Information was seen as brick-like (Dervin, 1983). An individual was engaged in an information-seeking activity only when they knew what he or she was seeking. The problem was to locate the item in some far-off library or archive and deliver it to the information seeker. Once the information had been found, the information seeker then took the information brick and placed it in whatever document he or she was writing—a report, an essay, or maybe a doctor's diagnostic memo.

So, narrowly defined, the human information condition is often marked by frustration and a lack of cognitive understanding when people engage in information behavior. To see undergraduate students suffer when seeking information for an essay, or poor people in need of information about living issues like job opportunities and training, security

A. Spink and C. Cole (eds), New Directions in Human Information Behavior, 3–10.
© *2006 Springer.*

issues at their front door, or the problems a patient has but cannot articulate to a doctor—this is the human information condition we address in this book. New more holistic directions in HIB are emerging that conceptualize the human information condition in a more holistic context and aim to help people to understand more about their own information behaviors.

We also seek to draw the research field of HIB more closely into the wider theoretical realm of the social sciences, so that we can utilize wider theories and models from sociology, psychology, communications, and anthropology in the study of the human information condition. The chapters in this book stretch our understanding of HIB to incorporate questions of evolution, social and spatial factors, multitasking and non-linear dimensions, and new organizational and digital directions. We then provide an initial integration of these new directions and identify further research opportunities. Our goal in developing this book has been facilitate intellectual challenges to assumptions and champion new ideas.

2. BOOK OUTLINE

This book has five sections.

Section 1: Chapter 1: Introduction

Chapter 1 provides an introduction to the book, setting out intentions, and summaries of each chapter. We have divided up the chapters into sections, each with a theme.

Section 2: Evolutionary and Social HIB Frameworks

Section 2 contains three chapters under the section title *Evolutionary and Social Frameworks*. These provide broad frameworks for studying, approaching, and analyzing HIB.

Chapter 2: Emerging Evolutionary Approach to Human Information Behavior—Amanda Spink and James Currier (University of Pittsburgh)

In Chapter 2, Spink and Currier begin a longitudinal investigation of the evolution of HIB over the course of human existence. Spink and Currier trace the evolution of HIB as evidenced in HIB studies from pre-historic times (cave paintings) to the near present. The authors write that the emerging evolutionary HIB perspective: "Explores and identifies information behaviors throughout the course of human existence by looking at specific eras while endeavoring to better understand the information behaviors of persons of those eras within both their own specific time contexts and the larger context of human existence".

This chapter provides an initial chronology of studies that examine HIB during different time periods from pre-historic times to the near present. The five ages examined are the Upper Paleolithic Era (10,000–70,000 years ago), Classical Greece

(8th Century–2nd Century B.C.), the Renaissance (1454–1699 A.D.), the Industrial Age (1700–1945 A.D.), and the Post-industrial Information Age (1946–21st Century).

Chapter 3: Information Behavior in Pre-literate Societies—Andrew D. Madden and Jared Bryson (University of Sheffield) and Joe Palimi (University of Papua New Guinea)

Chapter 3 highlights Madden, Bryson, and Palimi's studies that focus on a pre-industrial tribe in Papua New Guinea and provide an anthropological study of information uses in the tribe. The chapter starts from the personal perspective of Joe Palimi, who is a member of the Kope Tribe of the Western Highlands Province in the Central Highlands of Papua New Guinea. In their chapter, the authors:

1. explore some of the ways in which the demands of a pre-literate society deter-mined, and determine to a certain extent to this day, the information needs of its members, as well as shaping the information roles within that society; and
2. show how the identified information roles relate to life in a modern, literate society.

There are six main roles in Kope society: induction, dissemination, presentation, organization, interpretation, and preservation. The six roles are defined by the authors in terms of what information is used for in the society and how information is used. The authors also discuss how and why text has dominated the focus of information science and the consequences of this focus.

Chapter 4: Toward a Social Framework for Information Seeking—Eszter Hargittai and Amanda Hinnant (Northwestern University)

Chapter 3 by Hargittai and Hinnant evaluates current information needs and uses research from a sociological perspective. Hargittai and Hinnant start from the premise that the information riches of the information age and the new information technologies being developed to access this information may hit a digital divide—a barrier preventing certain populations in society from gaining access to them. In other words, mere *availability* of information neither equal *accessibility*, nor does it provide a realistic chance that people may come across the types of information of most interest or use to them. The barrier may be supported by the type of research done to study information seeking of users within the problem-solving perspective.

In this chapter, Hargittai and Hinnant draw on recent developments and challenges faced by the digital divide literature to gain a greater understanding of some of the ways in which work on HIB behavior should evolve. The authors integrate work from information science, sociology, and other disciplines to argue for a more holistic approach to the study of HIB. Specifically, the authors look at people's social attributes (demographic characteristics, their socio-economic status) which may influence what methods they employ for information seeking, searching and information use, how successful they may be in these endeavors, and the level of autonomy people enjoy in accessing different types of resources. The authors then consider challenges in the realm of both data collection and measurement, as well as difficulties in operationalizing variables of importance in the study of social factors relevant to information seeking.

Section 3: Spatial and Collaborative HIB Frameworks

Section 3 groups three chapters discussing spatial and collaborative HIB frameworks. Space and collaboration are treated both virtually and physically, from the space and collaboration on the Internet to sharing information in a doctor's waiting room.

Chapter 5: Mapping Textually Mediated Information Practice in Clinical Midwifery Care—Pamela McKenzie (University of Western Ontario)

Chapter 5 by Pamela McKenzie maps textually mediated information in clinical midwifery care. The author explores the concept of information practice through taped sessions between midwives and pregnant women, and the relations between texts and people in everyday local settings. In this case, the local setting is a midwifery clinic. McKenzie focuses on the interaction and the intersection of texts that structure the work and information flow carried out by the midwives with their patients.

The primary purpose of this chapter is to map the local and extra-local participants in clinical midwifery visits through an analysis of the texts used: to consider information sources not just as resources for participants, but as constituents of a larger social order. Texts can reveal a map of the social organization, information practice, how relations between people are organized, of both the creators of the texts and the users of the texts (the midwives). In this way, the social relations are both mediated and afforded by the presence, absence, structure, and use of those documents. The author situates information practices within a broader social practices context defined by texts. By providing an understanding of the web of texts and social relations within which individual information seekers in local contexts are located, the study of textual mediation can further reveal the broader contexts of information behavior in local settings.

Chapter 6: Information Grounds: Theoretical Basis and Empirical Findings on Information Flow in Social Settings—Karen E. Fisher and Charles M. Naumer (University of Washington)

In Chapter 6, Fisher and Naumer examine information flow and exchange in social settings. Fisher and Naumer write about information grounds, which is the location or place where information is exchanged. The authors are concerned with the wider view of HIB. They refer to Chatman's small worlds, looking closely at where, why, and how information exchange takes place between people in their small world. Information grounds are smaller still than small worlds, which is largely a sociological concept. Information grounds is the coffee shop, the waiting room, the hairdressers, etc., where diverse people come together to talk. The Internet chat line is also an information ground, and this is a virtual space that may become more and more important. Information is exchanged, frequently important information, but also information about small things that seem to matter the most.

Chapter 7: Information Sharing—Sanna Talja and Preben Hansen (University of Tampere)

In Chapter 7, Talja and Hansen's chapter examines information sharing and collaboration between individuals, and specifically the collaborative information behavior (CIB) in the work place and social settings. Talja and Hansen start from the premise that people naturally act and interact to discover solutions and interpret information in authentic collaborative work and everyday life settings. They examine CIB, which is defined as two or more actors who communicate to identify information for task performance or problem solving. However, they insert CIB into a more general social practice approach that embeds CIB in the work place and other social practices engaged in by humans. The authors also discuss "collaborative information spaces", where CIB is more likely to take place.

Section 4: Multitasking, Non-linear, Organizing, and Digital Frameworks

In Section 4, four chapters are grouped under the section title "Multitasking, Non-linear, Organizing, and Digital Frameworks". The authors of the chapters take the perspective that HIB is not static, not linear, and sometimes organized in memory via metaphor and should be aimed at a digital consumer more interested in information searching in an entertainment environment rather than libraries.

Chapter 8: Multitasking and Co-ordinating Framework for Human Information Behavior—Amanda Spink and Minsoo Park (University of Pittsburgh) and Charles Cole (McGill University)

In Chapter 8, Spink, Park, and Cole examine a new multitasking and co-ordinating framework for HIB. The authors start from the premise that while focusing on accomplishing one task, humans actually multitask, and that multitasking is a framework for conceptualizing HIB. The chapter discusses what is meant by multitasking. During multitasking, humans cognitively and physically co-ordinate multiple tasks through task switching. In this way, multitasking is conceptualized as a binding process that works with HIB to construct an information behavior process. A case study is also provided that explores the interplay between information and non-information tasks. Multitasking information behavior also provides a framework for co-ordinating and integrating the different levels within HIB. In the final part of the chapter, the authors outline an initial framework for HIB within a multitasking and co-ordination framework.

Chapter 9: A Non-linear Perspective on Information Seeking—Allen Foster (University of Wales, Aberystwyth)

In Chapter 9, Foster chapter explores non-linearity in HIB and advocates a non-linear perspective for information-seeking research. In a simplified, linear model of human problem-solving individuals work on one problem at a time, cumulatively building toward a solution to their information problem. This portrait of harmonious progression and development is disturbed when we recognize that HIB occurs as a complex dynamic interaction of core processes, contexts, with multiple user cognitive approaches at play.

As suggested by the developing HIB literature, a simple linear interpretation may not sufficiently explain the complexity of human information seeking. Foster compares non-linearity with the linear model exemplified by Kuhlthau's (1993) Information Search Process (ISP) model. Although the stages of the ISP model are present, the stages are more likely to occur in a highly recursive manner and people frequently combine stages or perform them in a different order from that suggested in Kuhlthau's model. Non-linear theory on the other hand represents complex dynamical systems. In the chapter, Foster explores a new perspective that seeks a holistic understanding of the inter-relationship of multiple individually complex variables that form HIB.

Chapter 10: A Cognitive Framework for Human Information Behavior: The Place of Metaphor in Human Information Organizing Behavior—Charles Cole and John Leide (McGill University)

In Chapter 10, Cole and Leide provide a new cognitive framework for human information organizing behavior (HIOB) as an offshoot of Spink and Currier's (in press) document organization-focused HIOB. The chapter focuses on metaphor instantiation as a methodology for creating user ad hoc categories, an ad hoc form of human information organization, or memory organization. In effect, metaphor instantiation is based on evidence that humans have an innate ability to facilitate the categorization of unfamiliar information stimuli by borrowing a category structure from somewhere else in memory. Cole and Leide report three case studies that explore the HIOB concept of metaphor instantiation as a mechanism that can be operationalized in some way, based on the subject's problem situation. This innate ad hoc categorization mechanism, once operationalized fully in further studies, may one day be used to facilitate human acquisition of data and information related to a new and unfamiliar subject area.

Chapter 11: The Digital Information Consumer—David Nicholas, Paul Huntington, Peter Williams, and Tom Dobrowolski (City University, London)

Chapter 11 discusses the concept of digital information and presents the results of Nicholas, Huntington, Williams, and Dobrowolski's evaluation of information behavior in large-scale digital environments, carried out primarily by employing evidence-based methods (logs) that mapped that behavior. They describe the key characteristics of the information behavior of the "new" digital information consumer. People used to do most of their searching in controlled, supervised, and mediated environments—typically through catalogs, bibliographies, and secondary services, much of which was in libraries. But no longer is it a case of searching static, archival systems in public or work places; people now search mobile systems, real-time systems, and interactive systems in the home or in the office. This is a big change.

Their studies examine log data that provides for real-time and continuous analysis, something that provides a fantastic opportunity to create a digital laboratory for the monitoring of changes in HIB. The authors discovered that information behavior in digital environments on the Web and in front of digital interactive television in touch-screen information kiosks, irrespective of the field or industry, has much in common. Both are largely shaped by the same things—the digital interface and its unique position in today's frenetic world. What the authors see in their log analysis is a form of behavior that has more in common with the media and entertainment worlds than the world of university libraries. In the logs, people search for fun or entertainment, because they are bored, or to obtain stimulation, or they simply just wish to feel in touch or connected.

Section 5: Chapter 12: Integrating Framework and Further Research

Chapter 12 provides an initial integrated HIB framework and offers an HIB perspective on further research. A preliminary model of HIB is offered.

References

Case, D. (2002). *Looking for Information: A Survey of Research on Information Seeking, Needs, and Behavior*. San Diego: Academic Press.

Dervin, B. (1983). An overview of sense-making research: Concepts, methods, and results to date. Paper Presented at the *Annual Meeting of the International Communication Association*, Dallas, TX.

Dervin, B. (1992). From the mind's eye of the "user": The sense-making qualitative–quantitative methodology. In J. D. Glazier & R. R. Powell (Eds.), *Qualitative Research in Information Management*, 61–84. Englewood, CO: Libraries Unlimited.

Kuhlthau, C. C. (1993). *Seeking Meaning: A Process Approach to Library and Information Services*. Norwood, NJ: Ablex.

Pirolli, P. & Card, S. (1999). Information foraging. *Psychological Review*, 106, 643–675.

Savolainen, R. (1995). Everyday life information seeking: approaching information seeking in the context of 'way of life'. *Library and Information Science Research*, 17, 259–294.

Spink, A. & Cole, C. (2001). Everyday life information seeking research. *Library and Information Science Research*, 23(4), 301–304.

Spink, A. & Cole, C. (2004). A human information behavior framework to the philosophy of information. *Library Trends*, 52(3), 373–380.

Spink, A. & Cole, C. (in press). Human information behavior: Integrating diverse approaches and information use. *Journal of the American Society for Information Science and Technology*.

Spink, A. & Currier, J. (in press). Towards an evolutionary perspective on human information behavior: An exploratory study. *Journal of Documentation*.

Wilson, T. D. (2000). Human information behaviour. *Informing Science*, 3(2), 49–56.

SECTION 2

Evolutionary and Social HIB Frameworks

Chapter 2

Emerging Evolutionary Approach to Human Information Behavior

Amanda Spink and James Currier
School of Information Sciences
University of Pittsburgh, USA

1. INTRODUCTION

Humans have been seeking, organizing, and using information for thousands of years. But, over the course of many millennia, how have human information behaviors (HIBs) changed and evolved? Did HIB changes mirror societal development as humans strove to fulfill needs and resolve problems of everyday life and survival? Eminent paleoanthropologist Richard Leakey, in considering the reason for variation and evolution among species, suggests that "... major evolutionary innovation ... has enabled the species to be in some way better, more efficient perhaps, than the preceding one" (Leakey and Lewin, 1992a, b, p. 247).

Additionally, discussing the evolution of systems within species, Leakey (1994) asserts that, "... evolution does not start from scratch; it builds on what already exists. As a result, some systems tend to become more complex through time". (p. 248). Longitudinal investigation of HIB, similarly, may illuminate whether HIBs have evolved and tend to become more complex over the course of human existence. Most HIB studies, models, and concepts, particularly within the field of library and information science (LIS), have focused on a contemporary view of human behavior; namely, post-1945 (Case, 2002; Spink & Currier, in press; Wilson, 2000).

This chapter explores the emerging evolutionary approach to an understanding of HIB. The emerging evolutionary approach represents a significant rethinking, new direction, and expansion for the HIB field. Research from this approach seeks to explore HIB throughout the evolutionary arc of human existence, particularly manifesting as information seeking, organization, and use behaviors. The emerging evolutionary approach has been developing within scientific disciplines that have adopted an evolutionary perspective to explore human behavior, including evolutionary biology, evolutionary psychology, and cognitive archeology. The emerging evolutionary exploration of HIB is broadening the scope of the field of HIB, particularly within LIS, creating interdisciplinarity with related fields using an evolutionary approach, and beginning an initial mapping of HIB across the long span of human existence.

In this chapter, we first discuss the emerging interdisciplinary and evolutionary approach to HIB. We then propose an initial chronology of studies investigating various

A. Spink and C. Cole (eds), New Directions in Human Information Behavior, 13–31.
© 2006 *Springer.*

aspects of HIB throughout the course of human existence. In conclusion, we discuss further HIB research directions from a more evolutionary perspective, as well as some implications of this approach.

Section 2 first lays out some important concepts and definitions to guide the reading of this chapter.

2. CURRENT CONCEPTUAL APPROACHES TO HIB

Some important HIB concepts are defined below including, *HIB*, *information seeking*, *information organizing*, and *information use*.

- Wilson (2000) provides a definition of *information behavior* as "the totality of human behavior in relation to sources and channels of information including both active and passive information seeking, and information use" (p. 49).
- Spink and Cole (2004) define *information seeking* as a sub-set of information behavior that includes the *purposive seeking of information in relation to a goal*.
- *Information organizing behavior* is the process of analyzing and classifying materials into defined categories (Cole & Leide, 2005; Spink & Cole, 2004).
- *Information use behavior* involves incorporating information into an individual's existing knowledge base (Spink & Cole, 2004).

Various conceptual approaches are currently used to study HIB. According to Spink and Cole (2004), the *information-seeking approach* has historically been the dominant area of study within LIS-focused HIB research. Other approaches such as *sense*-making (Dervin, 1992), *everyday life information seeking* (Savolainen, 1995), and *information foraging* (Pirolli & Card, 1999) have also developed to identify and study information finding behaviors. Spink and Cole (2004) suggest that the role of information use in information behavior has been unclear and offer an additional conceptualization based on a theory of information use. They also provide an initial framework for integrating these diverse approaches within an integrated model with consideration of information seeking/foraging/sense-making, organizing, and use behavior (Spink & Cole, 2004).

An analysis of the broad nature of HIB studies within LIS shows a primarily contemporary non-evolutionary focus (Spink & Currier, in press). However, Section 3 of the chapter discusses how the more evolutionary approach to human behavior developing in the broader social sciences is impacting the study of HIB, particularly within LIS.

3. EVOLUTIONARY INTERDISCIPLINARY APPROACHES TO HIB

Research outside the LIS field has explored aspects of how humans have used information and written materials over the ages (Spink & Currier, in press). Historians, for example, have examined the history of letter and diary writing as well as the ways in which people have used documents or how they as individuals have commented on their own use of documents (Augst, 2003; Bower, 1997; Breen, 1989; Bunkers & Huff, 1996; Ellis, 2002). Cressy (1987) explores how persons evolutionarily communicated with others and preserved their papers for posterity. Fleming (2001) studied graffiti and the writing arts of early modern England. Geary (1994) and Ulrich (1990) studied evolutionary diary writing.

The history of information behaviors is also related to the evolution of human behavior (Eibi-Eibesfeldt and Strachan, 1996). Many social sciences are developing fields of inquiry within a human evolutionary framework, including evolutionary biology, evolutionary psychology, and cognitive archeology. The objective of these scientific fields is to suggest explanations for the functioning and development of the human mind from a human evolutionary theoretical perspective, including information behavior (Barkow, Cosmides, & Tooby, 1992; Mithen, 1996). Cognitive archeologist Mithen (1996) studied Upper Paleolithic cultures, focusing on pre-historic cave art and the meaning that can be derived from what he and other researchers interpret as a method and mechanism for information storage. Mithen advocates an interdisciplinary approach to scientific inquiry and has stated that "almost all disciplines can contribute towards an understanding of the human mind" (Mithen, 1996, p. 10). Research and findings will be discussed in greater detail later in this chapter.

Kaplan (1992) is an evolutionary psychologist who has written about some of the issues involved in a synthesis of humans, evolution, and information (p. 582). Within a framework of "affective biases toward patterns of information" he states that, "... not only information in its own right, but the concern for information is considered a basic part of the human makeup" (p. 582). Kaplan sees "concern" as encompassing a broad range of human affective relationships vis-à-vis information, such as "the motivation to seek information" (p. 582). He asserts that a variety of "human affective relationships to information ... remain to be identified and conceptualized" (p. 582).

Kaplan (1992) offers a number of helpful threshold questions for thinking about a nexus of humans, information, and evolution: "It is reasonable to question whether this concern for information is a human characteristic of long standing, a matter of widespread interest, and importance for the species at large, or alternatively, simply a characteristic perversion of a small group of scholars. Is there any basis for believing that knowledge and the concern for knowledge have any role in the evolutionary scheme of things?" In a nutshell, Kaplan (1992) raises the issue of whether knowledge (i.e., information) has any relationship to human evolution. Intriguing and extraordinarily challenging questions like these raised by Kaplan, as well as numerous related others, will surface repeatedly throughout this chapter's consideration of the emerging evolutionary perspective of HIB. Such queries will also be evident within a fairly extensive list of questions for further research provided at the end of this chapter.

Evolutionary psychologists Barkow, Cosmides, and Tooby (1992) like Mithen are proponents of interdisciplinarity. They emphasize the ability of conceptual integration to create anchor points that enable the bridging of gaps that one's own and other fields may not be able to span by themselves. Such conceptual integration, they assert, generates powerful knowledge growth because it enables researchers to use knowledge gained in other disciplines to solve problems in their own (Barkow, Cosmides, & Tooby, 1992).

In attempting to provide explanations for the evolution of the human mind, evolutionary psychology researchers have studied cognition more from an information-processing viewpoint than a behavioral one. This information-processing approach focuses on how the mind functions; for example, how the left and right sides of the brain communicate or how fast neurons fire (Barkow, Cosmides, & Tooby, 1992).

Tooby and Cosmides (1989) view cognitive psychology and evolutionary biology as "sister disciplines" (p. 46). They assert that "the goal of evolutionary theory is to define the adaptive problems that organisms must be able to solve. The goal of psychological theory is to discover the information processing mechanisms that have evolved to solve them. Alone, each is incomplete for the understanding of human nature. Together they are powerful" (Tooby & Cosmides, 1989, pp. 46–47). Limited overlap exists between the evolutionary studies within the social sciences and HIB studies within LIS (Spink & Currier, in press).

The emerging evolutionary approach to HIB within LIS is situating HIB more closely to its evolutionary perspective siblings, evolutionary biology, evolutionary psychology, and cognitive archeology. This approach will more fully contribute to the understanding of the evolution of human behavior in general and further integrate HIB research at a fundamental, theoretical level with the social sciences and humanities (Spink & Currier, in press). It may also contribute to a more holistic understanding of the relationship between humans and information as well as the nexus among humankind, information, and human evolution.

The research integration described above is common scientific practice in the natural sciences as well as numerous other social science disciplines. Such "interdisciplinary splicing"—the joining and interweaving of conceptual and theoretical strands from various scientific disciplines and fields of inquiry into an integrated whole—can be profoundly useful and effective. Barkow, Cosmides, and Tooby (1992) assert, for example, that, "[E]vidence from evolutionary biology can help social psychologists generate new hypotheses about the design features of the information-processing mechanisms that govern social behavior" (p. 12). Tooby and Cosmides (1989) also suggest that "the promise of the evolutionary perspective lies . . . in its power to assist in the discovery, inventory, and analysis of innate psychological mechanisms" and "the key to understanding cultural processes must therefore lie in the discovery and subsequent mapping of the properties of these complex and specialized psychological mechanisms" (p. 30). In other words, look at data collected and see what insights emanate from the data.

Invoking the rationale for interdisciplinarity, Stonier (1997) discusses the challenges in "creating an information science", stating "that it requires expertise from a wide variety of traditional disciplines" (p. 4). A more interdisciplinary approach to HIB is also vital in providing a foundation for and achieving viable theoretical concepts like "information".

Stonier provides an interesting example supporting a nuanced but persuasive rationale for interdisciplinarity. His example comes from Nobel Prize-winning physicist Erwin Schrodinger's (1944) *What is Life?* book preface, cited by Stonier: "A scientist is supposed to have a complete and thorough knowledge . . . of *some* subjects, and, therefore, is usually expected not to write on any topic of which he is not a master". Schrodinger, however, argues that: ". . . The spread, both in width and depth of the multifarious branches of knowledge . . . has confronted us with a queer dilemma. We . . . are only now beginning to acquire reliable material for welding together the sum-total of all that is known into a whole; but, on the other hand, it has become next to impossible for a single mind fully to command more than a small specialized portion of it".

Stonier (1997) concludes: "I can see no escape from this dilemma . . . than that some of us should venture to embark on a synthesis of facts and theories . . . at the risk of making fools of ourselves" (p. 5). Likewise, an emerging perspective such as the evolutionary one proposed for HIB clearly does present challenges but also offers significant possibilities and potential upshots, such as potentially broadening the field of HIB. This perspective may also potentially foster a more interdisciplinary relationship with the other social sciences.

A more evolutionary perspective of HIB can make an important contribution as well toward an understanding of the human mind, as suggested via Mithen (1996) earlier. Just as evolutionary psychology is interested in mapping aspects of the information-processing components of the human mind; the key to better understanding HIB may involve identification and mapping of HIBs from a longitudinal perspective spanning the course of human evolution. The rationale for this approach is supported by Mithen's (1996) assertion that, "[W]e can only ever understand the present by knowing the past" (p. 10).

Similarly, Leakey's (1992) guiding principle is that the past is the key to our future. If other sciences and scientists are looking to the past to better understand the here and now—anthropology, archeology, biology, paleontology, psychology, etc.—it makes sense that this approach may also be beneficial for the field of HIB, given the overlap of research epistemologies and philosophies shared with these other sciences. It is logical to examine the past in order to understand the present. Psychologists have a saying that past behavior is the best predictor of future behavior. Though perhaps this maxim seems trite and simplistic, it does contain a kernel of insight vis-à-vis HIB: namely, to understand what HIBs *are* and *may be*, we need to investigate what they have *been*.

Section 4 of the chapter provides an initial chronology of studies investigating various aspects of HIB throughout human existence.

4. CHRONOLOGY OF STUDIES ILLUMINATING ASPECTS OF HIB OVER ERAS OF HUMAN EXISTENCE

In Figure 1, we provide an initial chronology of various studies that have explored various aspects of HIB from pre-historic ages to the 21st century. Our initial chronology shows research studies that contribute to our understanding of various aspects of HIB over human existence. The chronology provides a preliminary overview and more research is needed to identify further studies.

Many scientific disciplines have created chronologies showing the evolution of a human behavior. Mithen (1996) proposes a chronology for the evolution of human intelligence spanning the period from 100 million years ago (MYA) to 10,000 years ago (KYA). Settegast (1986) presents a chronology of cultural development from approximately 35,000 B.C. to 5000 B.C. Leakey and Lewin (1977) summarize the geological and paleontological history of the earth with a timeline running from the Azoic (without life) period to recent times (pp. 12–15).

Leakey and Lewin (1977) also employ a species timeline model ranging from the apes through early man to Homo sapiens in order to depict increases in mean brain size (pp. 198–199). Leakey and Lewin (1992a, b) and Leakey (1994) also use time-line chronologies to show human existence from 10 MYA to the present. Leakey (1994) discusses how French anthropologist and pre-historian Henri Breuil "... recorded, mapped, copied, and counted [Upper Paleolithic] images in the caves throughout

---→ Time --→

--→ Evolution ---→

Upper Paleolithic Era 10,000-70,000 Years Ago	Classical Greece 8th Century B.C. to 2nd Century B.C.	Renaissance 1454 A.D. to 1699 A.D.	Industrial Age 1700 A.D. to 1945 A.D.	Post-Industrial Information Age 1946-21st Century
Mithen (1988) – Art and Information Gathering	Payne (1993) – Information Collection and Transmission	Spink & Currier (in press) – Leonardo Da Vinci	Spink & Currier (in press) – Napoleon, Darwin, Casanova, Mill, Booker T. Washington, Freud, Payne-Gaposchkin	Madden, (2004)
Ouzman, Tacon, Mulvaney & Fullagar (2002) – Cave Art and Information	Russell (1999) – Information Gathering			Case (2002) - Post World War II Information Behaviors
Pfeiffer (1982) – Cave Art and Information Pfeiffer (1983) – Cave Art and Information				Wilson (2000) – Post World War II Information Behaviors

Figure 1. Initial chronology of studies illuminating various aspects of HIB
over of human existence.

Europe ... [and] ... developed a chronology for the evolution of art during the Upper Paleolithic" (p. 110). Chronologies like these are useful in portraying and suggesting shifts in human behavior and human evolution over time.

Ouzman et al. (2002) suggest several important roles for creating chronologies and chronological models in their own research area studying ancient rock-art. They discuss the need to create a more precise chronology of rock-art, which will thereby enable them to situate an ancient engraced bird footprint created by Aboriginal Australians. Furthermore, Ouzman et al. (2002) suggest that a chronology may help them to explain the time relationship between the ancient bird track and other drawings referred to as "ancient Bradshaw-like human figures" (p. 108). Finally, they argue that a more precise chronology may help them to better glean potential meanings from the rock-art and to note the significance of such art throughout various areas (p. 108).

Chronologies, like the one described by Ouzman et al., can be useful in helping to organize and make sense of data as well as facilitating the discovery of relationships and dissimilar features among data.

Our initial chronology in Figure 1 depicts the period of time from human pre-history, that is, 10,000–70,000 years ago, to the present. It is a horizontal, linear chronology, in the mode of most timeline models running from left (past) to right (more recent).

4.1 Constructs—Time and Evolution

Each time period depicted in Figure 1, for example, Upper Paleolithic Era, includes a list of HIB-relevant studies and their authors for that respective era. The constructs of time and evolution relate to each preceding and subsequent time periods' constructs of time and evolution in terms of a chronologically linear one, except for the Upper Paleolithic Era at the far left, which is the earliest time period represented in this particular figure. For example, the Industrial Age Era representing 1700–1945 A.D. is located between the earlier Renaissance Era to the left and the later Post-industrial Information Age to the right.

Two constructs used in this chronology are time and evolution. Time and evolution are human-created ontologies used to represent distinct but intangible conceptualizations of specific forces and properties of nature that impact and govern both the physical world and existence of humans and other organisms. Time is defined as "the indefinite continued progress of existence and events in the past, present, and future regarded as a whole" (New Oxford American Dictionary, 2001, p. 1774). Evolution is defined as "the process by which different kinds of living organisms are thought to have developed and diversified from earlier forms during the history of the earth" (New Oxford American Dictionary, 2001, p. 590).

Section 5 of the chapter discusses studies exploring various aspects of HIB during the Upper Paleolithic Era from 10,000 to 70,000 years ago.

5. UPPER PALEOLITHIC ERA—10,000–70,000 YEARS AGO

5.1 Cave Art

The Upper Paleolithic period represented in the initial chronology of studies of Figure 1 includes Mithen's (1988) study *Looking and Learning: Upper Palaeolithic Art and Information Gathering*. In this study, Mithen (1988) posits how and why early Upper Paleolithic hunters and gatherers may have collected, used, and stored information gained from studying animal tracks and predator–prey relationships in the form of cave art.

Other researchers have also posited a link between art, information, human behavior, and human evolution (Kaplan, 1992; Mithen, 1988, 1996; Pfeiffer, 1982). These studies have looked at global art, particularly cave paintings and rock art or rock engravings spanning various ages of human existence. In terms of the advent of art, the production of art occurred in Europe by around 30,000 years ago, in Africa by 27,500 years ago, and in Australia between 15,000 and 40,000 years ago or perhaps even beyond (Mithen, 1996).

Leakey (1994) asserts that, "Almost certainly, at least some elements of Ice Age art concerned the way Upper Paleolithic people organized their ideas about their world— an expression of their spiritual cosmos" (p. 112). Furthermore, as Kaplan cites from Pfeiffer's *The Creative Explosion* (1982), "[Pfeiffer] offers a persuasive argument for the hypothesis that [ancient cave paintings produced by humans] were means of storing and transmitting information central to the cultures that produced them. These various pieces of evidence, while far from overwhelming, suggest the likely significance of information to human evolution" (Kaplan, 1992, p. 583).

When examining and trying to divine meaning from cave art and rock art, it is vital to note that "many researchers argue for an overtly cautious approach . . . in assigning meaning to rock-art imagery [as] even apparently visually straightforward rock-art representations of humans, animals, everyday objects, and so forth cannot be verified with an absolute degree of confidence" (Ouzman et al., 2002, p. 103). According to Bahn (1998), a fundamental problem is that just because art looks to us like something straightforward and interpretable, we can never really know for sure what the meaning of that art is or the purpose for which it was created. (pp. 176–177). Bahn (1998) provides a cogent instance of the danger in over interpreting an image or marking: "a non-Aboriginal researcher ... identified a number of animal images using zoological reasoning, only to learn from an Aboriginal informant that, out of twenty-two images, he had been wrong about fifteen and only superficially right about the other seven!" (pp. 176–177).

Leakey (1994) also articulates the need for caution and provides a striking cultural example of the intrinsic limitations presented when endeavoring to interpret meaning and purpose from cave and rock-art: "The reasons for creating the [Lascaux cave art] bison and the circumstances under which bison were crafted are lost in time ... We do not know, perhaps even cannot know. As the South African archeologist David Lewis-Williams says of pre-historic art, 'Meaning is always culturally bound.' ... Even if we were to witness the slice of Upper Paleolithic life in which the cave paintings played their role, would we understand the meaning of the whole? I doubt it. We have only to think of the stories related in modern religions to appreciate the importance of cryptic symbols that may be meaningless outside the culture to which they belong. Think of the meaningfulness to a Christian of an image of a man holding a staff, with a lamb at his feet. And think of the absence of any such meaning to someone who has not heard the Christian story" (pp. 102–103).

We can never truly *know* with absolute certainty—short of time-traveling like H. G. Wells, an impossibility at present—the exact meanings envisioned or intended, and the specific behaviors and purposes manifested by ancient humans in creating cave art and rock art. Consider other art components and formats as well, like the Mona Lisa's enigmatic smile and Easter Island's *moai* rock statues, which have inspired generations to ponder their elusive meanings and purposes. What information was used in creating such art and what information, if any, was meant to be conveyed? A lack of time machines has not stopped historians, archeologists, anthropologists, and other scientists from studying the past and making "educated guesses", informed suggestions, and reasoned conclusions founded on scientific methods and principles of logic, analytical expertise, and evidence. Still, Leakey (1994) reminds us that "The ancient images we have today are fragments of an ancient story, and although the urge to know what they mean is great, it is wise to accept the probable limits of our understanding" (pp. 103–104). He further shines a spotlight on a Western bias in analyses of pre-historic art, as well as a dearth of focus on equally ancient if not even older pre-historic art in Africa (pp. 103–104).

The burden and incumbent responsibility upon researchers is to be aware of such biases as well as the ostensible limitations and ultimate barriers standing in the way of human knowledge and comprehension; all the while striving to elucidate and expand the bounds of our understanding of yesterday, as much as possible.

As Leakey (1994) concludes in his discussion of the language of human art, with a pragmatic but assured and reverent tone, "We may never know what the Tuc d'Audobert [cave] sculptor had in mind when they fashioned the bison, nor the painters at Lascaux when they drew the Unicorn, nor any of the Ice Age artists in what they did. But we can be sure that what they did was important in a very deep sense to the artists and to the people who saw the images in the generations afterward. The language of art is powerful to those who understand it, and puzzling to those who do not. What we do know is that here was the modern human mind at work, spinning symbolism and abstraction in a way that only *Homo sapiens* is capable of doing. Although we cannot yet be sure of the process by which modern humans evolved, we do know that it involved the emergence of the kind of mental world each of us experiences today" (p. 118).

5.2 Information Gathering

The identification of themes, such as information gathering, is an important aspect of information behavior-related research. Discovery and explanation of such themes and the mapping of information-related behaviors discussed earlier may not only aid the development of HIB, but also augment other sciences with an evolutionary perspective. Mithen's (1988) concluding remarks offer a well-crafted example of analysis that both qualifies and contributes to information behavior-related research: "Any attempt to provide one all-encompassing explanation for parietal and mobile paintings, engravings, bas-relief and sculpture produced over a 20,000-year period is hopelessly optimistic and will inevitably be flawed. However, what can be done is to identify themes each of which may help to explain a significant proportion of the imagery and which are not mutually exclusive. The information gathering theme discussed here is perhaps just one of many, in a complex but magnificent artistic tradition" (p. 323).

Mithen (1988) examines Upper Paleolithic art to consider "how it may have aided the Late Pleistocene hunter gatherers [to] adapt to their environment" and look at "the art as a medium for the transmission or storage of information" (p. 297). He notes, though, that the research done in this area has not really defined "information" as a concept and that little theory has been attached to the imagery studied. Mithen (1988) focuses on three aspects of information gathering behavior: Upper Paleolithic humans' use of tracks and signs made by animals, detailed observations made by humans once animals were spotted, and the use of animals as cues or clues to the whereabouts of other potential animal species resources. From his study and that of others, Mithen (1988) asserts that "[t]he gathering of information from the natural environment is an activity in which all modern hunter gatherers engage" (p. 297).

Clear parallels are evident between the language of HIB, with its focus on human information seeking, organization, and use, and Mithen's (1988) description of Upper Paleolithic human behavior—"once information has been collected [i.e., information seeking] in this manner, it will either be used directly, initiating a stalk or attempted kill [i.e., information use], or stored [i.e., information organizing] and exchanged with other hunters [i.e., information use]" (p. 297). Mithen (1988) also suggests that "Upper Palaeolithic art may be related to the cognitive development of the use of 'search' behavior" (p. 322).

5.3 Information Organizing and Using

Some researchers suggest that the intersection between rock art or cave paintings and oral stories can also be seen as a type of information organizing and information use behavior, among both past and present humans. As Mithen (1996) notes: "Once again the Aboriginal communities of Australia provide a good example. The wells in their landscape are where ancestral beings dug in the ground, the trees where they had placed their digging sticks and the deposits of red ochre where they had bled. John Pfeiffer has argued that the encompassing of the features of the landscape in a web of myths and stories is of great utility to the Aborigines, for it helps them to remember enormous quantities of geographic information" (p. 166).

Ouzman et al. (2002) examined a rock-engraved bird track of a now-extinct ostrich-size bird made by ancient Aboriginal Australians. They suggested what can be seen as possible information organizing and information use purposes for the engraving: "...perhaps both the most appealing and the most difficult to prove [point is]—that some aspects of Aboriginal history... have been passed down through oral history and imagery for many tens of thousand of years.... This is important in a global context when we seek to identify aspects of culture or experience that have been passed on to the present from very early stages of human development" (p. 108).

Indeed, in discussing cave paintings of the Upper Paleolithic Era, such as the famed Lascaux [France] cavern depictions, Pfeiffer (1982) also supports this idea of information organizing, stating that, "Confronted with an increasingly complex way of life and a pile-up of information, [the people of the Upper Paleolithic] were engaged in the first large-scale effort to organize knowledge for readier long-term retention and recall" (p. 215). Pfeiffer (1982) suggests that lack of a writing system, which would not be invented for 20,000 years, created an information need or problem, or as he calls it a "here-and-now emergency" (p. 123). This crisis created the need for cave painting in order "to transmit the expanding contents of 'the tribal encyclopedia' intact and indelibly from generation to generation" (Pfeiffer, 1982, p. 123).

In *The Prehistory of the Mind*, Mithen (1996) postulates an information organizing function to cave paintings. He also suggests their use as a technique for jogging and enhancing the memories of ancient humans: "Like the engraved pieces of bone, cave paintings also appear to have been used to store information about the natural world, or at least facilitate its recall by acting as a mnemonic device...I myself have suggested that much of the animal imagery within this art served to help recall information about the natural world stored within the mind. For instance, I have argued that the manner in which many of the animals were painted makes direct reference to the ways in which information was acquired about their movements and behaviour...".

Mithen continues "The way in which Upper Palaeolithic cave paintings may have functioned to help store information about the natural world is perhaps analogous to the way in which Wopkaimin hunter-horticulturalists of New Guinea use the bones from the animals they hunt...In summary, although the specific roles that pre-historic artifacts may have played in the management of information about the natural world remain unclear, there can be little doubt that many of them served to store, transmit, and retrieve information" (pp. 172–173).

Ancient art may also be viewed as the tangible embodiment of information seeking, organizing, and use behaviors related to the purpose of education. Mithen (1988) cites Pfeiffer's (1982) argument that "art may play a significant role in the education and development of young members of the Upper Palaeolithic groups" (p. 322). The combination of viewing the art while hearing myths and stories may have helped to imprint the crucial survival information contained in the myths into their memories (Mithen, 1988).

Section 6 of the chapter discusses studies exploring various aspects of HIB during Classical Greece from 8th Century B.C. to 2nd Century B.C.

6. CLASSICAL GREECE—8TH CENTURY–2ND CENTURY B.C.

Russell's (1999) *Information Gathering in Classical Greece* examines the information behaviors of persons from that influential era—well-known figures like military great Alexander, philosopher Plutarch, and military leader-cum-historian writer Xenophon. In addition, he addresses countless lesser-known and unknown spies, servants, slaves, prisoners, and other denizens of this period.

His study's focus has a twofold connotation of information gathering: (1) how Ancient Greeks sought, acquired, and used information and (2) within a specific context of the espionage-oriented, military and strategic intelligence procuring meaning of *information gathering* as well. Though Russell's area of concentration is the intelligence aspect of information, his work provides useful information behavior-relevant insights and reference points for an important period of time in terms of lasting global influence, offering few HIB-related studies.

Russell's (1999) research is also pertinent because it dovetails with the intent and aim of HIB's emerging evolutionary perspective for investigating HIB. This perspective explores and identifies information behaviors throughout the course of human existence by looking at specific eras while endeavoring to better understand the information behaviors of persons of those eras within both their own specific time contexts and the larger context of human existence.

As seen throughout this chapter's perusal of earlier eras like the Upper Paleolithic, it is important to acknowledge inherent limitations when looking at people, records, and artifacts from the past. For example, Russell (1999) underscores the parameters of his study as the Hellenic world of the fifth and fourth centuries B.C., because little information exists from before that time and what does is intermingled with myth. Issues of terminology can also be problematic, and Russell (1999), in fact, notes that the Greeks did not have specific terms for information and intelligence (p. 6).

Russell (1999) further expresses what his study cannot and can do: "It would be the height of folly to allege that a study of information gathering would in itself illuminate the motives behind decisions obscured by two and a half millennia, but it can at least establish parameters for the knowledge people would have or would not have possessed when they made the decisions. That is the ambition of this book: to define terms, to describe mechanisms, and, in effect, to produce an intelligence resource of use for specific studies" (pp. 1–2). Similarly, those developing the HIB evolutionary perspective (Spink & Cole, 2004; Spink & Currier, in press) are striving to define useful terminology and concepts, create taxonomies, identify information behaviors, provide a theoretical framework, and offer initial chronologies assembling pertinent studies that have been conducted and recommending areas for further research.

Perhaps, the most challenging feature in studying the past is whether evidence from the past exists. Another is whether one has access to that evidence. Like a scientific law, the need to engage in conjecture and speculation can be said to be inversely proportional to the quantity and quality of evidence available.

Unfortunately, for researchers, it is generally axiomatic that the further back in time one looks, the less material is available. Entropy after all—the tendency for a system to decline into disorder—also impacts and affects organic and inorganic things; things like rocks and cave walls, papyrus scrolls, and paper records and books, as well as living people. All decay, disintegrate, and are subject to destruction and disappearance over time. As Russell (1999) describes, "While early writers at times contained accounts of information gathering and intelligence, no extant work written before the fourth century contains a theoretical treatment of the subject" (p. 6).

Despite the challenges, thankfully for researchers and posterity, evidence does exist. Russell (1999) celebrates Herodotus and Thcydides for their contributions toward creating various aspects of historiography. But he especially singles out Xenophon as the first and sole Greek theorist who studied the gathering and evaluation of information as a field of its own (Russell, 1999).

Throughout *Information Gathering in Classical Greece,* Russell discusses the terrain and state of information gathering in the Classical Greek period. He describes how warring sides sought information and used it to avoid ambushes and surprise attacks, how leaders extracted information from captured prisoners, and the ways covert spies infiltrated enemy camps and lands to collect vital information that military generals and leaders desperately desired and needed for strategic planning and advantage. Russell (1999) also provides a model of Information flow to a central command with Alexander (356–323 B.C.) at the center. This model (1999) illustrates characteristics of the structural chain of military command from, as example, scouts to officers to Alexander. It also depicts the ebb and flow of information behaviors among those at the bottom, middle, and top of the era's hierarchical organization.

Russell (1999) notes that an awareness of the importance of information gathering increased between the 8th century (B.C.) and the middle of the 4th century (B.C.). This information gathering activity reached its apex with individuals like Xenophon, Aeneas Tacticus, and Alexander. (p. 226). Russell (1999) states that information-gathering processes tended to become more systematic over time, but finds "this was a function of political development rather than chronological evolution" (p. 226). Such findings may be beneficial in answering questions such as whether, when, why, and how HIBs evolve.

Payne's (1993) *Information collection and transmission in Classical Greece* share a number of similarities with Russell's (1999) study. However, she looks at the concept of information during this period with a broader lens than a focus on information as intelligence gathering. Payne (1993) surveys the ways and means by which information collection and transmission were conducted and effectuated in Classical Greece. She specifically examines the information collection and transmission behaviors of three important authors, Homer, Herodotus, and Theophrastus. Payne also delves into literary works about Alexander the Great, who was a pivotal focus of much of Russell's (1999) research.

Payne (1993) suggests that like present-day humans, those of the Classical Greek Era inhabited an information age, albeit one very different from ours. With the written word so ubiquitous today, it can be challenging but essential to remember and contemplate how recent a phenomenon writing really is, having emerged over the last several thousand years. The implications for information and attendant human behaviors in a milieu without writing are quite different from one with written modalities. Classical Greece was at the crossroads of a transition from an almost wholly oral culture to one, which became significantly literary. Payne (1993) finds that "this change had profound implications for the way information was collected and transmitted in the Classical Greek World" (p. 285).

Given that the Classical Greek world was undergoing an evolution from oral traditions of information collection and transmission to one that was a hybrid of oral and increasingly written formats, Payne's (1993) work is particularly relevant to examination and development of the emerging HIB evolutionary perspective. Moreover, in the vein of Spink and Currier's (in press) research, discussed in greater depth infra, which investigates the information behaviors of famous persons from the Middle Ages through the 20th century, Payne's (1993) findings support the conclusion that the subjects of her Classical Greek Era research did engage in information behaviors.

The persons examined in Payne's (1993) research encompass the specific cultural period referred to as Classical Greece. Payne sets the chronological boundaries for her inquiry, defines the Classical Greek period as ranging from "the emergence of Greece from the Dark Ages (c. 8th century B.C.) to its absorption into the larger Hellenistic world (late 4th century B.C.)" (p. 272).

The selection of this Classical Greece time period for study offers a chronological and longitudinal span that is sufficiently contained to facilitate understanding of a distinct system, yet sufficiently broad as well to depict the evolution, though not necessarily the evolutionary causes, of information seeking and use behaviors. As Payne (1993) notes: "Classical Greece was the site of an information explosion rivaling our own . . . It is the earliest one of which we have written documentation covering most aspects of life" (p. 272). Payne (1993) offers additional insight regarding why these figures were selected, stating that, "These men were also chosen because they are almost unique in the relatively large amounts of information about their sources found in their writings, or in the case of Alexander, those writing about him" (p. 272).

Herodotus and Theophrastus provide the most substantial instances of information behaviors in Payne's (1993) study. Herodotus (5th century B.C.) is particularly noteworthy as his composition *Histories* "is the earliest extant work we have which incorporated written information" (p. 275). Payne (1993) reveals that, "Herodotus himself tells us how he came by the information in his histories: Up to this point I have confined what I have written to the results of my own direct observation and research, and the views I have formed from them; but from now on the basis of my story will be the accounts given to me by the Egyptians themselves though here too, I shall put in one or two things which I have seen with my own eye" (pp. 275–276). Though Payne (1993) points out that Herodotus was referring specifically to study regarding Egypt, "the methods which he used to collect information for the entire book are outlined in this statement" (p. 276).

She goes on to say that a number of scholars assert that Herodotus fictitiously created the majority of the information he claimed as emanating from other sources. However, Payne (1993) adds that the majority of researchers believe Herodotus used a range of both written and oral sources and augmented that information with his own observations. (p. 276). Payne (1993) further states that by using a variety of information sources and endeavoring to explain notions of historical cause and effect, his efforts culminated in "a work that what is the first true work of history" (p. 276).

Herodotus collected his information from a variety of sources. These included logographers (historically oriented storytellers), city and temple archives, inscriptions such as those on monuments, and Egyptian priests (Payne, 1993). As Payne (1993) also describes, Herodotus "depended on his own observations, particularly where he could not get satisfactory information in any other manner... Complaining that he could get no information about the source of the Nile he says: I went as far as Elephantine to see what I could with my own eyes, but for the country still further south I had to be content with what I was told in answer to my questions" (p. 278).

The former military leader turned writer-historian Theophrastus (370–287 B.C.) also provides some illustrative examples of information behaviors in Payne's (1993) study. He was a student and colleague of Aristotle's and upon the death of Aristotle became the head of the Lyceum. Payne explains that [Theophrastus] is probably best known for his work "Characters", a series of sketches of famous people... [and]... The *Enquiry into Plants* is the earliest extant systematic treatment of botany. It contains information on the morphology, physiology, and habitat of over 500 plants many of them from areas it is known Theophrastus never visited (such as India)" (pp. 278–279). His information ostensibly came from observations, oral reports from a variety of informants, and a number of technical and non-technical writings (Payne, 1993, p. 279).

A summary of key findings from Payne's (1993) study includes the following: "In the case of Herodotus the information was collected from oral and written sources... Theophrastus is further removed from oral roots than Herodotus in that he makes increasing use of written sources. However, he did use oral reports used from a variety of informants, and his works seem to have been derived from notes used for public lectures... Alexander shows a greater use of written messages than Theophrastus, in part due to the nature of military information. He relied on the oral collection of information, but most of his transmissions were in written form" (p. 285).

As with Russell's (1999) Classical Greek study discussed supra, Payne (1993) acknowledges the challenges in researching a past era, especially one at the apex of transition from oral to written forms. She observes that, "The oral nature of information in the Classical Greek World and the differential survival of written materials make it difficult to trace the process of information collection and transmission during the Classical Period" (pp. 285–286).

Section 7 of the chapter discusses studies exploring various aspects of HIB during the Renaissance Era from 1454 A.D. to 1699 A.D.

7. RENAISSANCE ERA—1454–1699 A.D.

Spink and Currier (in press) analyzed the notebooks of the 15th century artist and inventor Leonardo Da Vinci (1452–1519). Da Vinci's (1998) notebooks indicated minimal discussion of his information behaviors. Da Vinci did, however, mention his collection of papers and articulated his future need to classify his papers and notebooks by subject (Da Vinci, 1998, p. vii). Sadly, Da Vinci's death cut short the completion of the classification of his notebooks.

Similar to other chronological eras discussed heretofore, more HIB-related research needs to be identified and conducted on Renaissance Era persons. Because this era is more recent than earlier eras like the Middle Ages and Classical Greece, more HIB-relevant studies for the Renaissance Era may have already been conducted and be "waiting for discovery" via the searching process and analytical investigation. Moreover, the advent of the printing press around 1455, at the beginning of the Renaissance Era, suggests the likelihood that more evidence in print form, related to the information behaviors of people during this time period, may potentially exist. The task for current and future researchers is to locate such evidence and thus further develop this likely pivotal HIB-pertinent period; an era that witnessed as never before the proliferation of information tools and mechanisms by means of the printing press.

Section 8 of the chapter discusses studies exploring various aspects of HIB during the Industrial Age from 1700 A.D. to 1945 A.D.

8. INDUSTRIAL AGE—1700–1945 A.D.

Spink and Currier (in press) examined the autobiographies, diaries, journals, and personal letters of a cross-section of persons of note from the industrial age, in order to identify instances in which such persons described their own information behaviors. These persons included military leaders like the French Emperor and military leader Napoleon Bonaparte (1769–1821), scientists such as Charles Darwin (1809–1882), the principal creator architect of evolutionary and natural selection theory, astronomer Cecilia Payne-Gaposchkin (1900–1979), and Sigmund Freud (1856–1939), the originator of psychoanalysis.

Spink and Currier (in press) examined whether these historical figures discussed their information-related behaviors and what types of information behaviors they wrote about information seeking, information organization, and/or information use. Spink and Currier (in press) identify examples of information seeking, organizing, and use behaviors, described by these past persons in their own words. For instance, the following quote indicates Napoleon's information-seeking behaviors: "While at Passau he will reconnoiter the road leading into Bohemia as far as possible in Bavarian territory and get information on the rest" (Bonaparte, 1999, p. 12).

Additionally, similar to some of the intelligence gathering information behaviors of Alexander the Great described earlier, in conjunction with maps, Napoleon discusses the importance of geographic information for successful military campaigns: "Order them especially to mark clearly the nature of different roads, in order to distinguish those which are practicable or impracticable for artillery" (Bonaparte, 1999, p. 15). Napoleon further explicitly decreed the method for seeking, organizing, and using such information: "When the army marches, the geographical engineers, who will have reconnoitered the country, will always be at headquarters in order to provide all necessary information. Their reconnaissance memoranda should always be written in the simplest style and be purely descriptive. They should never stray from their objective by introducing extraneous ideas" (Bonaparte, 1999, p. 160).

Charles Darwin (1958), credited with creating the quintessentially influential and seminal theory of evolution and natural selection, also provides some insights regarding his information behaviors, particularly in information organizing: "I have bought many books and at the ends I make an index of all the facts that concern my work; or, if the book is not my own, write out a separate abstract, and of such abstracts I have a large drawer full" (pp. 137–138). Furthermore: "Before beginning on any subject I look to all the short indexes and make a general and classified index, and by taking the one or more proper portfolios I have all the information collected during my life ready to use" (p. 138).

A more recent example reveals the information organizing and use behaviors of US educator Booker T. Washington (1856–1915): "Mrs. Raffner always encouraged and sympathized with me in all my efforts to get an education. It was while I was living with her that I began to get together my first library. I secured a dry-goods box, knocked out one side of it, put shelves in it, and began piling into it every kind of book that I could get my hands upon and called it my 'library'" (Washington, 1963, p. 32).

Another example, Astronomer Cecilia Payne-Gaposchkin (1900–1979) represents the most recent individual examined in the Spink and Currier (in press) HIB study. Her autobiography discusses her information seeking and organizing behaviors: "The Harvard plans called for a massive collection of data, information about as many stars as possible—which meant reaching stars as faint as possible. The next step was the systematic arrangement of the information which soon led to the discovery that the spectra could be placed in an orderly series" (Payne-Gaposchkin, 1996, p. 160).

9. FUTURE DIRECTIONS

This chapter documents the emerging evolutionary approach to HIB research. Spink and Currier (in press) underscore the need for more research to identify and map HIB across the spectrum of human existence. They suggest that this type of research "has implications for expanding the nature of our evolutionary understanding of information behavior and provides a broader context for the field of human information behavior" (p. 2). The emerging evolutionary approach to understanding HIB has wide ranging implications. A linkage to the social sciences evolutionary approaches to human behavior will strengthen and enhance HIB. Information has chiefly been conceptualized as a secondary need, that is to say, not a primary need like that of food and shelter. An evolutionary approach may support the elevation of information as a primary need, rather than a secondary need (Spink & Currier, in press).

In addition, insights into the information behaviors of past humans can shed light, on important and continually controversial issues such as how, why, and when the human race evolved. Perhaps foremost, the emerging evolutionary approach to HIB represents a shift toward a more holistic framework for HIB, not just as a modern or post-modern construct. In other words, the concepts of information seeking, organization, and use can be seen not as recent Industrial and Information age conceptualizations (Spink, 1995, 1999), but rather as millennia-spanning human behaviors that can be identified, mapped, and studied.

A more evolutionary approach to HIB promotes connections between the human past and present at all way stations along the human evolutionary path. This emerging approach has the potential to reshape the frame and refine the lens through which humans—we—are able to look at our past, present, and future behaviors in an information-relevant context. As Sagan (1979) opined, "We are the first species to have taken our evolution into our own hands" (p. 47). A more evolutionary approach to HIB continues that evolutionary process by proactively adapting and expanding our ideas and visions of HIB into the frontier of the quest for human knowledge through scientific inquiry.

Additional studies are needed to further develop the emerging more evolutionary approach to HIB and extend the chronology. The research perspective of HIB is also expanding to make the field more relevant and accessible for ordinary persons in order to assist with insights and better understanding into their own individual information behaviors and the evolution of humanity's information behaviors over the millennia.

In conclusion, we propose the following research questions that are emerging to challenge HIB research and guide the future direction of the field of evolutionary HIB:

1. What has been the chronicle and evolution of humans' information behaviors?
2. When did humans begin to develop HIBs?
3. Why did HIBs manifest and evolve in humans?
4. Have HIBs changed or developed over the centuries or past millennia?
5. Are humans' information behaviors genetically and/or environmentally derived?
6. How do information behaviors develop or evolve over a human lifetime?
7. What factors trigger changes in HIBs?
8. How does HIB evolve?
9. In what ways can the study of HIBs contribute toward a broader interdisciplinary and enhanced understanding of humankind?

References

Augst, T. (2003). *The Clerk's Tale: Young Men and Moral Life in Nineteenth-Century America*. Chicago: University of Chicago Press.

Bahn, P. (1998). *The Cambridge Illustrated History of Prehistoric Art*. New York: Cambridge University Press.

Barkow, J., Cosmides, L., & Tooby, J. (1992). *The Adapted Mind: Evolutionary Psychology and the Generation of Culture*. New York: Oxford University Press.

Bonaparte, N. (1999). In J. Luvaas (Ed.), *Napoleon on the Art of War*. New York: Simon & Schuster.

Bower, A. L. (1997). *Recipes for Reading: Community Cookbooks, Stories, Histories*. Amherst: University of Massachusetts Press.

Breen, T. H. (1989). *Imagining the Past: East Hampton Histories*. Reading, Massachusetts: Addison-Wesley Publishing Co., Inc.

Bunkers, S. L., & Huff, C. A. (Eds.) (1996). *Inscribing the Daily: Critical Essays on Women's Diaries*. Amherst: University of Massachusetts Press.

Case, D. (2002). *Looking for Information: A Survey of Research on Information Seeking, Needs, and Behavior*. San Diego: Academic Press.

Cole, C., & Leide, J. E. (2005). Human information organizing behavior. In A. Spink & C. Cole (Eds.), *New Directions in Human Information Behavior*. Springer: Berlin.

Cressy, D. (1987). *Coming Over: Migration and Communication Between England and New England in the Seventeenth Century*. Cambridge: Cambridge University Press.

Darwin, C. (1958). In N. Barlow (Ed.), *The Autobiography of Charles Darwin: 1809–1882*. New York: W.W. Norton, Inc.

Da Vinci, L. (1998). In I. A. Richter (Ed.), *The Notebooks of Leonardo Da Vinci*. Oxford: Oxford University Press.

Dervin, B. (1992). From the mind's eye of the user: The sense-making qualitative–quantitative Methodology. In J. Glazier & R. Powell (Eds.), *Qualitative Research in Information Management*, 61–84. Englewood, CO: Libraries Unlimited.

Eibi-Eibesfeldt, I., & Strachan, G. (1996). *Love and Hate: The Natural History of Behavior Patterns (Foundations of Human Behavior)*. Aldine de Gruyter: Berlin.

Ellis, J. (2002). *Founding Brothers: The Revolutionary Generation*. New York: Vintage Books.

Fleming, J. (2001). *Graffiti and the Writing Arts of Early Modern England*. Philadelphia: University of Pennsylvania Press.

Geary, P. J. (1994). *Phantoms of Remembrance: Memory and Oblivion at the End of the First Millennium*. Princeton, New Jersey: Princeton University Press.

Kaplan, S. (1992). Environmental preference in a knowledge-seeking, knowledge-using organism. In J. Barkow, L. Cosmides, & J. Tooby (Eds.), *The Adapted Mind: Evolutionary Psychology and the Generation of Culture,* 581–598. New York: Oxford University Press.

Leakey, R. (1994). *The Origin of Humankind*. New York: Basic Books.

Leakey, R., & Lewin, R. (1977). *Origins*: Rainbird Publishing.

Leakey, R., & Lewin, R. (1992a). *Origins: What New Discoveries Reveal About the Emergence of Our Species and Its Possible Future*. New York: E.P. Dutton.

Leakey, R., & Lewin, R. (1992b). *Origins Reconsidered: In Search of What Makes Us Human*. New York: Doubleday.

Madden, A. D. (2004). Evolution and information. *Journal of Documentation*, 60(1), 9–23.

Mithen, S. (1988). Looking and learning: upper palaeolithic art and information gathering. *World Archaeology*, 19(3), 297–327.

Mithen, S. (1996). *The Prehistory of the Mind: The Cognitive Origins of Art and Science*. London: Thames & Hudson.

Jewell E., & Abate F. (Eds.). (2001).*New Oxford American Dictionary*. New York: Oxford University Press.

Ouzman, S., Tacon, P., Mulvaney, K., & Fullagar, R. (2002). Extraordinary Engraved Bird Track from North Australia: Extinct Fauna, Dreaming Being and/or Aesthetic Masterpiece. *Cambridge Archaeological Journal*, 12(1), 103–112.

Payne, K. (1993). Information Collection and Transmission in Classical Greece. *Libri*, 43(4), 271–288.

Payne-Gaposchkin, C. (1996). In K. Haramundanis (Ed.), *Cecilia Payne-Gaposchkin: An Autobiography and Other Recollections*, 2nd Ed. Cambridge: Cambridge University Press.

Pfeiffer, J. (1982). *The Creative Explosion: An Inquiry into the Origins of Art and Religion*. New York: Harper & Row.

Pfeiffer, J. (1983). Was Europe's Fabulous Cave Art the Start of the Information Age? *Smithsonian*, 14, 36–45.

Pirolli, P., & Card, S. K. (1999). Information foraging. *Psychological Review*, 106, 643–675.

Russell, F. S. (1999). *Information Gathering in Classical Greece*. Ann Arbor, Michigan: University of Michigan Press.

Sagan, C. (1979). *Broca's Brain: Reflections on the Romance of Science*. New York: Random House.

Savolainen, R. (1995). Everyday life information seeking: Approaching information seeking in the context of way of life. *Library and Information Science Research*, 17, 259–294.

Schrodinger, E. (1944). What is life? (Cambridge University Press: 1992)

Settegast, M. (1986). *Plato Prehistorian: 10,000 to 5,000 B.C. in Myth and Archaeology*. Cambridge, Massachusetts: Rotenberg Press.

Spink, A. (1995). Information and sustainable development. *Libri*, 45, 203–208.

Spink, A. (1999). Information Science in Sustainable Development and De-industrialization. *Information Research: An Electronic Journal* [http://www.shef.ac.uk/~is/publications/infres], 5(1).

Spink, A., & Cole, C. (in press). Human information behavior: Integrating diverse approaches and information use. *Journal of the American Society for Information Science and Technology*.

Spink, A. & Cole, C. (2004). Introduction to information seeking research. Journal of the American Society for Information Science and Technology, 55(8), 657–659.

Spink, A., & Currier, J. (in press). Toward an evolutionary perspective for human information behavior: An exploratory study. *Journal of Documentation*.

Stonier, T. (1997). *Information and Meaning: An Evolutionary Perspective*. New York: Springer.

Tooby, J., & Cosmides, L. (1989). Evolutionary psychology and the generation of culture. Part I: Theoretical considerations. *Ethology and Sociobiology*, 10, 29–49.

Ulrich, L. T. (1990). *A Midwifes Tale: The Life of Martha Ballard: Based on Her Diary, 1785–1812*. New York: Vintage Books.

Washington, B. T. (1963). *Up from Slavery: An Autobiography*. Garden City, New York: Doubleday & Company, Inc.

Wilson, T. (2000). Human information behavior. *Informing Science*, 3(2), 49–55.

Chapter 3

Information Behavior in Pre-literate Societies

Andrew D. Madden and Jared Bryson
Department of Information Studies
University of Sheffield

Joe Palimi
School of Business Administration
University of Papua New Guinea

1. INTRODUCTION

Ong (1988, p. 10) refers to "the relentless dominance of textuality in the scholarly mind". As studies of Everyday Life Information Seeking (ELIS) show (Carey, McKechnie, & McKenzie, 2001; McKenzie, 2002), human information behavior (HIB) includes far more than just the use of text. Humans seeking information will generally seek it from other people before looking to a written source (Ellis, Cox, & Hall, 1993; Shenton, 2003). However, information behaviors associated with text are probably the easiest to examine and so have been the most studied. This chapter provides a new direction in HIB research by considering information behavior in societies where the seeker of information has no opportunity to resort to text.

For almost all of the thousand or so centuries that humans have been around, we have sought and exchanged information without using writing. This chapter looks at one society where, until recently, there was no awareness of writing. It discusses that society's relationships with information and uses examples from archeology and biology to put those relationships into a broader context.

In this chapter, we aim to:

* explore some of the ways in which the demands of a pre-literate society determined the information needs of its members and shaped information roles within that society;
* show how the information roles identified relate to life in a modern, literate society;
* discuss how and why text-based information sources have dominated the development of Information Science;
* explore some of the consequences of that dominance.

2. BACKGROUND

Information Science has been a pragmatic discipline. It grew from the need to organize documents in ways that facilitated retrieval; but the studies associated with this task have

A. Spink and C. Cole (eds), New Directions in Human Information Behavior, 33–53.
© 2006 *Springer.*

raised questions that impinged on several other disciplines, including computer science, business and management studies, education, and psychology. The themes explored in this chapter are something of a departure from existing Information Science literature. The first and third author of this chapter have, respectively, experience in biological and archeological sciences. Of most interest, however, is the background of the second author.

Joe Palimi is a member of the Kope Tribe (pronounced "Koppi") from the Western Highlands Province in the Central Highlands of Papua New Guinea. He studied for several years in Papua New Guinea, Australia, and the United Kingdom, but this chapter draws on his experiences as a member of a technologically unsophisticated society; and puts those experiences into the context of human and cultural evolution in general. As such, it accords with the views of Spink and Cole (in press) that Information Science, in addition to drawing on the disciplines listed above, can benefit from an anthropological perspective. In compiling this chapter, we are working with a definition of information suggested by Madden (2004): that is, that information is a stimulus that expands or amends the World View of whoever (or whatever) is being informed.

2.1 The Kope Tribe of Papua New Guinea

Anthropologists describe the most primitive unit of society as a *band*. Bands comprise around 25–100 members: they are usually hunter-gatherers and tend to be extended families. Bands are nomadic, without hierarchy, and none of their members has a specialized role. In regions where there is a rich supply of food, or where agriculture has begun to develop, bands may merge to form tribes (such as the Kope). These are substantially larger bodies of people, sharing the same language and usually with fixed villages. There is little more specialization than with bands, but there is a rudimentary hierarchy (Service, 1971).

The Kope is a tribe of around 5000 Melpa-speaking Melanesians based in the Western Highlands Province in the Central Highlands of Papua New Guinea. Traditionally, they were hunter-gatherers and subsistence farmers with a technology based on tools made from materials derived from plants, animals, and stones. The Kope tribe is divided into clans which comprise a number of settlements based on extended families. Polygamy was traditionally a common practice, so extended families can be very large. Family settlements may be several hundred meters apart, but there is always a central meeting house called the manga rapa or round house. This is usually the residence of the clan leader.

The manga rapa is the focal point of the community; and men of the clan would meet there frequently for business and social purposes. Most important decisions took place in the manga rapa. If any decisions required expenses however, they had to be cleared with the women of the tribe, who were custodians of the men's wealth (which usually took the form of pigs). The manga rapa was built at the end of a rectangular field (moka pena) the size of a football pitch. This was used for open-air meetings, dances, trading, etc.

The Kope's first contact with Western culture was in 1930 when some Australian prospectors wandered into their territory (Connolly & Anderson, 1987). The prospectors, the Leahy (pronounced *lay*) brothers, were the first white people the Kope had seen. Initially, the pale visitors were thought to be ghosts; but after the Kope had observed long enough to conclude that the men were human, they made themselves known. Several members of the tribe who were children at the time of this meeting are still alive, including Joe's father. Given the inaccessibility of the Western Highlands Province, contact with

Western society remained intermittent until after World War II when missionaries began to arrive. As a result, the tribe's culture remained largely unaffected until the late 1940s.

2.2 Information Uses in the Kope Tribe

In text-based societies, we read in order to be informed, inspired, educated, or entertained. In pre-literate societies, such divisions are alien. Tribal myths, histories, and technologies are remembered as stories, songs, and dances. Tellers of religious tales recount the origins of the tribe and its land; and in so doing may impart lessons on how to hunt, what to eat, and how to manage the environment. Tribal dances may be ritualized interpretations of technology, with the movements providing lessons in how to build a house or fashion a weapon (Guss, 1989). Alternatively, they may be used for organizing. In the Kope, for example, most dances are standard and unvarying. The exception is the war dance, which is used to help plan battle tactics.

From the perspective of a literate information scientist, however, tribal information can be regarded as performing three main functions for the Kope:

1. defining tribal identity,
2. preserving social networks, and
3. promulgation of practical skills.

2.2.1 Defining Tribal Identity Through History and Mythology

Like all other communities, the Kope are interested in news and gossip; and storytelling plays a significant part in their culture. However, traditionally, one of the more serious purposes of storytelling is the preservation of the tribe's history, which was remembered and passed on from generation to generation.

2.2.2 Preserving Social Networks

Kinship hierarchies in a polygamous society are both complex and important. The clan provides a system of mutual support, but with it come reciprocal obligations. To avoid or resolve conflicts, it is necessary to be able to recall accurately the links and associations between relatives. Marriages between clans are forbidden, but not marriages between tribes: even warring tribes.

2.2.3 Promulgation of Practical Skills, Including Hunting, House-Building, and Agronomy

Before their contact with Western culture, the Kope were, of necessity, generalists. The clan groups were too small to support specialists, so all the skills required for survival had to be acquired by all members of the tribe. Since plant and animal materials were commonly used, not only for food, but also for building and toolmaking, the Kope have a very detailed knowledge of the local flora and fauna and their uses. Such an in-depth applied knowledge of botany and zoology amongst all members of a pre-literate society seems widespread. Lévi-Strauss (1966) cites numerous incidences of Western biologists being astounded by the ability of native peoples to classify and to identify large numbers of indigenous organisms.

3. TRIBAL POLITICS

Leadership amongst the Kope has never been hereditary: leaders were chosen on merit. The tight network of family connections helped to make the biases and motivations of aspiring leaders' common knowledge, and their skills would have been on display to all. The main role of the tribal leader was to represent his tribe in inter-tribal negotiations. In consequence, the most important skill for a chief was oratory. He would need to be well versed in local history and politics, but not only was his knowledge important, so too was the skill with which he presented it.

Strathern (1984) contrasts this with the practice in the Eastern Highlands of Papua New Guinea, where leadership was tied up with prowess in warfare, rather than leadership through trading and exchange. As a result, where the hierarchies in the Eastern Highlands were destroyed by contact with Europeans, those in the Western Highlands were "... *in a sense, enhanced ... The oral history of politics was preserved, developed, and constantly brought into play*" (Strathern, 1984, p. 23).

It could be argued that a key difference between the cultures of the Eastern and Western Highlands was that, while the Eastern tribes prized military prowess, their Western counterparts recognized the value of knowledge and information.

4. PRESENTATION OF INFORMATION

Because the tribe's history and politics were widely known, a leader (or "Big Man") was judged, not by the information he gave, but by the way in which it was presented. Like all politicians, Kope orators make considerable use of wit, metaphor, and simile, allowing them to present information in a way that suits their case, while being entertaining. Such use of imagery in presenting information helps to place it in a context selected by the presenter. Use of inappropriate imagery, however, makes the message uninformative. As an example of this, the first missionaries to visit the Kope had considerable difficulty in explaining their beliefs to a people who had never had sheep. The idea of "The Lamb of God" proved to be more confusing than enlightening. Given that the Kope's usual sacrificial animal was a small pig (Strathern, 1984), a more appropriate description of Jesus would have been the "Piglet of God".

5. INITIATION AND RELIGION

Although the Kope no longer practice initiation ceremonies, many neighboring tribes still do. Such ceremonies usually involve teaching the initiates necessary survival skills and testing their knowledge of the tribe's traditions and beliefs. Under pressure from missionaries, many indigenous religions in the Highlands of Papua New Guinea were discouraged (Strathern, 1984). Prior to the arrival of the missionaries, however, the Kope did have a well-established religion based on ancestor worship (Ross, 1936). As with other aspects of Kope culture, however, religious roles were not hereditary. Because there was no partitioning of knowledge into history, arts, technology, and religion, activities and rites that, to the literate observer, might seem religious, could combine spiritual and mnemonic functions. All however, were important in allowing all participants to feel integrated into the tribe.

6. REPOSITORIES OF KNOWLEDGE

As has traditionally been the case in most societies, the elderly are repositories of tribal knowledge. Even today, with many Kope living and working around the world, tribal links are strong. From a Kope perspective, if someone is not part of a tribe, then he or she is nobody. The people who hold the memory of the tribe's culture to a large extent shape the identity of all members of the tribe. In a sense, this role contributed to the tribe's religion. Like many societies, the Kope were ancestor worshippers. Knowledgeable, wise, and skillful members of the tribe could therefore be consulted, even after death.

7. INFORMATION ROLES IN THE KOPE TRIBE

The various information sources and flows discussed above can be summarized by arguing that the flow of information from source to target depends on a number of information roles within the Kope community that determine how information is used, and what it is used for.

- *Induction*—The passing on of the knowledge and skills needed to make a person a fully contributing member of the tribe. To be inducted into tribal society, children need to have an understanding of the tribe's culture, and sufficient knowledge of the local environment to provide for themselves and any families they may have. In the Kope, a boy, once inducted, was permitted to enter the manga rapa and join in the discussions relating to clan business.
- *Dissemination*—The spreading of news and stories. This may be local gossip, concerning the activities of tribal members; it may be news brought back from traders about the goings on in neighboring tribes; or it may be reports from hunters and gatherers about the movements of prey or the location of useful plants.
- *Presentation*—The ability to select and express information in a way that best suits the interests of a representative and those of his family, or of the clan that he represents.
- *Organization*—The sharing of information to co-ordinate group activities, such as hunting, warfare, and trade.
- *Interpretation*—The ability to derive information. Most obviously, this is done by trackers who "read" the landscape in order to determine the movements of prey; but it is also valuable in social interactions for interpreting motives and anticipating actions.
- *Preservation*—The retention of tribal history, culture, and expertise by the elderly.

The Kope is only one tribe, and caution should be exercised if generalizing from a single instance; but the roles described above have obvious parallels in most societies. Some of these are discussed below.

8. DERIVED INFORMATION

Of the six information roles listed above, five are related to the exchange of information. Interpretation is the exception and relates to innate abilities. Indeed, from the perspective of the information scientist, an appropriate definition of intelligence would be "the ability to derive useful information from the environment", whether the environment be physical, social, economic, or cultural. This ability, coupled with an intimate understanding of the environment and the nuances of change, facilitates serendipitous acquisition of information (Foster & Ford, 2003) and is especially important in a society that depends on hunting and gathering, where survival can depend on derived information.

Spink and Cole (in press), in summarizing theories of sense-making (e.g., Dervin, 1992, 1999) suggest that such theorizing about the world may be hard-wired. This view accords with that of Gibson (1986), who argues that humans perceive their environment and the objects it contains, not in terms of measurable qualities, such as height, weight, color, etc., but in terms of what useful service they may perform. So, a barren hillock is not seen as being 100 m high, it is "high enough to help me see above the trees"; a stone is not thought of as 1 kg in weight, it is "heavy enough for me to crack nuts with"; and a dark red soil is not considered to be reflecting light of approximately 750 nm, but "will be good for marking my face and body with". In other words, people view their surroundings in terms of what actions they afford.

Gibson (1986) refers to the properties that allow these actions, as affordances. Such behavior is an example of hard-wired theorizing in infants, who first notice the affordance or meaning of an object and then learn its particular qualities or attributes (e.g., the substance, surface, color, and form of the object) (Madden et al., 2003).

From the perspective of a Kope hunter, changes in the environment afford information concerning an animal's whereabouts. So, a Kope hunter may look at a fallen fruit beneath a tree. He is not interested in the type of fruit, but in what might have been eating it. If there are bite marks, he will learn what creature is in the tree above him. Or the hunter, on finding the puppies of a wild dog, may feel the lair to see how warm it is. He is not interested in the temperature as an absolute property of the lair, but because it will help him to learn about the movements of the mother. If the lair is warm, the hunter will infer that the mother has only just left to find food and will not be back for a while. If it is cold, she may return soon, so he leaves quickly.

Carruthers (2000) argues that scientific reasoning has its roots in the art of tracking. Both the scientist and the tracker infer from the observed to the unobserved; and thus derive information about the world.

9. INTRA- AND INTER-GENERATIONAL COMMUNICATION

Of the five information roles associated with the exchange of information amongst the Kope, three deal with the sharing of information amongst contemporaries (dissemination, presentation, and organization) while the remaining two relate to the transmission of information to future generations. One of the key differences between tribal society and industrial/post-industrial societies is the level of specialization. The Kope were, of necessity, generalists. Age and sex played a part in the roles a Kope may be able to fulfill; but all members of the tribe had an understanding and appreciation of every task, making them well able to judge whether or not they were being adequately performed. This included the information roles listed above. A Kope's assessment of information would, to a large degree, be based on his or her evaluation of the person providing it.

In the modern world, in contrast, people specialize in one or more of the roles. Huge industries have arisen around the dissemination of news and stories. Advertizers, legal representatives, and politicians go to considerable efforts to present information in ways that best suit the interests of themselves or their clients. Managers, consultants, and systems analysts are paid great sums of money to ensure that organizational information reaches the right people at the right time. Teachers and lecturers are paid rather less money to ensure that students are inculcated with the knowledge and values needed to function appropriately and effectively in society.

This latter information role, induction, has arguably grown in scope with increasing levels of specialization. For the Kope, induction into the community usually meant the initiation of children into adulthood; hence the above description of induction being an instance of inter-generational information exchange. In our society, however, with growing numbers of communities of interest, induction can be intra-generational.

The nature of a community will determine the nature of any form of induction. Professional communities, for example, will normally require prospective members to have appropriate qualifications. These will be determined by the community's representative body and administered by those responsible for induction. The jargon and other arcane language of many expert communities have led to their being perceived as:

"Priestly groups [which] effect and maintain power by possessing significant cultural secrets. Training in the codes and rituals of these secrets is characteristically arduous, often lengthy, and reserved to elites" (Marvin, 1988, p. 39).

Preservation is the information role most commonly associated with Information Science. It involves librarians, archivists, and museum curators, and will be discussed more fully later in this chapter.

10. MACRO- AND MICRO-INFORMATION STUDIES

Although specialists now perform each of the six information roles discussed above, people in ELIS, within their own "small world" (Spink and Cole, in press), will still perform all of these roles to some degree. It may be useful, therefore, for the information scientist to borrow from the economist and refer to macro- and micro-information situations. In macro situations, for example, specialist information roles are developed and refined; and processes are introduced to ensure that information can be retrieved that is appropriate and of adequate quality. Methods can be developed and standards established, so that professional presenters, disseminators, etc. can assess the work of their counterparts across the world. In micro-information situations, in contrast, people would have the ability to assess the communities and environments in which they live and work.

11. REPOSITORIES OF KNOWLEDGE AND CULTURAL TRANSMISSION

Culture, to an anthropologist, is "Information affecting their phenotype acquired by individuals by imitation or teaching" (Boyd & Richerson, 1985). Culture therefore refers not only to the artistic expression of a civilization, but also to all the practices that define it, from its belief systems to the way it prepares its vegetables. The success with which aspects of a culture are transmitted from one generation to the next helps to determine the stability and durability of a civilization. As will be discussed later, there are many instances of technology playing a role in cultural transmission; but the most readily available means of passing on culture in a pre-literate society is to rely on the memory of older generations.

Care of the elderly has a long history within human and pre-human society. Archeologists in France, for example, have found a hominid jawbone 150–200 thousand years old (from the Middle Pleistocene period) which provides evidence of an individual being kept alive for some time after most of his or her teeth had been lost (Lebel et al., 2001). Behavior of this sort is mirrored today in tribal societies such as Papua New Guinea, where old, virtually toothless Papua New Guineans eat food that is chewed by their children and spat into a bowl (Diamond, 2001).

That such behavior should have remained a feature of human society for so long, suggests that it has evolutionary significance; an idea recently given support by studies of historic data from Canada and Finland. Lahdenperä et al. (2004) found that, if a woman survives beyond menopause, her offspring is likely to have more children of their own, and those children are more likely to survive beyond childhood. Consequently, genes that increase the chance of surviving beyond reproductive age in women are being selected. Since many of these genes will be the same for both men and women, longevity is likely to increase throughout the population.

Lahdenperä et al. (2004) do not suggest reasons why the presence of a post-reproductive mother increases the likelihood of children surviving to adulthood. One probable reason for this is the accumulated knowledge of the grandmother. Evidence from Kenya suggests that this is the case with elephants. McComb et al. (2001) have found that family units of elephants display greater social confidence if they have older matriarchs. This appears to be linked to the fact that older females are able to remember the calls of a greater number of elephants. If elephants hear a call they do not recognize, they display defensive behavior. The frequency of such behavior was lowest amongst groups led by older matriarchs, who, the authors infer, are acting as repositories of social knowledge.

Joe Palimi notes the exceptional clarity of recall of the older, illiterate members of his tribe. Even in literate societies, however, where memory loss is regarded as a common feature of old age, it tends to be short-term memory that is impaired. Nelson (2003), in discussing the role of autobiographical memory, stresses the role of communal narratives in defining and sustaining cultures. Throughout most of human history, culture changed very slowly; so what was learned in childhood would serve throughout the whole of life, without there being a need to keep learning new skills and stories. Arguably therefore, there is more selection pressure for people to remember for a long time, than for them to carry on learning into old age.

The role of the elderly as repositories of public knowledge not only plays a part in preserving tribal identity, but also is of considerable practical importance. At times, tribal survival can depend on the knowledge of the elderly. Diamond (2001) recalls a visit, in 1976, to one of the Solomon Islands, where he learned that tree species were categorized according to whether they were inedible, fully edible, or only to be eaten in famine times.

None of his middle-aged informants could tell him which trees fell into the latter category, so they introduced him to a woman who had been a child in 1910 when a particularly destructive cyclone struck the island. Many of the trees bearing "fully edible" fruit had been destroyed, so the islanders had resorted to eating foods that, though nutritious, were presumably less palatable. The old woman was the only person in the community who had lived through the disaster and was the only person who could recall what foodstuffs they had resorted to. Had there been a similar disaster therefore, the old woman's memory may have saved the tribe from starvation.

12. CULTURAL TRANSMISSION THROUGH SIGNS

It is widely acknowledged that, in pre-literate cultures, hearing was the sense most commonly associated with exchange of information (McLuhan, 1964; Ong, 1988; Shanks & Tilley, 1987). According to McLuhan (1964):

"The dominant organ of sensory and social orientation in the pre-alphabet societies was the ear—'hearing was believing.' The phonetic alphabet forced the magic world of the ear to yield to the neutral world of the eye. Man was given an eye for an ear" (p. 44).

Certainly, most of the information roles identified above would have involved auditory rather then visual transmission of information; and preservation of information would have depended on frequent and formulaic repetition. Memory, to a pre-literate:

"... is not so much a thing as an act, a gestalt uniting bard and audience in a shared consciousness. This phenomenon has little in common with that desiccated thing we literates call "memory." In the world before writing, memory is the social act of remembering. It is commemoration" (Hobart & Schiffman, 1998, p. 15).

Nevertheless, McLuhan's emphasis perhaps understates the role of the visual. Color and imagery commonly play a part in pre-literate cultures, not only in ritual, but also in the exchange of information. During a tribal war for example, a member of the enemy tribe with relatives among the Kope may stick his tongue out at them. This would inform them that they are moving toward an ambush and so should approach with caution. Alternatively, the relative may hand over a knotted leaf. The Kope recipient would then know that he was a target for assassination.

Other means of transmitting information visually amongst the Kope include the use of body paint, for example, black for war, red for funerals, or blue for a widow in mourning. People also wear ornaments. A Big Man may advertize his wealth by wearing a necklace of small bamboo tubes, with each tube representing a quantity of wealth (usually measured in pigs or shell money).

Another example of the use of signs is the placing of markers to delineate the boundaries of regions. If a wanderer steps beyond the marker, he or she may be in trouble, perhaps because a crop has just been planted and the farmer does not wish it to be trampled, or perhaps because they are walking on taboo ground and will offend the spirits. If a Kope sees a certain type of leaf tied to a stake or a tree beside a path, he or she will know that entry to that path is restricted.

Such manipulation of the landscape as a means of marking routes is by no means a solely human practice. Wood mice, for example, have been found to distribute markers (twigs, leaves, etc.) when exploring. If they are startled, the mice will dash for cover. The markers help them to return quickly to the site of their earlier exploration (Stopka & Macdonald, 2003). Humans, like wood mice, use such devices as an *aide memoir*; but humans also use them to convey information to others from their culture. Those capable of interpreting the devices, therefore, can benefit from the experience of the explorer without needing to do the exploring themselves.

13. UNRELIABILITY OF CULTURAL TRANSMISSION

When a society becomes sufficiently stable, it begins to manipulate the landscape by producing permanent structures. Many of these, such as residences and storehouses, have an obvious function. Other structures, often the largest and most ornate ones, are less easy to understand, except for people from the society that created them. As a means of transmitting information from generation to generation, they were only effective when reinforced by the rituals, or "social act of remembering" that imbued them with meaning.

It has been common throughout human history and pre-history for some societies to dominate and ultimately assimilate other societies. One means of doing so is the prohibition of the rituals that gave identity to the dominated society. An oral culture, and the identities of those belonging to that culture, resides:

> "in the living memories of successive living people who are young and then old and then die . . . [and is preserved by] the rhythmic word organized cunningly in verbal and metrical patterns which were unique enough to retain their shape" (Havelock, 1963, pp. 42–43).

If such mnemonic rituals and rhymes are suppressed or prevented therefore, after a few generations the communal memory will be lost, and with it, the meaning assigned to the material representations of that culture.

An archeologist, given the relics of that culture in situ may, and by applying various techniques and by analogy with apparently similar cultures, attempt to discern some of the meanings that were attached to those relics. In the absence of written records, however, any picture that emerges will be sketchy and possibly misleading. Imagine, for example, an archeologist, ignorant of Christianity, coming across the ruins of ancient churches in Western Europe. One obvious feature common to all the ruins would be their east to west orientation. It would not be unreasonable to assume that this related in some way to the passage of the sun throughout the day.

Such fundamentally attractive, but demonstratively inaccurate attributions of meaning are not unknown in archeology, and remain current in popular consciousness long after they have been abandoned by archeologists. One of the most famous examples is that of Stonehenge, the well-known megalithic monument in the South West of England. This example of ritualized landscape from a pre-literate society was constructed over many generations during the early Bronze Age (ca. 3000–1500 B.C.), with each generation introducing additional features and with them, more associated meaning to the landscape.

In the 1960s, it was noted that several astronomical alignments coincided with certain key features of Stonehenge. This led to the theory that Stonehenge must have acted as a form of observatory. However, subsequent research revealed that these alignments are fortuitous (English Heritage, 1996, p. 20); so:

> "despite strong popular belief... Stonehenge did not incorporate precise astronomical alignments and did not function as an ancient 'observatory'" (Ruggles, 1996, p. 15).

Although archeologists cannot say what Stonehenge meant to its builders, they have good reason to suppose that it meant a great deal. Four to five hundred years after the first Stonehenge was built, huge stones from Wales were added to it (English Heritage, 1996). How Bronze Age technology could have quarried stones weighing up to 4 tonnes, and then moved those hundreds of kilometers, is the subject of much speculation. What is not in dispute is the fact that it would have required a great deal of effort; so it is not unreasonable to suppose that Stonehenge was considered important by those who built or commissioned it. Knowledge of why it was important however, like most of the monuments of pre-history, died many centuries ago.

14. WRITING AND CULTURAL TRANSMISSION

Writing, in contrast, provided a memory that did not fade. Even today, over 5000 years after their creation, records of transactions can be read '(Schmandt-Besserat, 1997). Without those records, the different interests of the transacting parties would have been represented by their own memories and the memories of witnesses, all of which would have been subject to change, to bias and, of course, to death.

Writing did not only offer a way of preserving transactions and accounts however. By 2900 B.C. (around 300 years before the builders of Stonehenge moved stones from Wales), it had developed to a level where it could also provide a means of preserving and disseminating histories and legends (Schmandt-Besserat, 1997). Once preserved in this way, they became canon. They became the standard against which all other versions of histories and legends could be compared. Documents could be copied and distributed around a realm and would provide fixed reference points. A central administration would know that its instructions were being relayed precisely, to all parts of the realm, without undergoing change through inaccurate recall (either accidental or deliberate).

Groups of people, making "parallel use of texts, both to structure the internal behavior of the groups' members and to provide solidarity against the outside world" are described by Stock (1983, p. 90), as "textual communities". Most obviously today, they include adherents to the world's major religions; but legal codes, written constitutions, bodies of rules, and the standard texts of many academic disciplines, produce other examples of textual communities.

15. REACTIONS TO WRITING AMONG PRE-LITERATES

When and how writing began is the subject of much discussion amongst archeologists. Of necessity, its origins were in pre-literate society and are therefore the subject of myth rather than history. What myths there are, however, are instructive. Our writing system has its roots around 4000 years ago in Mesopotamia. According to a Sumerian myth, writing was the invention of Enmerkar, the lord of Kulaba. He sent an emissary to another lord to ask for materials to help rebuild the residence of the Goddess Inanna. The emissary traveled back and forth between the two lords, passing on their messages verbatim; until 1 day Enmerkar's instructions proved too difficult to memorize. The lord of Kulaba then promptly invented writing and the messages were committed to clay tablets rather than to the memory of the emissary (Schmandt-Besserat, 1997). As Schmandt-Besserat notes, however, Enmerkar lived around 2700 B.C. when writing had been common practice for 500 years.

Perhaps the best-known myth surrounding the origin of writing is that recounted to Phaedrus by Socrates (Plato, 2002). According to Socrates, the Egyptian God Theuth invented writing, and demonstrated it to the God Thamous (or Amon). Writing, Theuth explained, would "increase the intelligence of the people of Egypt and improve their memories".

Both accounts stress the role of writing as a support for memory. In Plato's story, Socrates famously goes on to express reservations about the value of writing; but modern accounts of pre-literate people encountering writing for the first time show a rapid appreciation of its value. Joe Palimi recalls an encounter that took place while he was a student. While on vacation from university in the 1980s, he sat beneath a tree, reading a novel. An old man, after watching him for over an hour, came and asked what he was doing. The man may have been aware of the existence of reading, but had never seen it being done. Joe explained that the book contained representations of words and that he was listening to those words. Over the next few days, Joe recounted the story in the novel to the old man, who was both amazed and angry. Why, he wondered, had not the white man come sooner so that he too could have learned this secret?

Lévi-Strauss (1974) tells of his experiences with the Nambikwara tribe of Brazil in the 1930s, and recalls their response on seeing him write. Most members of the tribe were content merely to draw wavy horizontal lines in imitation of his writing:

> "... but the chief had further ambitions. No doubt he was the only one who had grasped the purpose of writing ... if I asked for information on a given point, he did not supply it verbally but drew wavy lines on his paper and presented them to me ... As soon as he had got the company together, he took from a basket a piece of

paper covered with wavy lines and made a show of reading it.... Was he perhaps hoping to delude himself? More probably he wanted to ... convince [his companions] that he was ... in alliance with the white man and shared his secrets" (Lévi-Strauss, 1974, p. 388).

If these accounts are put into the context of the six information roles identified earlier, it is interesting to note that two of them (the myth of Enmerkar and the account of the Nambikwara chief) recognize the value of writing as a means of accurately transmitting organizational information. As stated in the previous section, it was only after many years that writing was used to preserve histories and legends.

16. PRE-LITERATE AND POST-LITERATE CONSCIOUSNESS

The myth of Theuth and Thamous is an invention of Plato (2002), but it was written in a society where, although writing was a widely used tool, the culture was primarily oral. Speech was an extension of the speaker, and the idea of externalizing it remained alien to such an extent that, even as late as the end of the fourth century A.D., St. Jerome (the patron saint of libraries and librarians) was considered remarkable because he read without speaking the words out loud (Manguel, 1994). However:

"At some time towards the end of the fifth century before Christ, it became possible for a few Greeks to talk about their 'souls' as though they had selves or personalities which were autonomous and not fragments of the atmosphere nor of a cosmic life force, but what we might call entities or real substances" (Havelock, 1963, p. 197).

Havelock attributes this change to the switch from an orally memorized tradition to one in which memory is supplemented by text. Around 100 years later, Plato, through the persona of Socrates, criticized writing because it would make people "remember things by relying on marks made by others, from outside themselves, not on their own inner resources" (Plato, 2002, p. 69).

As we saw earlier, the use of route markers amongst pre-literates already made this possible to some extent, by allowing people to benefit from the explorations of others. Writing expanded this facility to levels that even Lévi-Strauss's canny Nambikwara chief would have found difficult to grasp. Havelock implies that there was a change in the nature of consciousness arising from textuality, but Dennett (1993) states it. A post-literate consciousness, Dennett (1993) argues:

"... can exist only in an environment that has not just language and social interaction, but writing and diagramming as well, simply because the demands on memory and pattern recognition for its implementation require the brain to "off-load" some of its memories into buffers in the environment" (p. 220).

Before the development of text, knowledge was inseparable from the knower. As societies became literate however, it became possible to stand aside from what was known and to review it. Carruthers (2000), in considering the roots of scientific reasoning, argues that there is no difference between the cognitive abilities of the hunter tracking prey, and the scientist drawing inferences from data. What is different, however, is the extent to which scientific activity can draw on external resources; in particular, the prop of the written word.

A pre-literate hunter-gatherer, for example, cannot learn from the writings of a zoologist. He can draw only on his experience and the experience of those in his tribe that taught him. But his teachers, in turn, are drawing on the collected memories of a limited community. Zoologists, in contrast, have learned a great deal from the recorded observations of pre-literate trackers from many hunter-gatherer communities.

17. RESPECT FOR WRITING

To a society in transition from orality to literacy, writing could be seen to give life to memories that otherwise may have died out in a few generations; it provided an impartial witness to business transactions; and statements of law and belief became an immortal presence that outlived the law givers and priests. Those few who could read and write, therefore, were in a powerful position. Their mouths gave voice to the words of Gods and rulers. Given the close association in oral societies between the knower and the knowledge, and between the speaker and the words, some of the respect due to Gods and kings would have been accorded to those who spoke their words. The same awe was accorded to the writings themselves. Joe Palimi describes an incident in the 1950s when one of his clansmen burned a piece of paper. The tribal elders promptly cursed the man.

The paper had details of the contributions expected from each clan toward the cost of a new van, and the man who burnt the paper considered them unfair. But most dealings with the outside world came through missionaries, who had introduced the Kope to the written word in the form of the Bible. Since none of the elders could read, they had no way of knowing whether the piece of paper bore something sacred or something trivial. Those Kope clansmen in the 1950s were in the same position as most people who have lived in a society undergoing the change from orality to literacy. Literacy, throughout most of history, has been rare. Those initiated into the knowledge stored in written documents guarded that knowledge. In temple libraries in ancient Mesopotamia, for example, inscriptions at the end of religious and scientific texts often carried the restriction that only those who were competent should be shown the religious and scientific text, but they were not to be shown to the uninitiated (Black, 2004).

For the illiterate majority, documents bearing text became a symbol of knowledge, power, and sacredness. In a purely oral culture, the symbols of knowledge, power, and sacredness had, associated with them, rituals and communal acts of remembering that involved the whole community; but now, the full power of the symbol could only be accessed through a literate intermediary. The painstaking reproduction of texts meant that, for centuries, only the most significant of documents were copied and preserved. A single copy of the Bible might take up to 3 years to produce (Gutenberg Digital, 2004). Then, between 1452 and 1455, one man in Mainz, Germany, produced around 200 Bibles (Presser, 1974).

The invention by Johannes Gutenberg of the printing press with moveable type turned the production of textual documents into a large-scale commercial enterprise. Within 50 years, books were being printed in almost every European country. By 1500, more than 10 million copies of 40,000 different books had been printed (Presser, 1974). The introduction of the steam press in the early 19th century, followed by the invention of Linotype in 1884 made printed texts widely available and affordable. In the industrialized world, reading and writing were no longer associated with an influential few, but were being taught at all levels of society. Literate intermediaries became commonplace.

Although the advent of printing provided increased opportunities for reading, the barriers to publication remained formidable. People being published were often exceptionally talented and were certainly educated far beyond the norm. (Being wealthy, well connected, and male also significantly contributed to the chance of publication of course). Furthermore, a published work generally represented the efforts of a community, usually comprising not only the author, but also editors and financiers. Consequently, it was in the interests of several people to ensure that the work could be defended. Published documents, therefore, were usually considered reliable at the time of going to press. Where they expressed opinions, they were the opinions of influential people.

Published documents became artifacts that represent knowledge. A person making a contested statement can often satisfy the demand that they "*prove it!*" by pointing to an appropriate text. The association between knowledge and publication is such that the deliberate destruction of texts is considered shocking. The burning of books, such as that carried out in Nazi, Germany in May 1933, has become a modern symbol of barbarism; but people are upset by rather less extreme incidences of the destruction of texts.

In 1992, for example, while Andrew Madden was working as a biologist at the Natural Resources Institute in Kent, UK, a new librarian was appointed. Within weeks of his appointment, skips were hired and were soon filled with books and papers. Tim Cullen, the librarian in question, still recalls with frustration, the outcry that ensued. Those documents, some of his critics argued, went back decades and were part of the Institute's long tradition. Tim Cullen's response was to point out that the documents had not been looked at for decades; no one had wanted them when he had offered them around, and he needed to make space for texts that would be looked at. To those who protested however, published texts, regardless of their content, remained a symbol of knowledge.

18. ONLINE PUBLISHING

One year earlier, in 1991, the World Wide Web was released (Berners-Lee, 1999), making it possible to disseminate documents among a potential readership that rapidly grew into hundreds of millions. Where previously the opportunities for reaching a worldwide readership were limited to very few people, now the barriers to publication became trivial.

McLuhan (1964) discusses the tendency of people to accommodate to new technologies by relating them to existing, familiar ones, and the Internet is clearly no exception. The perception of the Internet as a bookstore or library is widespread, even amongst expert users (Ratzan, 2000). In an unpublished survey in March 2003, Madden asked 176 students at a Sheffield school to indicate on a five-point Likert scale, the extent to which they agreed or disagreed with a series of statements about the Internet. Eighty-six percentage of the students (aged 11–16 years) agreed that "The Internet is like a library". When the same questionnaire was circulated amongst delegates of the "Internet

Librarian" International 2003 Conference, only 10 of the 29 respondents disagreed with the statement (though nine neither agreed nor disagreed).

Clearly, therefore, even some experienced users of the Internet are inclined to regard it as some kind of electronic book collection. With that perception comes the risk that people transfer to the Internet the respect that they accord to books.

19. INFORMATION ROLES AND THE INTERNET

Text, as has been stated, developed from providing a useful means of exchanging organizational information to become, in time, a reliable way of preserving information. It was this latter role that led to text-based information sources being held in such high regard. With real (as opposed to virtual) text, there are certain, widely recognized indicators of quality associated with the presentation of information. As has been said, the fact that something has been published is an indication that several people have assigned value to the text.

Aspects of presentation, however, are also considered when judging the information transmitted by a text. So, for example, if, next to the paperback edition of a text, there is a leather-bound version with expensive paper, it suggests that the text is particularly valued. While the quality of a book's binding does not guarantee the quality of its contents, it seems reasonable to suppose that there is a correlation. There are probably more leather-bound editions of Plato sold than of pulp Westerns.

With the Internet, however, there are no such conventions. A sophisticated, well laid out Website may be the product of a professional publisher, or it may have been produced by a technically competent 15 years old with pirate software, who copied the design from another Website. Even the worst of books, in contrast, has been subject to some quality control (unless published through a vanity press). Experienced users of the Internet will be aware of this: inexperienced users, believing the Internet to be some sort of electronic library, may not. Such an unquestioning acceptance of professional-looking documents on the Web helps to account for the numerous cases of naïve Web users who, following the directions in a hoax e-mail, go to a Website that resembles their bank's, and enter all their bank details. Admittedly, such people are at the more credulous end of the spectrum of inexperienced Web users. A more common response is one of disappointment and frustration at the number of unhelpful, misleading, and plainly inaccurate sites.

The Web, though, is not primarily used as a means of preserving information, but as a means of exchanging it. It is used for the presentation and dissemination of information; and uses the information exchanged for the purposes of induction and organization. Rather than comparing the Web to a library, it would be more meaningful to regard it as a collection of monologs. Madden (2003), for example, has suggested that a more appropriate analogy than a library would be a bar-room, because most of its users are men, and most of the talk is of sex and sport. However, "among the bar-room bores are many people who come to do business and many others who can talk knowledgeably and enthusiastically about their interests" (Madden, 2003, p. 18).

Although documents on the Web are preserved; for many (perhaps most) the preservation is incidental. Whereas the authors of traditionally published texts need to convince a real audience of the text's merits before it will be printed, many (perhaps most) authors of documents on the Web are speaking to a wholly imagined audience. What the author says is of interest to him or her; which is reason enough to say it. At one time, it was sufficient for people in information professions to concentrate on the organization and retrieval of documents. Now, it is increasingly important that they consider means of evaluating them.

20. WRITING AND INFORMATION SCIENCE

The influence of written information sources on society is hard to overstate. Indeed, Diamond (1998) argues convincingly that writing, by providing an effective means of transferring knowledge from generation to generation, has been a major factor in explaining the dominance of Western culture on the world. As a result of the influence of text, it is not uncommon to equate text with information, hence, the frequent claim that the Internet has contributed to "information overload". This equation is even common amongst Information Scientists (particularly those in the Information Retrieval community) many of whom ignore the suggestion by Meadow and Yuan (1997) that textual documents be regarded as "potential information".

The close association of text with information was reinforced when Shannon (1949), in modeling the transmission of signals, referred to the content of signals as "information". Text is, after all, a signal; and the application of Shannon's mathematics facilitated the transmission and receipt of text. However, when information is understood in this way, there is no requirement for it to be meaningful to the recipient.

Such a view of information is in marked contrast to the definition used in this chapter.

With derived information, for example, nothing is communicated: any meaning is assigned by the person who receives the information. The assumption that there is a connection between information and communication, however, is widespread in the Information Sciences; but as Madden (2004) implied, the two, although associated, are not inseparably so.

21. INFORMATION FORAGING

Sandstrom (1994) and Pirolli and Card (1999) drew analogies between information seeking behavior and the behavior of animals foraging for food. To survive, an animal in search of food must successfully offset any gains made from finding food, against any effort involved in seeking it. Pirolli and Card built on this analogy to develop a sophisticated and much publicized mathematical model. To find food, an animal must derive information (from scent, sound, tracks, etc.) from the environment. Superficially therefore, the idea of information foraging may be thought relevant to this chapter; but one consequence of working with the broad concept of information used here is that it is not readily amenable to mathematical modeling.

Pirolli and Card (1999) take mathematical models developed in studies of animal foraging behavior (known as optimal foraging models) and adapt them to help describe information-seeking behavior. In their model, rather than balancing the reward of food against the effort of finding it, they looked at the benefit (in terms of valuable information) against the cost (in terms of time). For a mathematical model to be tested, however, it has to rely on measurable units. Optimal foraging models assess the costs and benefits of seeking food in terms of energy losses and energy gains. To test the models, these energy flows must be calculated. This is not an easy task, but there is a range of established techniques available that produce objective measures.

Pirolli and Card (1999) assess the cost of information foraging in terms of time taken to find "valuable information", and they describe the benefit as "the total net amount of valuable information gained". They do not explicitly provide a means of measuring the forager's gain in valuable information, but their later experiments imply that they consider "valuable information" to equate to documents deemed relevant by the searchers. In short, therefore, as Spink and Cole (in press) suggest Pirolli and Card (1999) have developed a system to study document foraging, but it ignores many interesting aspects of information seeking.

22. DISCUSSION

Information Science, though a new discipline, deals with old practices. HIB predates writing by a hundred thousand years or so. Writing and associated activities, however, have been hugely influential information technologies that have literally defined cultures. Spink and Currier (2005) address the related issues of evolutionary HIB in another chapter of this book.

This chapter focuses on the Kope, a tribe in Papua New Guinea that was, until recently, isolated and relied almost totally on oral exchanges of information. In their culture, knowledge was held in common by all adult members of the tribe and was not separated into discrete areas. Consequently, technical information was often conveyed with religious and historic information in the form of stories, dances, and chants. Nevertheless, despite the extent to which information and the exchange of information were integrated into the Kopi's pre-literate culture, it has been possible to identify six information roles amongst them: induction, dissemination, presentation, organization, interpretation, and preservation.

It was argued that these roles have parallels in literate societies, but that some of these roles (in particular, those associated with the organization, dissemination, and preservation of information) are more effectively performed with text. Hence, the rapidity with which writing and associated technologies have been absorbed by cultures exposed to them. The power of text to preserve culturally defining information led textual records to be accorded respect, especially in societies where literacy was uncommon. The development of printing and the consequent increase in availability of written documents helped to increase literacy, but the cost of publication meant that most authors had to convince a critical audience of the value of their work before they could be provided with the resources needed to publish.

In ELIS situations, most people continue to exchange information within their communities, performing all the information roles carried out by the Kope and using knowledge of their informants and their environments to evaluate the information. Where information is derived from published sources, however, it is often evaluated by proxy.

Editors, publishers, etc., consider the texts to be worthwhile, so the information seeker credits the text with some value as a result.

The Internet creates problems for information seekers wishing to evaluate its contents because there is no personal link with the informing author, and there is often no evaluation by proxy prior to publication. Such problems are compounded by the widely held view that documents on Websites are information, which leads many information seekers to give more consideration to a statement that is written down on the Internet than they would to a similar spoken comment. However, the Internet, because most of its users are men, and most of the talk is of sex and sport, is more like a bar-room than the library collection most people consider it to be.

23. CONCLUSION

Most of the story of humanity, though unwritten, has involved flows of information within and between communities. Although there are good reasons for the dominance of text in Information Science, its use represents only a small part of HIB. As was discussed earlier, not all information is associated with communication: much of it is derived. Where it is communicated, text has value in releasing "unheard-of potentials of the word" (Ong, 1988, p. 74). In considering exchanges of information between humans, however, it is important to remember that the main tool of communication is the word, not the letter.

References

Berners-Lee, T. (1999). *Weaving the Web*. London. UK: Orion Publishing.

Black, J. (2004). Lost libraries of Mesopotamia. In J. Raven (Ed.), *Lost Libraries: The Destruction of Great Book Collections Since Antiquity*, Chapter 2. London, UK: Palgrave Macmillan Ltd.

Boyd, R., & Richerson, P. J. (1985). *Culture and the Evolutionary Process*. Chicago: University of Chicago Press.

Carey, R. F., McKechnie, E. F., & McKenzie, P. J. (2001). Gaining access to everyday life information seeking. *Library and Information Science Research*, 23, 319–334.

Carruthers, P. (2000). The roots of scientific reasoning: Infancy, modularity and the art of tracking. In P. Carruthers, S. Stich, & M. Siegal (Eds.), *The Cognitive Basis of Science*, Chapter 4. Cambridge, UK: Cambridge University Press.

Connolly, B., & Anderson, R. (1987). *First Contact: New Guinea Highlanders Encounter the Outsider World*. New York: Viking Penguin.

Dennett, D. C. (1993). *Consciousness Explained*. London: Penguin.

Dervin, B. (1992). From the mind's eye of the user: The sense-making qualitative–quantitative methodology. In J. Glazier & R. Powell (Eds.), *Qualitative Research in Information Management*, 61–84. Englewood, CO: Libraries Unlimited.

Dervin, B. (1999). On studying information seeking methodologically: The implications of connecting metatheory to method. *Information Processing and Management*, 35, 727–750.

Diamond, J. (1998). *Guns, Germs and Steel*. London, UK: Vintage.

Diamond, J. (2001). Unwritten knowledge. *Nature*, 410, 521.

Ellis, D., Cox, D., & Hall, K. (1993). A comparison of the information seeking patterns of researchers in the physical and social sciences. *Journal of Documentation*, 49(4), 356–369.

English Heritage (1996). In K. Osborne (Ed.), *Stonehenge and Neighbouring Monuments*. London, UK: English Heritage.

Foster, A., & Ford, N. (2003). Serendipity and information seeking: An empirical study. *Journal of Documentation*, 59(3), 321–340.

Gibson, J. J. (1986). *The Ecological Approach to Visual Perception*. Hillsdale, NJ: Laurence Erlbaum Associates.

Guss, D. M. (1989). *To Weave and Sing: Art, Symbol, and Narrative in the South American Rain Forest*. Berkeley: University of California Press.

Gutenberg Digital (2004). University Library, Göttingen, Germany. http://www.gutenbergdigital.de/gudi/eframes/texte/framere/b42_2.htm (accessed 19/11/04).

Havelock, E. A. (1963). *Preface to Plato*. Cambridge, MA: Harvard University Press.

Hobart, M. E., & Schiffman, Z. S. (1998). *Information Ages: Literacy, Numeracy, and the Computer Revolution*. Maryland: John Hopkins University Press.

Lahdenperä, M., Lummaa, V., Helle, S., Tremblay, M., & Russell, A. F. (2004). Fitness benefits of prolonged post-reproductive lifespan in women. *Nature*, 428, 178–181.

Lebel, S., Trinkaus, E., Faure, M., Fernandez, P., Guérin, R. D., Mercier, N., Valladas, H., & Wagner, G. (2001). Comparative morphology and paleobiology of middle pleistocene human remains from the Bau De l'Aubesier, Vaucluse, France. *Proceedings of the National Academy of Sciences*, 98, 11097–11102.

Lévi-Strauss, C. (1966). *Savage Mind*. Chicago: University of Chicago Press.

Lévi-Strauss, C. (1974). *Tristes Tropiques*. London, UK: Jonathan Cape.

Madden, A. D. (2003). Soapbox: Evaluating Websites. *Library and Information Update*, 2(4), 18.

Madden, A. D. (2004). Evolution and information. *Journal of Documentation*, 60(1), 9–23.

Madden, A., Ford, N., Miller, D., & Levy, P. (2003). How do schoolchildren search the Internet? Teachers' perceptions. In A. Martin & H. Rader (Eds.), *Information and IT Literacy: Enabling Learning in the 21st Century*. London: Facet.

Manguel, A. (1994). *A History of Reading*. London, UK: Flamingo.

Marvin, C. (1988). *When Old Technologies were New*. Oxford, UK: Oxford University Press.

McComb, K., Moss, C., Durant, S. M., Baker, L., & Sayialel, S. (2001). Matriarchs as repositories of social knowledge in African elephants. *Science*, 292, 491–494.

McKenzie, P. J. (2002). A model of information practices in accounts of everyday-life information seeking. *Journal of Documentation*, 59(1), 19–40.

McLuhan, M. (1964). *Understanding Media: The Extensions of Man*. Cambridge, MA: First MIT Press.

Meadow, C. T., & Yuan, W. (1997). Measuring the Impact of Information: Defining the Concepts. *Information Processing and Management*, 33(6), 697–714.

Nelson, K. (2003). Self and social functions: Individual autobiographical memory and collective narrative. *Memory*, 11(2), 125–136.

Ong, W. (1988). *Orality and Literacy: The Technologizing of the Word*. Routledge, London.

Pirolli, P., & Card, S. K. (1999). Information foraging. *Psychological Review*, 106, 643–675.

Plato (2002). *Phaedrus* (Translated by R. Waterfield). Oxford, UK: Oxford University Press.

Presser, H. (1974). *Gutenberg-Museum of the City of Mainz—World Museum of Printing*. Munich, Germany: Verlag.

Ratzan, L. (2000). Making sense of the web: A metaphorical approach. *Information Research*, 6(1). http://informationr.net/ir/6-1/paper85.html (accessed 28/10/04).

Ross, W. (1936). Ethnological notes on Mt Hagen tribes (mandated territory of New Guinea). *Anthropos*, 31, 341–363.

Ruggles, C. (1996). Archaeoastronomy in Europe. In C. Walker (Ed.), *Astronomy Before the Telescope*, Chapter 1.London, UK: British Museum Press.

Sandstrom, P. E. (1994). An optimal foraging approach to information seeking and use. *Library Quarterly*, 64, 414–449.

Schmandt-Besserat, D. (1997). *How Writing Came About*. Texas: University of Texas Press.

Service, E. R. (1971). *Primitive Social Organization: An Evolutionary Perspective*, 2nd Ed. New York: Random House.

Shanks, M., & Tilley, C. (1987). *Social Theory and Archaeology*. London, UK: Polity Press.

Shannon, C. (1949). *The Mathematical Theory of Communication*. Urbana, IL: The University of Illinois Press.

Shenton, A. (2003). Youngsters' use of other people as information-seeking method. *Journal of Librarianship and Information Science*, 34, 219–233.

Spink, A., & Cole, C. (in press). Human information behavior: Integrating diverse approaches and information use. *Journal of the American Society for Information Science and Technology*.

Spink, A., & Currier, J. (2005). Emerging evolutionary approach to human information behavior. In A. Spink & C. Cole (Eds.), *New Directions in Human Information Behavior*. Springer.

Stock, B. (1983). *The Implications of Literacy*. Princeton: Princeton University Press.

Stopka, P., & Macdonald, D. W. (2003). Way-marking behavior: An aid to spatial navigation in the wood mouse (*Apodemus sylvaticus*). *BMC Ecology*, 3(3). http://www.biomedcentral.com/1472-6785/3/3 (accessed 22/10/04).

Strathern, A. (1984). *A Line of Power*. London: Tavistock Publications.

Chapter 4

Toward a Social Framework for Information Seeking

Eszter Hargittai and Amanda Hinnant
Department of Communication Studies
Northwestern University

1. INTRODUCTION

Since the increasing spread of the Internet across the population at large, there has been much commentary about how we live in an information age (Castells, 1996). The idea that we live in a knowledge society predates the 1990s mass diffusion of information technologies (IT) and has been of interest to social scientists for decades (Bell, 1976; Reich, 1992). However, it is only recently that a myriad of IT have spread across all segments of the population, branching to every imaginable daily activity, putting them in the forefront of academic and popular discussions and debates alike (Howard & Jones, 2003; Katz & Rice, 2002; Wellman & Haythornthwaite, 2002). Given this wide-ranging significance and relevance, it is of utmost importance to focus research on the specifics of how people seek, search for, access, find and make use of information, or human information behavior (HIB) (Spink & Cole, in press).

Undoubtedly, the rapid spread of IT to an increasing portion of the population has made more information readily available to people than ever before. This aspect of IT prompted early commentators to express much enthusiasm for these technologies (Barlow, 1997; Dizard, 1997). Concurrently, however, others expressed concern that the riches provided by the new resources would not be distributed equally among different segments of the population (Anderson et al., 1995; DiMaggio et al., 2004). These concerns are related to the idea that mere *availability* of information does not equal *accessibility*, nor does it necessarily provide a realistic chance that people may come across the types of information of most interest or use to them (Hargittai, 2000).

Consequently, to ensure equal access and that people find the information they need, library and information science (LIS) researchers must strive for a better understanding of how people are accessing information and how this may differ across populations. HIB broadens our understanding of how people react to information by focusing in on specific groups and trying to understand the social framework of their information condition.

In this chapter, we then focus on new directions in the development of a social framework for understanding the information behavior of well-targeted groups in society. That is, we explore how one's social positioning influences one's information behavior which, in turn, influences the information-seeking behavior of the populations studied. We concentrate especially on HIB through IT, but base our discussion in a more general

A. Spink and C. Cole (eds), New Directions in Human Information Behavior, 55–70.
© 2006 *Springer.*

framework of HIB behavior encompassing other sources. We integrate work from information science, sociology, and other disciplines to argue for a more holistic approach to the study of HIB. We outline both conceptual and methodological challenges facing the field of HIB and, for each, suggest specific directions for future research.

In addition to drawing on research in the fields of information science, we also discuss contributions made to the topic at hand by the literature on the digital divide stemming from various social science disciplines (DiMaggio et al., 2004; van Dijk, 1999, 2005). We aim to show that these areas have much to gain from each other and have some important commonalities that are worth exploring together. As the research program on the "digital divide" has moved toward looking at the various dimensions of digital inequality, some researchers have started to incorporate studies related to information seeking into their agenda including explorations of skill (Hargittai, 2002a, b, 2003; Mossberger, Tolbert, & Stansbury, 2003) and IT competency (Bunz, 2004).

In this chapter, we draw on recent developments and challenges faced by the digital divide literature to gain a greater understanding of some of the ways in which work on HIB behavior should evolve.

2. CHAPTER ROAD MAP

We start in Section 3 by presenting a conceptual framework for studying the social aspects of HIB. We begin that section by discussing the ways in which people's social attributes (demographic characteristics, their socio-economic status) may influence what methods they employ for information seeking, searching, and information use, and how successful they may be in these endeavors.

Next, we explore how the context of the user's actions matters. We consider several types of context that may be relevant to the topic at hand, from the level of autonomy people enjoy in accessing different types of resources to the extent to which they can draw on social support networks for assistance. Finally, we delineate the different types of HIB in which people may engage from the various goals and purposes that may guide their behavior to the types of sources and means they may employ in an attempt to satisfy their information objectives.

In Section 4, the methodological section, we consider challenges in the realm of both data collection and measurement. We start by a discussion of sampling concerns as we feel it will be important for the field to expand the populations under study. We then explore what methods may be most appropriate for some of the proposed research. Finally, we elaborate on some of the difficulties in operationalizing variables that we deem important in the study of social factors relevant to information seeking. For each of these points, we draw on existing literature to suggest strides that have already been made in advancing the research agenda and outline challenges that remain. We end our chapter by summarizing why we believe it is important to consider the social factors of information seeking in studies of HIB.

3. CONCEPTUAL FRAMEWORK

Much of the existing work on information seeking has focused on the technical and cognitive aspects of the behavior often ignoring or only briefly mentioning the relevant social factors in the process (Case, 2002; Marchionini, 1995). For example, Spink (2002) notes in her Introduction to a Special Issue on Web Search in the *Journal of the American Society for Information Science and Technology* that "Social and organizational impacts and aspects of the Web are not well represented in this special issue. A further special issue, including social and organizational Web research is much needed" (p. 65). Here, we take this observation seriously and consider the social aspects of both Web research and information seeking more generally.

Since Spink (2002), researchers in LIS have expanded their perspective on what should be studied in information-seeking research, making information seeking itself but one part of a broader picture, which they call HIB. Information seeking is now just purposive information seeking as information-seeking research has traditionally examined the problem situation of the user, and the purposive information seeking done to solve the problem.

A particularly important milestone in this evolution from information seeking to a broader HIB approach is everyday life information seeking (ELIS) which focuses on the "small worlds" of the group being studied, particularly the social aspects or social situation of the studied group. Chatman (1991), for example, studied the social aspects of janitors, their small world which was divided into insiders and outsiders. Insiders share the same perspective, and this perspective has cultural, social, and occupational aspects (Houtari & Chatman, 2001). These aspects in turn are more important than any information coming at the small world from the outside that does not coincide with these aspects. The ELIS perspective examines and values the social context in which information is accepted or not accepted in a specific community group.

In this section, we start by making a case for the inclusion of people's social attributes in studies of information behavior. We discuss why ignoring variables such as gender, age, and socio-economic status may lead us to draw mistaken conclusions about the HIB of the population at large. We draw on earlier work that linked such factors to differences among people's ability to perform various information-seeking tasks. We continue by considering the various types of contexts in which people may seek, search, and use information and how these contexts may influence their behavior. We also reflect on the different goals and purposes that lead people to seek information, and how research should be conscious of all these factors for a better understanding of HIB.

3.1 Social Attributes

Few studies in the information-seeking literature elaborate on subjects' social attributes such as gender, age, race, ethnicity, education, and income. This is partly due to the fact that variance on some of these factors is often not present in the samples used by researchers to study related questions. Most studies in information seeking have traditionally looked at academics, students, or university library patrons, because these populations are readily available for study.

In a LIS study of the information-seeking channels used by African Americans living in a subsidized housing complex in Dallas Texas, Spink and Cole (2001) concluded that these residents lived in relative isolation, but nonetheless they had what was called an Information Environment that could be studied and had specific characteristics. Agada

(1999) explored the information-use environment of African-American inner-city gate-keepers and noted that the needs in such a community and approaches to information seeking were different from those experienced in more privileged milieus. A user's socio-economic background may well influence his or her information-seeking behavior high-lighting the importance of focusing on related variables in our explorations of HIB if we are to develop an understanding of HIB that reaches past very particular privileged communities of people.

Given the large number of studies administered on undergraduate or graduate students, variables such as age and education are held constant (Case, 2002). Nonetheless, even in such studies, ignoring other attributes such as gender may lead to drawing the wrong conclusions about certain sub-populations.

Work exploring possible gender differences in computer and Internet use has often found differences between how male and female users integrate these media into their lives (Boneva, Kraut, & Frohlich, 2001; Liff & Shepherd, 2004; Schumacher & Morahan-Martin, 2000). Although these studies did not focus on information seeking *per se*, their findings that men and women perceive and use these technologies differently may have important implications for how people of different genders perform information-seeking tasks using IT.

HIB broadens the perspective on studies about possible differences between men and women and how they use IT. Are women more likely as compared to men to turn to their social networks for information? Do women incorporate and interpret material differently from men? These are relevant questions especially as IT services with important collaborative features become more widespread. The increasing spread of and reliance on IT in organizations may lead to changes in how responsibilities are allocated and work is conducted. Might the incorporation of IT services have different results depending on the particular workforce due to interaction effects of gender? If it is a variable we ignore in our analyses then we will never know how generalizable certain findings are across population groups.

Age is another factor that should not be ignored in studies looking at how people find material of interest to them. There may well be generational differences in how people approach information-seeking tasks so ignoring this attribute of users will result in faulty generalizations about how different people may undertake a search task. However, it is not enough to make a simple assumption about the effects of age on information-seeking behavior.

Older people are sometimes believed to be shy or slow with IT, but such approaches are rarely based on rigorous empirical evidence. Assumptions like this are, at times, considered as the only possible explanation of the particular ways in which the elderly use IT. However, the few related studies that do take a nuanced look at the mediating effects of age seem to suggest alternative explanations. Hargittai (2003), looking at the online behavior of one hundred adults in age ranging from 18 to 81, found that although older users were more likely to make typographical and spelling mistakes during the study, the effect of age disappeared once the statistical models controlled for use of a computer at work and experience with the Internet. Similarly, she found that although older users were less likely to find certain types of material online, once the statistical analyses controlled for types of search methods used in certain instances, the effects of age disappeared on successful searching ability. Conversely, young people are often assumed to be the most savvy IT users. Yet empirical evidence exists to disprove this assumption. Nielsen (2005) found that teenagers were less successful than their adult counterparts in finding certain types of content on the Web.

It seems that design and social conditions of use (e.g., the availability of support and training) can alleviate generational differences. But we can only learn the in-depth reasons for differences in information-seeking behavior if we collect and include in our analyses enough detailed information about our participants, their demographic characteristics, the conditions of their use and experiences, and details about their information behavior.

To be sure, some studies have moved past undergraduate populations for studies of information behavior, but even in these cases variables such as race or income are controlled for by focusing on a narrow group of people affiliated with an institution of higher learning, a particular business environment or patrons of a library (Case, 2002). Restricting variation on factors such as education and income potentially limits our ability to draw conclusions about the relationship of these attributes to the information behavior under study. Findings from the few studies that have explored information seeking among less privileged populations underscore the importance of including these groups in our work (Agada, 1999; Chatman, 1996; Spink & Cole, 2001).

3.2 Context of Information-Seeking Behavior

Information-seeking does not occur in isolation from one's surroundings. These surroundings encompass a wide variety of factors that influence people's information behavior. In this section, we discuss why the availability of resources, whether physical or social, should be a part of the framework that we use to explore the nuances of HIB.

3.2.1 Autonomy

Hargittai (2003), while writing about Web-use skills in particular, defined "autonomy of use" as "one's freedom to use the technology when, where and for what purposes one wishes" (p. 64). This definition can be expanded to encompass autonomy of use regarding other media and sources of information. The main concern is the extent to which the person seeking information has the freedom and flexibility to consult the necessary sources at his or her leisure and convenience.

Few studies of information seeking using computers are conducted in users' usual natural environment where the subjects have at their disposal the particular features of their everyday surroundings. If we do not collect and take into consideration data about users' typical IT access and experiences, we may be missing important information relevant for an in-depth understanding of HIB. Having a network-connected machine at home where a user has round-the-clock access to the medium is arguably different from having access at a university terminal to which access is restricted by library or laboratory hours in addition to the travel time to and from the location.

In fact, some studies have presented empirical evidence of how ease of home access to a network-connected machine is associated with differentiated online activities (Hargittai & Hinnant, 2005; Howard, Rainie, & Jones, 2001). These studies have found that users with home access are more likely to visit so-called "capital-enhancing" Websites (Howard, Rainie, & Jones, 2001) and are more knowledgeable about the Web than those who do not go online at home (Hargittai & Hinnant, 2005). Capital-enhancing Websites are Websites that have the potential to contribute to one's human capital, for example, job searches, health-information seeking, and utilization of government services (DiMaggio & Hargittai, 2002) (see below for further discussion).

Another aspect of autonomy concerns the location of resources in the household (or other site). Families (and various organizations) may take different approaches to the integration of IT into their spaces. Some may purposefully position technologies so they can be monitored by others in the user's vicinity. This can influence the ways in which people go about their information seeking and thus the types of habits and skills they develop. The home terminal may be in a family room where the user is never alone in viewing Websites, or library machines may be lined up next to each other so closely that others sitting nearby can view one's screen restricting the exploration of certain types of material. In contrast, if the machine at home is in a private room or an employee has a terminal in a private office then the user will have much more freedom in exploring all that the medium has to offer.

Autonomy of use is relevant with respect to other information sources as well. Whether one is in need of accessing resources through the phone or in person, the level of privacy afforded in the particular environment may have significant implications for how one may address the situation. The reasons for the various degrees of autonomy in the use of information sources can be economic, social, or cultural in origin. Whether due to financial constraints, legal reasons for monitoring user behavior, or cultural beliefs that suggest communal use of resources, differences in one's freedom to access information sources when, where, and how one wants to can influence the types of information behavior in which people engage and the types of approaches they develop.

Thus, ignoring this concept in our studies of information seeking likely excludes important variables with significant implications for HIB.

3.2.2 Social Support

Another important factor influencing users' information-seeking behavior concerns the availability of social support networks to help address users' needs and interests. People's information behavior does not happen in isolation of others. Social theorists have long been interested in the myriad of advantages one can accrue from one's social surroundings (Bourdieu, 1986; Coleman, 1988). Growing up in a certain milieu affords one not only certain economic resources, but also social and cultural ones on which one can draw—whether directly or indirectly—to further one's goals. Given that asking others for guidance is an important source of advice for people seeking information, the ease of access to networks and the attributes of said networks have important implications for how people approach and address their information needs.

Although a considerable body of literature has developed around exploring how people draw on their networks for information, much of this research has focused on communication within organizations (e.g., Contractor & Monge, 2002) with much less attention paid to people's individual everyday life information behavior.

The literature on the diffusion of innovations long ago identified the importance of social networks in the process (Rogers, 1995). Whether the adoption of certain products or practices, people rely on trusted sources in their personal networks to try new approaches to tasks in their everyday lives. Regarding the importance of available support for the use of IT, one study of home computer diffusion found that those without friends or neighbors to call upon for help with the technology were more likely to abandon its use than those who had people to consult with challenges (Murdock, Hartmann, & Gray, 1992). Demographic characteristics discussed earlier in this section are also relevant in these nuanced measures of the conditions under which people utilize IT. For example, Kiesler et al. (2000) found that teenagers were the most likely in families to contact technical support for assistance with IT difficulties.

3.2.3 Goals and Purposes

Much initial literature in the field focused on information seeking for occupational or study purposes. The recently developed ELIS approach has highlighted the significant point that much important information seeking happens in people's everyday lives unrelated to their work (Savolainen, 1995). Rather, people engage in active and passive information-seeking behavior throughout their daily lives relating to activities from the seemingly mundane tasks of getting weather or sports information to the extremely serious actions of researching immediate health concerns. The types of information sought constitute an important part of the process and should be considered with care in studies of information seeking.

Often studies examining people's ability to find various types of content using particular interfaces or the Web present participants with trivia questions whose inclusion in the study seems haphazard. Rather, researchers should make conscious effort in identifying their proposed queries. Since many of these studies already take place in artificial settings, asking respondents to look for material they would likely never encounter in daily life adds another layer of abstraction to the research projects. Of course, if the goal is to have subjects look for something they would never have encountered otherwise then the trivia questions may be justified, but this should be stated up front in the project. In other instances, however, it would help further our research agenda to pick tasks that are conceptually motivated.

One proposed classification of activities draws a distinction between "capital-enhancing" and recreational activities (DiMaggio & Hargittai, 2002). These authors argue that there are conceptual reasons for distinguishing between information-seeking behavior that has the potential to contribute to one's human capital (e.g., job searches, health-information seeking, utilization of government services) and information seeking that has recreational motivations (e.g., visiting gaming sites, following sport scores).

While an argument can be made that equitable access to the former should be of concern to policy makers, it would be harder to justify policy intervention for activities in the latter category. Consequently, researchers may want to take care in considering such a distinction in types of information sought when assigning tasks to respondents or when collecting data about the information-seeking behavior of people in natural settings. Other categories that may be relevant to consider separately could include information gathering for purchasing purposes or informing oneself about possible participation in computer-mediated communication (although even these could likely be organized according to the classification proposed above).

In this section, we have discussed the ways in which the conceptual framework for research on HIB must expand its reach to include social factors. Now we turn to addressing some of the methodological challenges posed by these propositions.

4. METHODOLOGICAL FRAMEWORK

It is one thing to recognize the conceptual ways in which a field must evolve; it is another to find the right methodological tools to carry out the developing research agenda. In this section, we outline some of the challenges we face as we refine the variables in our models of information-seeking behavior. In particular, we address sampling issues and specific measurements of concepts introduced in the previous section. Although many of the approaches we mention have already been employed by some researchers, what we consider a main challenge to the field is to integrate the advances in the various areas into new studies that improve on earlier work on several dimensions (i.e., better sampling methodology coupled with more in-depth studies).

We will have to draw on diverse methodologies recognizing the strengths and weaknesses of each. Given the challenges and limitations of each methodology, multimethod studies may be the most fruitful.

4.1 More Diverse Populations

As we discussed in the previous section, much research in information seeking is conducted on convenience samples of undergraduate or graduate students at research universities. Such sampling techniques can be justified if a study is only about very select populations (especially relevant, e.g., in the case of patrons of libraries), but must be expanded and diversified if we are to comment on the information-seeking behavior of more general populations. Too often authors apologize for the limitations in their sampling techniques by suggesting that theirs is a study exploratory in nature. While this is a necessary first step in the development of a new field, eventually the exploratory studies have to move to another level and be administered on samples that allow more generalization for a field to gain legitimacy.

It is too limiting to operationalize novice vs. expert users as beginning vs. advanced graduate students in an information science program (e.g., Ford, Miller, & Moss, 2001) when less than 5% of the population has graduate degrees and even college degrees are held by a minority of American adults. For a study to claim legitimately that it is exploring the practices of novice vs. expert users the researchers should reach out to populations with much less experience with the services under study than any student at a university would possess.

One way to categorize novice users is to consider subjects' overall experiences with the medium and services under study. For example, researchers may look at the number of years someone has been a user or the amount of time people spend with the medium on a weekly basis. Howard, Rainie, and Jones (2001) did just that distinguishing between "newcomers" and "veterans" where the former had been online for less than a year before the study while the latter had been users for at least 3 years. These authors distinguished among the participants in their study further by considering additional information about daily usage and designating the most frequent users who had also been online for several years as "netizens". This particular project was conducted on a random sample of American adult Internet users making the findings of the analyses much more generalizable than studies conducted on very select non-random groups of people.

To be sure, we are not suggesting that experience measures be used as a proxy for abilities. To the contrary, Hargittai (2005) found that years of use or amount of time spent online are weak predictors of people's actual skills. In fact, she found that the former explains only a third, the latter only a sixth of the variance in actual abilities compared to the stronger—albeit still limited—explanatory power of composite variables based on survey measures of skill. The idea is to use variance in the user experience variable to guarantee a diverse sample in our studies.

4.2 New Methods of Data Collection

Surveys can be helpful, but this field can often benefit more from other less traditional methods. Interesting and informative data can be derived from large-scale log analyses (Goldfarb, 2002; Spink, Wolfram, & Jansen, 2001; Spink et al., 2002). Although such data can be hard to find as they are often proprietary, access to just one dataset can be quite fruitful and lead to numerous publications. Jansen and Pooch (2001) offer a helpful review of Web search studies, many of them based on log analyses.

For an in-depth understanding of people's information-seeking behavior, in-person observations and interviews can be especially insightful (Hargittai, 2002a, b; Rieh, 2004). Such studies are not uncommon in the LIS literature, but more often than not they are conducted in artificial settings and with a very particular set of tasks not necessarily reflecting conceptual motivations. A particular challenge of related approaches is finding the appropriate tools for the collection and analysis of data. These should also be related to the ultimate goals of the study. Whether one video-tapes the subjects or records snapshots of the actions on a computer screen should be motivated by what data will be the most helpful for addressing the research questions.

Carey, McKechnie, and McKenzie (2001) explore the new challenges posed by conducting in-person observations in research on ELIS. Unlike much qualitative research in the area that ignores details about how researchers can gain access to particular populations under study, Carey, Mckechnie, and Mckenzie (2001) give a detailed account of gaining and maintaining access to three specific groups: pregnant women, support groups, and children. As they note, most studies do not present the reader with much information about the modes of data collection, a shortcoming future studies should address.

We have mentioned the importance of social support networks to the full understanding of HIB. Social network analysis often requires its own particular data gathering approach—a matrix with in and out links of participating actors or nodes—an approach that could prove invaluable for uncovering patterns of information behavior among members of a network that are currently difficult for LIS researchers to see lacking appropriate datasets.

4.3 New Measurements

Given the ever-changing nature of IT and the myriad of services offered by new technologies, and given the new directions in which we believe research in the field should proceed, it is important to develop new measurements that meet the conceptual needs of progress for our research agenda. Here, we describe possible new measures for concepts discussed earlier in the chapter such as skill, digital literacy, autonomy of use, and social support networks.

4.3.1 Skill and Digital Literacy

One way to compare HIB across population groups is to examine the extent to which different people possess the necessary skills to perform certain types of tasks having to do with information seeking, evaluation, and use. The measures of performance will depend on the specifics of the study, but the following are some possible variables researchers may consider as indicators of skill and digital literacy: (a) success rate with tasks; (b) amount of time spent on tasks; (c) number of steps taken to achieve certain goals; (d) number of resources used to find information; (e) quality of information found; and (f) the ability to evaluate the located information.

While some of these measures are fairly straight forward (e.g., one can measure time in seconds or minutes), others can be much more nuanced and complicated, and may require the development of new coding and analysis techniques. It behooves the LIS research community to publish new methodologies so energy is not spent on reinventing the wheel with every project. Jansen and Pooch's (2001) review piece about Web searching studies provides an important service to the community by presenting a summary table of variables that had been used in previous studies about search queries (p. 243) giving other researchers in the field guidelines for the types of variables that have proved to be helpful in past work. Hargittai (2004) published a separate article just on the coding and classification scheme she employed in her study of 100 randomly sampled adult Internet users' online actions. The complexity of the method attests to the fact that it would be a waste of resources for each researcher in the field to come up with their own unique coding mechanism.

4.3.2 Autonomy

In Section 3.2.1, we discussed the importance of considering how one's autonomy in information seeking may influence one's behavior. There are numerous ways in which one might collect information about people's autonomy. In her work on how a diverse sample of adult Internet users finds information online, Hargittai (2003) measured autonomy of use in two ways: (1) the number of locations in which Internet users had access to a network-connected machine; and (2) whether users had an Internet connection at work, which they were very free to use for the activities of their choice. Although her study was conducted in a lab environment, multiple regression analyses that included information on these variables predicting success with various information-seeking tasks suggested a statistically significant relationship between autonomy of use and online information-seeking skills.

Operationalizing autonomy of use as the number of locations of access or the freedom to use the medium at work are just two possibilities. Other potentially important factors that emerged through interview data in the above-cited study (Hargittai, 2003) also suggested a need for considering the number and types of people with whom a user may have to share IT-resources in the home or elsewhere.

For example, parents sometimes find themselves with limited access to their home terminals due to their teenage children's monopolization of the medium. Since home access is usually the most autonomous regarding the type of material one may view (i.e., less likelihood of third-party surveillance, higher chance of finding time to browse freely without time constraints), considering the limits that may be put on it is important. In fact, some studies have already found these measures to have significant influence on the types of uses to which people put the medium indicating that those with home use are more likely to visit Websites with capital-enhancing content (Hargittai & Hinnant, 2005; Howard, Rainie, & Jones, 2001).

4.3.3 Social Support

In the previous section on new methods of data collection, we suggested that LIS researchers may want to start collecting matrix data appropriate for social network analysis. In addition to that particular method, there are other ways in which one might assess the importance of social support networks to HIB. For one, social psychologists have developed relevant indexes for measuring general social support (Cohen et al., 1984). Regarding measurements related to information seeking, in particular, possibilities include: (a) the types of ties or relationships available for informational purposes; (b) the number of ties or relationships in one's immediate or more distant network; (c) the amount of contact one has with knowledgeable relations in one's network; and (d) the level of expertise in one's network. These are just a few possibilities and researchers should experiment with others by including additional options in their surveys.

4.4 Concerns Regarding Measurement Validity

There are various ways in which the particular setting of a study or the type of data collection may influence the validity and thus the quality of measurements about HIB. Here, we consider just some examples to highlight the importance of the careful considerations that must go into decisions about what particular measures to use to collect data about HIB. Although a number of projects on HIB look at people's actual actions in study settings, measures are often collected using proxies. This can be problematic as we often know little about the validity of such proxy measures. Not only might there be validity concerns regarding the measure in general, but it may be that the measure is a good reflection for one sub-sample of the population while a bad one for another.

One study found significant gender differences in the validity of a proxy measure for online abilities (Hargittai & Shafer, 2003). The study considered how well survey measures of Web-use skill reflected people's actual online expertise. It is rare that researchers look at measures of perceived abilities in the context of actual abilities. The results of this one study indicated that despite exhibiting similar levels of *actual online skill*, women tended to *perceive* their skills as significantly lower than men perceived their own skills. So while the proxy measures of Web-use skill may be a good predictor of *men's* online abilities, the measures work poorly as a proxy for *women's* online abilities.

This stream of research is related to an even broader area of inquiry regarding gender differences in attitudes about and abilities regarding math and science fields (Benbow & Stanley, 1980; Etzkowitz, Kemelgor, & Uzzi, 2000; Hyde, Fennema, & Lamon, 1990; Margolis & Fisher, 2002). Correll (2001), for example, found that net of actual abilities young women found themselves to be less skilled in math and science than their male counterparts. This in turn influenced their propensity to pursue math and science careers. Similarly, research has found that nuanced details about a study's context—for example, what participants understand to be the goal of the study—may influence participants' performance and achievements on tests across racial categories (Osborne, 2001; Steele, 1997; Steele & Aronson, 1995).

Although the focus of these projects was not on HIB *per se*, these examples highlight relevant methodological challenges for the field. If significant differences exist across demographic groups regarding perceptions of abilities and actions then using proxies to measure behavior or neglecting to consider the particular circumstances of the study may lead to misleading findings in some instances.

5. CONCLUSION

In this chapter, we have outlined conceptual and methodological frameworks for incorporating social factors into the study of HIB. As the field matures, it will be increasingly important to approach our research questions in a more holistic manner and to include more nuanced measures of HIB than much of existing work has done so. We have offered specific recommendations on how to do this. Here, we call attention to a few additional points we deem worthy of consideration.

As IT evolve and the different services spread to an ever growing number of devices, it will be increasingly difficult to distinguish certain services based on the machines on which they run. That is, while in the 1990s it made sense to restrict the study of Internet use to Web access using computers, in the 21st century it becomes increasingly limiting to make assumptions about what devices people use to access different information sources. As phones and personal digital assistants gain functionality, it will be important to include a diverse set of equipments in our studies. As we argued earlier, conducting studies on subjects in research labs already adds an artificial component to the data collection process, but requiring participants in a project to use devices they do not normally consult for services will make findings especially difficult to interpret and generalize.

While we have mainly focused on the use of IT in this chapter, it is important to recognize and remember that much HIB continues to take place through more traditional channels. Incorporation of diverse media and a focus on the importance of social networks—whether accessed through IT, in person or through other means—will remain crucial for an all-encompassing understanding of HIB.

Finally, we would like to mention that many of the social factors whose importance we discussed in this chapter can be included in studies both as independent and dependent variables. Researchers will want to be careful with how they approach the various social attributes we discussed and should let the conceptual questions guide how variables are incorporated into future studies. For example, while skill can be considered a dependent variable where one examines the predictors of differential abilities (Hargittai, 2003; Mossberger, Tolbert, & Stansbury, 2003), it can also serve as an independent variable when one looks at its implications for different types of uses (Hargittai & Hinnant, 2005).

While the research agenda related to HIB has made some significant strides in the past few decades, as we have argued in this chapter, the field faces new challenges as it matures. In particular, we have focused on the importance of incorporating social factors into our analyses. By considering particular socio-economic features of the populations under study and by expanding the characteristics of the groups whose behavior we investigate, we will gain a better, more encompassing and more generalizable understanding of HIB.

References

Agada, J. (1999). Inner-city gatekeepers: An exploratory survey of their information use environment. *Journal of the American Society for Information Science and Technology*, 50(1), 74–85.

Anderson, R. H., Bikson, T. K., Law, S. A., & Mitchell, B. M. (1995). *Universal Access to E-Mail—Feasibility and Societal Implications*. Santa Monica, California: RAND.

Barlow, J. P. (1997). The best of all possible worlds. *Communications of the ACM*, 40(2), 68–74.

Bell, D. (1976). *The Coming of the Post-Industrial Society*. New York: Basic Books.

Benbow, C. P., & Stanley, J. C. (1980). Sex differences in mathematical ability: Fact or artifact? *Science*, 210(4475), 1262–1264.

Boneva, B., Kraut, R., & Frohlich, D. (2001). Using e-mail for personal relationships: The difference gender makes. *American Behavioral Scientist*, 45(3), 530–549.

Bourdieu, P. (1986). The forms of capital. In J. G. Richardson (Ed.), *Handbook of Theory and Research for the Sociology of Education*, 241–258. New York: Greenwood Press.

Bunz, U. (2004). The computer-email-Web fluency scale: Development and validation. *International Journal of Human-Computer Interaction*, 17(4), 477–504.

Carey, R. F., McKechnie, L. E. F., & McKenzie, P. J. (2001). Gaining access to everyday life information seeking. *Library and Information Science Research*, 23(4), 335–349.

Case, D. (2002). *Looking for Information: A Survey of Research on Information Seeking, Needs, and Behavior*. San Diego: Academic Press.

Castells, M. (1996). *The Rise of the Network Society. Vol. 1 of The Information Age: Economy, Society and Culture*. Boston: Blackwell.

Chatman, E. (1991). Life in a small world: Applicability of gratification theory to information seeking behavior. *Journal of the American Society for Information Science and Technology*, 42, 438–449.

Chatman, E. (1996). The impoverished life-world of outsiders. *Journal of the American Society for Information Science and Technology*, 47(3), 193–206.

Cohen, S., Mermelstein, R., Kamarck, T., & Hoberman, H. (1984). Measuring the functional components of social support. In I. G. Sarason, & B. R. Sarason (Eds.), *Social Support: Theory, Research and Applications*, 73–94. T he Hague: Martines Niijfhoff.

Coleman, J. (1988). Social capital in the creation of human capital. *American Journal of Sociology*, 94, S95–S120.

Contractor, N., & Monge, P. (2002). Managing knowledge networks. *Management Communication Quarterly*, 16, 249–258.

Correll, S. J. (2001). Gender and the career choice process: The role of biased self-assessments. *American Journal of Sociology*, 106(6), 1691–1730.

DiMaggio, P., & Hargittai, E. (2002). The new digital inequality: Social stratification among Internet users. *American Sociological Association Annual Meetings*. Chicago, IL.

DiMaggio, P., Hargittai, E., Celeste, C., & Shafer, S. (2004). Digital inequality: From unequal access to differentiated use. In K. Neckerman (Ed.), *Social Inequality*, 355–400. New York: Russell Sage Foundation.

Dizard, W. (1997). *MegaNet: How the Global Communications Network will Connect Everyone on Earth*. Boulder, CO: Westview.

Etzkowitz, H., Kemelgor, C., & Uzzi, B. (2000). *Athena Unbound: The Advancement of Women in Science and Technology*. Cambridge: Cambridge University Press.

Ford, N., Miller, D., & Moss, N. (2001). The role of individual differences in Internet searching: An empirical study. *Journal of the American Society for Information Science and Technology*, 52(12), 1049–1066.

Goldfarb, A. (2002). Analyzing Website choice using Clickstream data. In M. R. Baye (Ed.), *Advances in Applied Microeconomics v.11: The Economics of the Internet and E-commerce*, 209–230. Elsevier Science Ltd: London.

Hargittai, E. (2000). Open portals or closed gates? Channeling content on the world wide Web. *Poetics*, 27, 233–253.

Hargittai, E. (2002a). Beyond logs and surveys: In-depth measures of people's web use skills. *Journal of the American Society for Information Science and Technology Perspectives*, 53(14), 1239–1244.

Hargittai, E. (2002b). Second-level digital divide: Differences in people's online skills. *First Monday*, 7(4).

Hargittai, E. (2003). *How Wide a Web? Inequalities in Accessing Information Online*. Princeton, NJ: Sociology Department, Princeton University.

Hargittai, E. (2004). Classifying and coding online actions. *Social Science Computer Review*, 22(2), 210–227.

Hargittai, E. (2005). Survey measures of web-oriented digital literacy. *Social Science Computer Review*, 23.

Hargittai, E., & Hinnant, A. (2005). *New Dimensions of the Digital Divide: Differences in Young Adults' Use of the Internet*. Washington, DC: Eastern Sociological Society.

Hargittai, E., & Shafer, S. (2003). Refining the "digital divide": Gender differences in web-use skill.*Culture and Society Workshop*, Northwestern University: Chicago.

Houtari, M.-L., & Chatman, E. (2001). Using everyday life information seeking to explain organizational behavior. *Library and Information Science Research*, 23, 351–366.

Howard, P. E. N., & Jones, S. (2003). *Society Online*. Thousand Oaks, California: Sage Publications.

Howard, P. N., Rainie, L., & Jones, S. (2001). Days and nights on the Internet: The impact of a diffusing technology. *American Behavioral Scientist*, 45(3), 383–404.

Hyde, J. S., Fennema, E., & Lamon, S. J. (1990). Gender differences in mathematics performance: A meta-analysis. *Psychological Bulletin*, 107(2), 139–155.

Jansen, B. J., & Pooch, U. (2001). A review of web searching studies and a framework for future research. *Journal of the American Society for Information Science and Technology*, 52(3), 235–246.

Katz, J. E., & Rice, R. E. (2002). *Social Consequences of Internet Use: Access, Involvement and Interaction*. Cambridge, MA: MIT Press.

Kiesler, S., Zdaniuk, B., Lundmark, V., & Kraut, R. (2000). Troubles with the Internet: The dynamics of help at home. *Human-Computer Interaction*, 15(4), 323–351.

Liff, S., & Shepherd, A. (2004). *An Evolving Gender Digital Divide? Internet Issue Brief*, 2: 1–17. Oxford: Oxford Internet Institute.

Marchionini, G. (1995). *Information Seeking in Electronic Environments*. New York: Cambridge University Press.

Margolis, J., & Fisher, A. (2002). *Unlocking the Clubhouse: Women in Computing*. Cambridge, MA: MIT Press.

Mossberger, K., Tolbert, C. J., & Stansbury, M. (2003). *Virtual Inequality: Beyond the Digital Divide*. Washington, DC: Georgetown University Press.

Murdock, G., Hartmann, P., & Gray, P. (1992). Contextualizing home computing: Resources and practices. In R. Silverstone, & E. Hirsch (Eds.), *Consuming Technologies*, 146–160. New York, NY: Routledge.

Nielsen, J. (2005). *Usability of Websites for Teenagers*. Alertbox: Nielsen Norman Group.

Osborne, J. W. (2001). Testing stereotype threat: Does anxiety explain race and sex differences in achievement? *Contemporary Educational Psychology*, 26(3), 291–310.

Reich, R. (1992). *The Work of Nations: Preparing Ourselves for 21st-Century Capitalism*. New York: Vintage Books.

Rieh, S. Y. (2004). On the web at home: Information seeking and web searching in the home environment. *Journal of the American Society for Information Science and Technology*, 55, 743–753.

Rogers, E. (1995). *Diffusion of Innovations*. New York: Free Press.

Savolainen, R. (1995). Everyday life information seeking: Approaching information seeking in the context of way of life. *Library and Information Science Research*, 17, 259–294.

Schumacher, P., & Morahan-Martin, J. (2000). Gender, Internet and computer attitudes and experiences. *Computers in Human Behavior*, 16(1), 13–29.

Spink, A. (2002). Introduction to the special issue on web research. *Journal of the American Society for Information Science and Technology*, 53(2), 65–66.

Spink, A., & Cole, C. (2001). Information and poverty: Information-seeking channels used by African American low-income households. *Library and Information Science Research*, 23(1), 45–65.

Spink, A., & Cole, C. (in press). Human information behavior: Integrating diverse approaches and information use. *Journal of the American Society for Information Science and Technology*.

Spink, A., Jansen, B. J., Wolfram, D., & Saracevic, T. (2002). From e-sex to e-commerce: Web search changes. *IEEE Computer*, 35(3), 107–109.

Spink, A., Wolfram, D., & Jansen, B. J. (2001). Searching the web: The public and their queries. *Journal of the American Society for Information Science and Technology*, 52(3), 226–234.

Steele, C. (1997). A threat in the air: How stereotypes shape intellectual I identity and performance. *American Psychologist*, 52(6), 613–629.

Steele, C. M., & Aronson, J. (1995). Stereotype threat and the intellectual test performance of African Americans. *Journal of Personality and Social Psychology*, 69(5), 797–811.

van Dijk, J. A. G. M. (1999). *The Network Society: Social Aspects of New Media*. London: Sage.

van Dijk, J. A. G. M. (2005). *The Deepening Divide: Inequality in the Information Society*. London: Sage.

Wellman, B., & Haythornthwaite, C. (2002). *The Internet in Everyday Life*. Oxford: Blackwell Publishers.

SECTION 3

Spatial and Collaborative HIB Frameworks

Chapter 5

Mapping Textually Mediated Information Practice in Clinical Midwifery Care

Pamela J. McKenzie
Faculty of Information and Media Studies
University of Western Ontario

1. INTRODUCTION

This chapter provides, via an analysis of document use in a midwifery clinic, an ethnographic study of information behavior in an institutional context. An analysis inspired by institutional ethnography offers much to the study of information behavior. In particular, it permits a study of the ways that "information" is negotiated and constituted through the actions of individuals within a broader social context, whether or not they are present in the local setting.

This chapter goes beyond even Wilson's (1999) broad definition of *information behavior* "those activities a person may engage in when identifying his or her own needs for information, searching for such information in any way, and using or transferring that information" (p. 249) to seek a more inclusive understanding of *information practices* situated within broader social practices. This orientation requires working at the edges of Spink and Cole's (2004) definition of *information behavior* as including passive or undetermined information behavior (Case, 2002).

The role of documents in clinical care has long been recognized. In particular, the clinical record has been analyzed extensively since Garfinkel's observation that "[r]eporting procedures, their results, and the uses of those results, are integral features of the same social orders they describe" (Garfinkel, 1967, p. 192). Studies of documents in clinical settings have considered the ways that the clinical record contributes to medical work (Berg, 1996), its role in the social construction of the patient or client (Bowler, 1995; Macintyre, 1978) and the constitution of the work of care providers (Berg & Bowker, 1996), the narrative structure of operative reports (Pettinari, 1988), and the accomplishment of accountability in radiological records (Yakel, 2001).

Researchers have studied the affordances of the paper medical record (Fitzpatrick, 2000; Heath & Luff, 1996) and have analyzed how this and other clinical records are used and the implications of these uses for the creation of electronic clinical documents (Gorman et al., 2000; Reddy et al., 2002). Three studies (Fitzpatrick, 2000; Gorman et al., 2000; Reddy et al., 2002) looked at the role of a variety of information sources in clinical decision-making and problem solving. These included documents and bundles

A. Spink and C. Cole (eds), New Directions in Human Information Behavior, 73–92.
© 2006 *Springer.*

of documents ranging from formal paper and electronic records to informal documents such as sticky notes affixed to the record and notes scrawled on gauze dressing wrappers.

Despite their differing perspectives, these studies all share a focus on texts as actively constructing and in turn being constructed by a social setting. The present work seeks to contribute to this discussion by exploring the relations between texts and people in everyday local settings by focusing on "the interaction and intersection of the diverse texts that constitute work in a given domain" (Davenport & Cronin, 1998, p. 266).

I adopt Dorothy Smith's perspective on documents within a social setting. Smith (1990) argues not only that texts are active, but also that they reveal the social organization of their creators and users:

> "Texts are not seen as inert extra-temporal blobs of meaning, the fixity of which enables the reader to forget the actual back and forth work on the piece or pieces of paper in front of her that constitute the text as a body of meaning existing outside time and all at once. [. . .] The text is analyzed for its characteristically textual form of participation in social relations. The interest is in the social organization of those relations and penetrating them, discovering them, opening them up from within, through the text. The text enters the laboratory, so to speak, carrying the threads and shreds of the relations it is organized by and organizes. The text before the analyst, then, is not used as a specimen or sample, but as a means of access, a direct line to the relations it organizes" (pp. 3–4).

Although a sequence of social action may begin with the activities of individual participants in a local setting, these activities can be traced through the text to the extra-local sites of power to which they extend. Analysis therefore begins from the standpoint of the individual in her everyday/every night life, and the activity of each local subject is studied as a component of the more extended social relation. As part of this process "the researcher must discover and map the missing pieces of the social relation" (Campbell & Gregor, 2002, p. 44). The primary purpose of this chapter is therefore to map the local and extra-local participants in clinical midwifery visits through an analysis of the texts used; to consider information sources not just as resources for participants, but as constituents of a larger social order.

Such a mapping is complemented by a consideration of the ways that the *activation* of texts, or "the human involvement in the capacity of texts to coordinate action and get things done in specific ways" (Campbell & Gregor, 2002, p. 33), can accomplish the goals and objectives of extra-local interests in local settings. This chapter's second purpose is to provide specific examples that illustrate "the socially organized practices, including sequences of talk, that are integral to the discursive process" (Smith, 1990, p. 215) of the prenatal clinical visit. I make use here of Smith's definition of discourse, which:

> "refers to a field of relations that includes not only texts and their intertextual conversation, but the activities of people in actual sites who produce them and use them and take up the conceptual frames they circulate. This notion of discourse never loses the presence of the subject who activates the text in any local moment of its use" (DeVault & McCoy, 2002, p. 772, note 2).

Although Smith's institutional ethnography method has been used in a variety of professional and human service disciplines, particularly education and nursing, her work has not yet been widely adopted in library and information science. To date two dissertations have taken institutional ethnography perspectives on the study of librarians' work (Lundberg, 1991; Stooke, 2004). Lundberg's has not resulted in publications but Stooke's, completed only 4 months before the submission of this chapter, will likely result in at least one article geared specifically for an LIS audience.

The rest of the chapter reports a study of clinical midwifery visits which recorded the interactions between the midwife and the pregnant woman. The midwifery visits are analyzed from the point of view of Smith's (1990) concept of "socially organized practices". Local and extra-local participants are identified from recorded evidence of the use and discussion of texts, and are then mapped in a series of document maps.

2. THE STUDY AND METHODS

This chapter is based on an ongoing study of communication and information exchange in midwife–client visits in the Canadian province of Ontario. The research has been funded by the Social Sciences and Humanities Research Council of Canada and a pilot study co-researched by Jacquelyn Burkell was funded by the Faculty of Information and Media Studies of The University of Western Ontario.

Midwifery is a licensed and publicly funded profession in Ontario. Midwives provide primary prenatal care, attend home or hospital births for low-risk women, and provide 6 weeks of post-partum follow-up. In this regard, prenatal midwifery visits stand in sharp contrast to the high-risk critical-care environments investigated by Gorman et al. (2000) and Reddy et al. (2002). High-risk midwifery cases involve a consultation with or a transfer of care to an obstetrician (Hawkins & Knox, 2003). The midwifery model of care is based on the client's right to make informed choices about all aspects of her care. The exchange of information is integral to midwifery practice and the clinical midwifery visit is therefore a rich field for studying several facets of information behavior.

2.1 Data Collection

Data collection for this study involves two phases. First, I record, but am not present to observe, a clinical midwifery visit. Second, I conduct a separate follow-up interview with each willing participant in which she responds to several background questions and then listens to the audiotape of the visit and provides her comments on it. Data collection is ongoing. To date, 31 midwife–client pairs have participated from a total of 11 midwifery practices in seven southern Ontario communities. The communities constitute a stratified purposive sample.

Seven clinical visits took place in the city of Toronto (3 practices, with a community population of over 2 million and access to a number of tertiary-care teaching hospitals), nine visits took place in ||large-city practices (2 practices, 300,000–900,000 people and access to one or more teaching hospitals), 10 visits took place in practices located in smaller cities (4 practices, 100,000–300,000 population and no teaching hospital), and five visits took places in practices located in small towns and villages (2 practices, population under 50,000, with a small local hospital or access to a hospital in a neighboring community only).

Recruitment has taken place on a regional basis. For each period of data collection, I identified a single geographic region containing communities representing one or more strata and approached all midwifery practices in the region. Within each region, I recruited a convenience sample of willing practices, then willing midwives within each practice, and finally willing clients of those midwives. Some practices refused, and even once practices and midwives agreed to participate there were cases in which no clients were willing.

Data collection and analysis conform to ethical guidelines on research on human subjects of The University of Western Ontario and the Social Science and Humanities Research Council of Canada. In order to protect anonymity and confidentiality, codes are used throughout. The same code is used consistently to represent the same participant.

Of the visits recorded to date, two have been post-partum visits and the other 29 prenatal, with clients ranging from 14 to 40 weeks pregnant at the time of the recorded visit. All were repeat visits rather than the lengthy initial "booking" visit in which the pregnant woman is introduced to the midwife, the midwifery practice and often to the midwifery model of care, gives her complete medical and obstetrical history and may have a full physical examination. This chapter analyzes evidence from the 29 prenatal clinic visits of the use of documents within those visits.

Many studies of the role of records in clinical practice have had access to those records (Berg, 1996; Fitzpatrick, 2000; Heath & Luff, 1996; Pettinari, 1988; Yakel, 2001). Findings are therefore based on an analysis of the records themselves in conjunction with observation and/or interviews. The present analysis is based on evidence available from audio recordings of prenatal clinical visits at which the researcher was not present. One of the properties of paper is that its use is often audible: a rhythmic sound indicates a systematic turning of pages while rustling and shuffling sounds suggest rummaging through papers and files. When combined with dialogue and other contextual clues, the sounds of paper can prove instructive in analyzing the use of documents in prenatal clinical practice.

I present two forms of analysis. I created document maps using the model function in QSR N-Vivo, version 2.0 163. The maps depict the range of documents whose use is evident in the recordings of the prenatal visits. Most documents described in this way were physically present, although others were simply mentioned without being present. Figures 1–4 each represent a portion of the full map (Figure 5) of all of the documents and the various individuals and agencies to whom they provide connections. While these maps provide a starting place for the analysis of the contributions of texts to the information work of midwives and pregnant women in the clinical context, they are far from complete.

The more detailed textual analysis of specific examples related to each figure serves as a beginning step in the more complete analysis allowed by the adoption of Smith's perspective on textually mediated practice. Excerpts were therefore chosen not for their representativeness but because they provided clear examples of textually mediated information practices and because they illustrated the contributions of extra-local actors.

3. THE CLINICAL CONTEXT

At its most fundamental, a prenatal clinical visit is an interpersonal transaction between the midwife and the pregnant woman. Indeed, much of the research on communication and information behavior in this context focuses on that interaction (Levy, 1999; Linell & Bredmar, 1996; McKenzie, 2004; Olsson & Jansson, 2001). The 29 prenatal visits involved anywhere from two to five people. Clients came alone or were attended by a male or female partner or some other support person, for example, a mother or sister. In many cases, the client's child or children also came along. On occasion, one or more midwifery students participated in prenatal visits as part of their clinical training.

The considerable interpersonal communication and exchange of information was mediated in a variety of ways by documents. Practices of reading and writing:

"in which the record is turned to, leafed through, read, used for jottings, communicated through, dispatched, form a crucial site in the sociotechnical organization of medical work. Without these practices, the record would be dead, disconnected, without any relevance. These activities are what bring it to life—and what allow it to have its mediating role in the organization of medical work. Without the interrelation of people and paperwork, in other words, doctors could not be doctors and nurses could not be nurses" (Berg, 1996, p. 501).

Like the hospital environments observed by Gorman et al. (2000) and Fitzpatrick (2000), the midwifery clinics housed a variety of documents. The examining rooms in which prenatal visits took place varied in size, layout, and contents between and within practices. In some clinics, each room was used exclusively by one midwife while in others two or more midwives shared an examining room. Each room had a desk and chair for the midwife, two or more chairs for the client and her support people, and an examining bed. Walls of some examining rooms were hung with educational posters, for example, illustrating fetal development.

The midwife's desk housed the day's pile of client file folders. File drawers or the desk surface held forms and handouts, and if a single midwife made exclusive use of the room, all of her client charts might be located in a locked drawer there. Bookshelves above the desk might house the midwife's personal collection of professional books, which included volumes such as textbooks on anatomy, physiology, nursing, or midwifery practice, the Canadian pharmacopeia, and books on natural or herbal remedies. In some practices, a staff room held an integrated professional collection of such materials for the entire practice.

A number of other documents were present in the clinic. Most practices held a client library consisting of one or more bookshelves bearing books, videos, and/or DVDs relating to pregnancy, childbirth, parenting, and holistic health. Waiting areas displayed pamphlets, flyers, and business cards from local businesses and agencies. The practice administrator's desk housed a large desk calendar, commonly with a column for each midwife. Current client files and business records might also be kept there as well as educational handouts for clients.

Figure 1 illustrates the kinds of documents whose consultation of or referral to was evident from the recordings of the 29 prenatal visits.

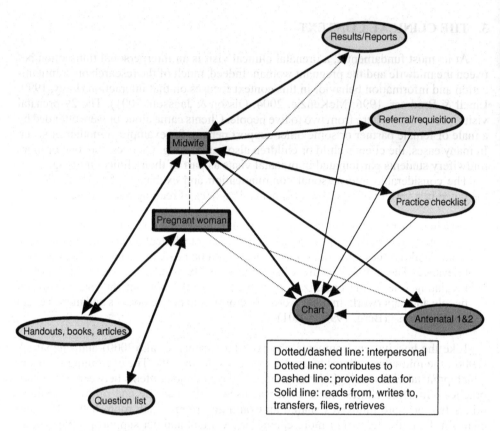

Figure 1. All documents present in prenatal visits.

In all figures, rectangles represent people, organizations, or agencies and ovals represent documents. Dark gray shapes with black borders indicate people or documents physically present in every prenatal visit. Light gray shapes represent those that may or may not be present, and white shapes bordered in light gray indicate documents or people contributing to the visit but not physically present in any of the prenatal visits.

First, midwives gave clients handouts, such as a detailed information package introducing the philosophy and scope of midwifery care in this practice or a selection of articles on a topic on which the woman would make a decision. These were compiled of locally written texts and/or photocopies of published articles and other documents.

Midwife 19: I'll just pass that to you [Partner], some sheets about newborn medication.

Handouts were given to the client under various circumstances, either if she requested them or at specific times during the pregnancy. For example, the introduction to midwifery care might be given at the initial booking visit.

Second, the recordings provided evidence of documents of outside authorship being brought to the discussion by a participant. The documents themselves may have been present in the visit, as in this example in which a midwife and client jointly consulted a source from the midwife's professional library that was located on the shelf above her desk:

Midwife 13: There's an actual, [rustling noise, some banging of movement] not a, medical condition, it's more like a state of the body and it's called acidosis. And, it is, brought on and, people that are not pregnant as well, by, a diet that's high in acid and low in alkaline foods. [sound of pages turning, client coughs]. **So.** We can make a copy **for** you, before you go if you like cause it **lists** the foods that are acid-forming and alkaline-forming... And I think **that** might be the ticket. [pages rustling].

Client   13: Hmm. [sounds of pages turning, no talking for several seconds.] (inaudible) **Shell**fish is even that acid-forming? Wow. **Poul**try? [...]

Midwife 13: Well I can photocopy that for you. [paper rustling]

Client   13: Yeah, thanks. Acidosis.

Although the physical presence of a document provided the opportunity to analyze the sounds made by the document's use, a text did not have to be physically present to contribute directly to the visit. For example, there are several examples of reader's advisory. After asking the pregnant woman if she planned to breastfeed, the midwife offered the following suggestion:

Midwife 19: There are some good [breastfeeding] resources in our library

Client   19: Mhmm

Midwife 19: *The womanly art of breastfeeding, Bestfeeding, Jack Newman's guide to breastfeeding.* The La Leche League resources, some medical-based resources and *Bestfeeding*'s a nice big **basic** book.

Client   19: Okay

In the next case, the pregnant woman recommended a novel to the midwife, one featuring a midwife as the protagonist. The participants went on to discuss the book at some length:

Client   7: I'm reading *The baby catcher*. Did you read that yet?

Midwife 7: No

Client   7: Oh my God. It's ...

Midwife 7: Is it good?

Client   7: Yeah.

A variety of documents of outside authorship played a significant role in the work of midwives and pregnant women in prenatal visits. The remainder of this chapter will consider those documents that were created or inscribed within the visit itself or were created for use there. It is in these documents that the ties to the broader social order are most evident.

4. LOCAL PRACTICES OF INSCRIPTION

A small number of documents were mentioned and used at every prenatal visit. These are illustrated in Figure 2.

The pregnant woman's chart was uniformly housed in a file folder, often of a color with a particular organizational significance. For example, all charts might have the same color or a different color might be associated with each midwife's client charts. Although the contents of the client files varied from woman to woman and from practice to practice, all practices made use of the Ontario Antenatal Record (Ontario Ministry of Health and Long-Term Care, 2000). Part I of the record is used at the booking visit to record the woman's history and assessment, and Part II is used at subsequent visits. References to the Antenatal Record in this chapter therefore refer to Part II. In addition, each practice used practice-specific tracking sheets and checklists of various types. The checklist is used to make notes and record discussion topics. It complements, supplements, or replaces the lists of discussion topics on the Antenatal Record.

The Ontario Antenatal Record (Ontario Ministry of Health and Long-Term Care, 2000) deserves particular attention for the ways it shapes the information exchange between the midwife and the pregnant woman. For example, the general structure of prenatal visits mirrors in large part the structure of the record (Davies & McKenzie, 2004). Prenatal visits generally begin with a recording of the date, the gestational age of the fetus, the woman's weight, and the results of her urine test. From there discussion commonly moves to matters of concern to the pregnant woman and proceeds to issues related to the stage of pregnancy, particularly those on which the pregnant woman will need to make decisions. The visit commonly finishes with a physical examination and a brief discussion

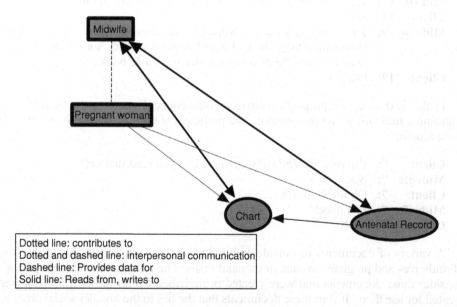

Figure 2. Documents always present.

of the next appointment (Hawkins & Knox, 2003). In other terms, "participants in local settings find their actions coordinated by the requirements of working with the text" (Campbell & Gregor, 2002, p. 32).

As the hub of the pregnant woman's file, the Antenatal Record co-ordinates and records the work of the various participants and functions in several ways as a boundary object—an object with "different meanings in different social worlds but [whose] structure is common enough to more than one world to make them recognizable, a means of translation" (Star & Griesemer, 1989, p. 393). The Antenatal Record serves as a standardized form on which a participants with potentially different goals can communicate the information needed by all, an ideal type describing standard features of a pregnancy (for example, fetal size at various weeks' gestation), a repository housing and coordinating data from other records, and a temporal boundary object, coordinating multiple temporalities as well as multiple communities of practice (Davies & McKenzie, 2004).

The Antenatal Record is in turn shaped by the visit as details are negotiated, recorded, or left unrecorded. Central to the study of textual practice is the inscription of documentary traces (Latour & Woolgar, 1986; Smith, 1990) during the process of doing the work. Filling out a form, however, is "not a neutral undertaking, but one in which organizational policy and a variety of taken-for-granted assumptions are brought into the helping relation. In that sense, the activation of the text in question is a procedure both for conducting a health care program and for exercising organizational power" (Campbell & Gregor, 2002, p. 34).

The act of filling out the form "accomplishes the objectification of the client" (Campbell & Gregor, 2002, p. 35) in ways that have material consequences. Bowler (1995) and Macintyre (1978) found that record makers' stereotyped views of pregnant women affected the ways in which they asked questions and recorded answers on forms. For example, the question of whether the pregnancy was planned was presented differently to married and unmarried women, and the companion question of whether the woman was happy to be pregnant was asked differently (or not at all) depending on the response recorded for the first question. Married women were therefore much more likely to be documented as being happy about their pregnancies than were single women, regardless of whether they had actually been asked this question. The forms filled out in this manner then went on to provide clues to the woman's identity and attitudes for later care providers. The routine practices of record makers "could be consequential not only for the statistics produced from the records but also for the pregnancy careers and experiences of individual women" (Macintyre, 1978, p. 602).

In the following example, the pregnant woman is reporting on her urine test, taken with a dip-strip that changes color in the presence of glucose or protein. In midwifery care, the client routinely conducts this test herself and interprets the result, which she reports orally to the midwife.

Midwife 4: Did you do your urine today?

Client 4: Yeah. So [glucose] was um, [sighing] nor, it was normal and slightly trace for the protein.

Midwife 4: Okay

Client 4: But

Midwife 4: More normal?

Client	4:	More normal
Midwife	4:	O.k. Often they kind of spill together
Client	4:	Yeah
Midwife	4:	just kind of around the edges a bit
Client	4:	Yeah
Midwife	4:	between the green and the yellow. We'll call it normal.

Of note here is the fact that the Antenatal Record was not developed by midwives, but rather by a sub-committee of the Ontario Medical Association which included representatives from a variety of medical specialties (obstetrics and gynecology, general and family practice, pediatrics, anesthesiology, and rural medicine), and from the OMA's Board of Directors and Committee on Women's Issues. The record is "widely used throughout the province" although its use is "not mandatory" (Ontario Medical Association Subcommittee on the Antenatal Record, 2000). It was evident in every practice I visited and no midwife described its use as optional. Sharpe (2004) characterizes its use as "required" (p. 160). See the passage quoted below in the conclusion).

Thus, the form does not "appear from nowhere . . . " but:

"should rather be understood as having been produced to intend the interpretive practices and usages of the succeeding phases of the relation. The text-reader moment is contained as a potentiality in the text itself. . . . [I]f we are to analyze textual materials for their properties as organizers of social relations, methods of textual analysis are required which explicate the active power of the text as it is realized or activated by a competent reader" (Smith, 1990, p. 222).

A competent reader would, therefore, read and inscribe the record in possession of considerable contextual knowledge. By recording this potentially ambiguous result as "normal" rather than "trace" the midwife's reading and writing demonstrates competence with regard to several issues: the specificity of the urine test strips, the acceptable tolerance for "normal" in various communities, and the consequences of recording one assessment or the other. Although the midwife may informally remind herself or her colleagues to reconsider this reading in light of later tests (either by making a mental note to herself or by attaching a sticky note to the client's record), she has chosen not to include an anomalous result on the official record. This client's Antenatal Record will be seen and used by other midwives in the practice and, if complications develop, by the obstetricians with whom the client consults or to whom her care is transferred. When seeing a care provider who has access to the records created by others, "the patient already, to some extent, is what the records say she is" (Macintyre, 1978, p. 607).

Rather than seeing this as an example of sloppy or inaccurate charting, it is more useful to regard this example as evidence that, in addition to clinical competence, the midwife must possess competence in all of these contextual matters in order to inscribe and interpret the record:

"[C]linic records, such as they are, are not something clinic personnel get away with, but . . . indeed, the records consist of procedures and consequences of clinical activities as a medico-legal enterprise" (Garfinkel, 1967, p. 198, emphasis in original).

As Berg and Bowker (1997) have found, medical records represent both the patient and the work done on the patient. They can inscribe the patient into certain prescribed procedures and temporalities (e.g., Berg, 1996). "The social relation of which the [client and the practitioner] are part originates outside the room where the interview takes place. [The document] carries the organizational aspect of the relation into the interaction . . . ". (Campbell & Gregor, 2002, p. 35). An example of this can be seen in the following excerpt:

> **Midwife 25:** [rustling papers] You're right on 50th percentile, we'd expect about a seven and a half pound baby.

The Antenatal Record contains a *Symphysis fundus height diagram*, a chart for estimating the size of the fetus by measuring the size of the woman's abdomen: "At each visit after 20 weeks, the symphysis fundus height in cm may be plotted on this graph. Discrepancies in growth should be evaluated" (Ontario Medical Association Subcommittee on the Antenatal Record, 2000). This linkage of size and time in a graphical format functions as a standard, allowing the woman's current measurement to be compared to a norm, as in this case, and also to her own previous measurement. The rule of thumb—that the symphysis fundus height in centimeters is approximately equal to the number of weeks gestation—is illustrated graphically on the chart, although the source of the normative data is documented neither on the Record itself nor in the instructions for its use. The inclusion of percentile lines on the chart means that the midwife can follow and predict a trend, using past measurements to infer a pattern likely to persist into the future (Davies & McKenzie, 2004). In this way, data recorded at this visit are linked to norms and standards developed elsewhere and themselves persist beyond the local setting and are carried through the record into the succeeding phases of the relation.

5. THE EXTRA-LOCAL USE OF LOCAL INSCRIPTIONS I: WITHIN THE CLINIC

Documents created or inscribed within the local setting may move physically and organizationally beyond its temporal and spatial boundaries in several ways. The client's clinical records follow her from visit to visit regardless of which midwife she sees. The documents within it play a pivotal role in the communication between the current midwife and the other midwives who have provided or will provide care for the client. Figure 3 illustrates the relationships observed between the current midwife past and future midwives, the client, and her records.

The transcripts provided several examples of the discussion of inscriptions made by midwives who had seen the current client previously but were not present at this visit. In the first case, this is the client's first visit with this midwife. Until now she has been seeing the midwife who was present at her previous birth.

> **Midwife 11:** I think we need to expect that [your labor] **will** be fast? Because, I mean, what she's written here is "five hours".

In order to read and understand the contents of a clinical document, a clinician requires knowledge of the author(s) of the report as well as knowledge of tacit documentary

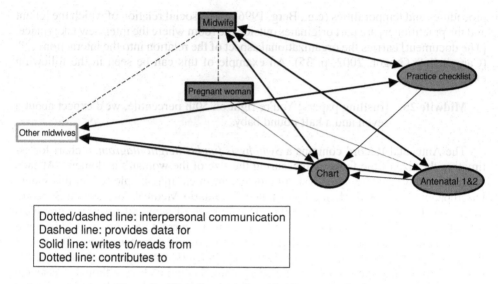

Dotted/dashed line: interpersonal communication
Dashed line: provides data for
Solid line: writes to/reads from
Dotted line: contributes to

Figure 3. Clinical records in midwife communication.

practices and the relationship of entries to one another (Garfinkel, 1967; Heath & Luff, 1996):

"The very *possibility* of understanding the record's entries is based on a shared, practical, and entitled understanding of common tasks, experiences, and expectations. The entries' brevity and (seeming) incompleteness 'works' since the reader knows the specifics of the writer's situation, what (s)he is concerned with, or requires" (Berg, 1996, p. 513, emphasis in original.)

Identification of other writers by their handwriting provides contextual information. For example, that person's history, experience, and charting practices. Knowing the author of the inscription, the midwife is able to infer a shared meaning of a "fast labor" that corresponds to standards accepted by different kinds of practitioners (Martin, 1987; Thomas, 1992). As Fitzpatrick (2000) observed, the official chart is not the full working clinical record. Although it provides the focus:

"it does not represent the totality of the record at work; the working record is made up of an evolving complex network of relationships among the multiple parts and the people who use them. Various degrees of formality co-exist in this working record. Some parts are formally sanctioned forms that will end up in the archived version of the record. . . . Others are forms that have been developed locally to meet specific needs" (Fitzpatrick, 2000, n.p.).

As the Antenatal Record was designed by physicians, its list of suggested discussion topics does not include those topics particular to midwifery care. For example, the principal midwife at each birth is assisted by a back-up care provider. The Antenatal II does not include this item in its checklist of topics for discussion. In the next example, the previous midwife has attached a note to the record to alert the current midwife to discussion topics not listed on the form.

Midwife 9:   I got a little note here, and I'm trying to read what this says . . . [sound of paper rustling] I can nearly
Client   9:   [reading] Role of, [says letters] b, u
Midwife 9:   back up midwife.

The sticky note functions as an adjunct to the record, extending its use in ways that correspond to the needs of the local users. Midwives provided many more examples and descriptions of the various uses of sticky notes and similar communications in follow-up interviews.

Conversely, inscriptions made in the course of the current visit will extend forward in time to contribute to the next visit. Prenatal midwifery visits routinely ended with a trip to see the practice administrator to book the next visit:

Midwife 14:   So, we'll book you to come in a month. Let's just go to the front and I'll book you in.

The midwife's statement here demonstrates an awareness of the standard visit frequency—once per month for the first 26 weeks of pregnancy, once every 2 weeks until week 36, and then once a week until the birth (Hawkins & Knox, 2003, pp. 91–92)—and of the gestational age of this client's pregnancy. The Antenatal Record would provide the midwife with the gestational age, which she has combined with her knowledge of the standard and translated into a date for the next visit.

Booking an appointment involves writing the client's name in the practice calendar, on the correct date and in the column for the midwife she will see next. This task is usually undertaken by the practice administrator but sometimes by the midwife, as in this case when the administrator was away from her desk. In addition, midwives and clients had personal date books into which they wrote dates and times for upcoming appointments. This particular inscription moves the next visit from something belonging solely to the practice, to something to be accounted for in the overall lives of the midwife and client.

This act of booking a visit ties the client visit back to the organizational management of the practice itself. In some practices, the administrator would prepare for each new clinic day by photocopying the day's calendar page for each midwife and highlighting the names of that midwife's clients with a fluorescent marker. I observed these calendar photocopy pages on midwives' desks, fastened with an elastic band to the top of her stack of the day's client charts. In this way, the post-visit inscription into the practice calendar is transformed into the midwife's pre-visit planning tool and reminder list for the next visit. (For a similar example, see Fitzpatrick, 2000). Taken further, the act of booking can be seen to be linked to documents concerned with the deployment of human resources in the clinic: from practice vacation schedules to the regulatory documents governing midwifery caseloads. This seemingly simple act of writing a name in a calendar in a particular location in fact provides a "direct line" to the broader social order.

6. THE EXTRA-LOCAL USE OF LOCAL INSCRIPTIONS II:
BEYOND THE PRACTICE

Physical movement may take records beyond the clinic itself. Several practices encourage the pregnant woman to carry her records as she approaches her expected due date.

Client   23: I forgot my folder. Sorry.
Midwife 23: That's okay, we just have to remember to update since those are the originals you have.

In addition, some forms are filled out within the confines of the visit with the intention that they will be used elsewhere. A prime example is the case of referral to another care provider or a requisition for a test or procedure. These forms serve as boundary objects (Star & Griesemer, 1989), which are used by some external care provider who then communicates back to the midwife and thereby to the client through a result or a report. Figure 4 illustrates this relationship:

The inscription of a requisition may set into motion an entirely new set of documentary practices for the external care provider, of which the local participants in the clinical

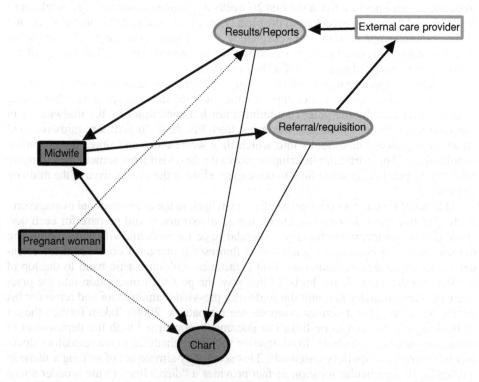

Figure 4. Referrals and requisitions.

midwifery visit may not be fully aware. Both the interpretation of clinical images and the creation of reports:

"are bounded by the generation of records. A radiological requisition begins these processes and a signed radiographical report signals their completion. During the course of the interpretation of an image, other records and information are created and used. These records include the new images, indexes to displayed images, preliminary book entries, prior images, previous reports, and various temporary notes that the radiologists make for themselves" (Yakel, 2001, p. 236).

Different levels of competence in the practices of reading and writing these reports can result in barriers in the midwife–client interaction:

Midwife 6: It's pretty brief what they, what they actually wrote, sometimes they're a lot more, umm, verbose, ah, this one just says, uh "single fetus in a cephalic presentation", so head-down, "placenta posterior and clear of the os, fluid volume".

Client   6: What's "clear of the os" mean?

Midwife 6: Clear of the os is clear, the os is the opening. So,

Client   6: Oh, okay!

Midwife 6: So

Client   6: That's good then. Yeah

Midwife 6: there's, the placenta is nowhere near the opening,

Client   6: Okay.

Midwife 6: so that's great.

Midwife 6: And fluid volume is normal, the measurements are all, what you'd expect [. . .]

Midwife 6: It says it's "a routine anatomic survey. Complete and appears within normal limits".

Client   6: Okay. All right.

Midwife 6: No concerns [. . .]

Client   6: I was just kind of worried about, you know, they checked, for the brain, and

Midwife 6: Yes!

Client   6: how things stand?

Midwife 6: Yes, they check all those things

Client   6: all that stuff?

Midwife 6: They have no (inaudible)

Client   6: No signs of Down's Syndrome, or anything like that?

Midwife 6: They look for, they measure the nuchal folds,

Client   6: Ummhmm

Midwife 6: and that's one of the indicators that they look for Down's. They look at the heart and the structure and, you know, sometimes there's heart problems that go along with Down's. They check the brain, they check for three-vessel cord because that sometimes goes with some kidney problems and other things. They check for the kidneys, the stomach, the bladder, all those things are what they routinely check for, and

                         sometimes they will list everything that they looked at, this time it just
                         says that, "a routine survey, complete
Client   **6:** Right
Midwife   **6:** and within normal limits".

This interchange demonstrates the differences between the radiologist writing the report, the client, and the midwife, in terms of "what the subject knows how to do as a reader and what the subject knows how to do in reading, and in so doing also displays the organizing capacity of the text, its capacity to operate as a constituent of social relations" (Smith, 1990, p. 5). The radiologist has made use of descriptive economies that "exploit the reader's ability to draw the necessary inferences from particular items and their configuration within the entry" (Heath & Luff, 1996, p. 356). In radiological reports in particular, such parsimonious language may be used as a strategy to create conservative and risk-averse reports (Yakel, 2001, p. 242).

    When different types of health care professionals all use the same records, "the brevity and conciseness *required* for the record to work at the same time necessitates continuous repair work" (Berg, 1996, p. 514). Here, the midwife is demonstrating familiarity with both the conventions of the radiologists writing the report and with the exigencies of communicating with a client. She intervenes immediately to reassure the client of the meaning of normal values and benign findings and she explains radiological reporting conventions. This work is most evident when it becomes clear that the terms "routine anatomic survey, complete and appears within normal limits" did not for this client rule out the potential for abnormalities, in particular Down's syndrome. The midwife responds to the client's concerns by explaining the radiologists' definition of "routine anatomic survey" and demystifying the meaning of "normal".

    Frontline human service workers such as midwives are often required in this way to serve as intermediaries between systems and people. In this role, "they negotiate the disjuncture between rational, impersonal 'ways with words' and embodied, personal 'ways with words' many times during a workshift. Indeed, they do not necessarily experience the disjuncture as one 'line of fault' but rather as a network of recurring, disorienting fractures" (Stooke, 2004, p. 41).

    In the next case, the mere physical absence of a document provides evidence of extralocal practices. This client is pregnant for the second time. She received her previous prenatal care from another midwifery practice, and gave birth by Caesarian section at Hospital A. Between 1996 and 1999, the province of Ontario's Health Services Restructuring Commission "directed that 33 public hospital sites no longer be used as hospitals as well as recommending to the Minister of Health that six psychiatric hospital sites and six private hospital sites be closed" (Ontario Health Services Restructuring Commission, 1999, p. 9). Hospital A was one of these.

Midwife 12: I had uh, some difficulty getting your, um operative report from, the
                     midwife. At the clinic? The midwife, it's [midwife name],
Client   **12:** Mhmm
Midwife 12: right? She's on leave
Client   **12:** Mhmm

Midwife 12:   for a while and um the folks over at her clinic thought it would be too much trouble to look through boxes to look for the operative report. So, my next place to check is [Hospital B] and hopefully the records from [Hospital A] have been transferred there

What manifests itself to local participants as an information-seeking barrier in fact carries the threads of a large number of social relations. For example, it hints at the relationships between midwifery clinics, the need for leaves and holidays including midwife burnout, illnesses, and midwives' own maternity leaves, the relationship between midwives and hospitals, and the restructuring of hospital services and the implications for hospital records management. All of these relationships and more are made visible through the absence of a single document.

7. CONCLUSION

This chapter has shown how audiorecordings can provide evidence of the uses of documents in local clinical settings. Figure 5 provides a complete map of the documents

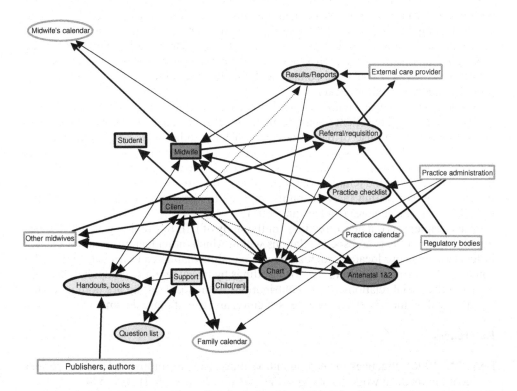

Figure 5. Textually mediated relationships evident in visit transcripts.

explicitly used or mentioned in the 29 prenatal clinical visits and illustrates the extra-local actors whose participation in the local setting is effected through the documents.

Other relationships clearly exist but are not documented here because the recordings did not provide explicit evidence of them, for example, the relationship between the mid-wife and various regulatory bodies, the role of regulatory bodies as authors and publishers of handouts and books, or the role of support staff in physically managing and filing documents and transferring them from one professional to another. This diagram will continue to evolve as more data are gathered and analysis proceeds. There is evidence in field notes, for example, that midwives' diplomas and current College of Midwifery registration certificates were prominently displayed in the practice. These documents and their particular placement are indicators of a variety of relations, regulations, and conventions.

While mapping the individuals and documents contributing in various ways to the antenatal visit is a necessary prerequisite to understanding the broader social relations, it is not in itself sufficient. Further analysis using Smith's approach to the role of texts in mediating social relations will uncover more subtle and farther-reaching relationships than the mapping of documents alone provides.

For example, a practicing midwife observed that, because the Antenatal Record was developed by the Ontario Medical Association, "as government regulated registered mid-wives, we have become implicated in [obstetrical] discourse by the required use of the Antenatal 1 and Antenatal 2 forms" (Sharpe, 2004, p. 160). The follow-up interviews with midwives provide much more data regarding midwives' actual use of these documents. During the interviews several midwives pulled out charts, forms, and records and described and demonstrated how they work with them. Further analysis will identify the ways in which midwives function as agents of the extra-local biomedical agenda and the means by which they resist and comply with this function in their roles as information providers and information seekers.

Although the analysis in this chapter has focused mainly on the midwife as an information provider and the client as an information seeker, the client is likewise implicated. Her own reading and use of parent advice books and other texts will shape both her information needs and the ways that she approaches the relationship with her midwife. Extra-local actors, brought into the pregnant woman's life through texts and other means, may provide models and templates of acceptable information behavior. The woman must likewise negotiate within the constraints imposed by these models in the information work in which she engages (McKenzie, 2003).

This chapter sets out new directions for the study of HIB by providing an understanding of the web of texts and social relations within which individual information seekers in local contexts are located. Such study of textual mediation can uncover the broader contexts of information behavior in local settings by revealing more completely the elements of the social relations whose contributions to the local setting are both mediated and afforded by the presence, absence, structure, and use of those documents.

References

Berg, M. (1996). Practices of reading and writing: The constitutive role of the patient record in medical work. *Sociology of Health and Illness*, 18(4), 499–524.
Berg, M., & Bowker, G. (1997). The multiple bodies of the medical record: Towards a sociology of an artifact. *Sociological Quarterly*, 38(3), 513–537.

Bowler, I. (1995). Further notes on record taking and making in maternity care: The case of South Asian descent women. *Sociological Review*, 43, 36–51.

Campbell, M., & Gregor, F. (2002). *Mapping Social Relations: A Primer in Doing Institutional Ethnography*. Aurora, ON: Garamond.

Case, D. O. (2002). *Looking for Information: A Survey of Research on Information Seeking, Needs, and Behavior.* New York: Academic Press.

Davenport, E., & Cronin, B. (1998). Some thoughts on >just for you= service in the context of domain expertise. *Journal of Education for Library and Information Science*, 39(4), 264–274.

Davies, E., & McKenzie, P. J. (2004). Preparing for opening night: Temporal boundary objects in textually-mediated professional practice. *Information Research*, 10(1) paper 211. Available at http://InformationR.net/ir/10-1/paper211.html.

DeVault, M., & McCoy, L. (2002). Institutional ethnography: Using interviews to investigate ruling relations. In J. Gubrium & J. Holstein (Eds.), *Handbook of Interview Research*, 751–776. Thousand Oaks, CA: Sage.

Fitzpatrick, G. (2000). Understanding the paper health record in practice: Implications for EHRs. *CD-ROM Proceedings of the Health Informatics Conference (HIC)*, n.p. Adelaide, Australia. Available at http://www.dstc.edu.au/Research/Projects/EWP/HIC_20_fitzpatrick_dist.pdf.

Garfinkel, H. (1967). Good organizational reasons for "bad" clinical records. In H. Garfinkel (Ed.), *Studies in Ethnomethodology*, 186–207. Englewood Cliffs, NJ: Prentice-Hall.

Gorman, P., Ash, J., Lavelle, M., Lyman, J., Delcambre, L., Maier, D., Weaver, M., & Bowers, S. (2000). Bundles in the wild: Managing information to solve problems and maintain situation awareness. *Library Trends*, 49(2), 266–289.

Hawkins, M., & Knox, S. (2003). *The Midwifery Option: A Canadian Guide to the Birth Experience.* Toronto: HarperCollins.

Heath, C., & Luff, P. (1996). Documents and professional practice: "Bad" organisational reasons for "good" clinical records. *Computer Supported Collaborative Work 1996*, 354–363. Cambridge, MA: ACM.

Latour, B., & Woolgar, S. (1986). *Laboratory Life: The [Social] Construction of Scientific Facts*. Princeton, NJ: Princeton University Press.

Levy, V. (1999). Protective steering: A grounded theory study of the processes by which midwives facilitate informed choices during pregnancy. *Journal of Advanced Nursing*, 29, 104–112.

Linell, P., & Bredmar, M. (1996). Reconstructing topical sensitivity: Aspects of facework in talks between midwives and expectant mothers. *Research on Language and Social Interaction*, 29, 347–379.

Lundberg, N. J. (1991). *The Social Organization of Birth Control Information in Public Libraries.* Unpublished Doctoral Dissertation. London, Ontario: The University of Western Ontario.

Macintyre, S. (1978). Some notes on record taking and making in an antenatal clinic. *Sociological Review*, 26, 595–611.

Martin, E. (1987). *The Woman in the Body: A Cultural Analysis of Reproduction.* Boston: Beacon Press.

McKenzie, P. J. (2003). Justifying cognitive authority decisions: Discursive strategies of information seekers. *Library Quarterly*, 73, 261–288.

McKenzie, P. J. (2004). Positioning theory and the negotiation of information needs in a clinical midwifery setting. *Journal of the American Society for Information Science*, 55(8), 685–694.

Olsson, P., & Jansson, L. (2001). Patterns in midwives' and expectant/new parents' ways of relating to one another in ante- and postnatal consultations. *Scandinavian Journal of Caring Sciences*, 15, 113–122.

Ontario Health Services Restructuring Commission. (1999). *Better Hospitals, Better Health Care for the Future: Summary Report on Hospital Restructuring, 1996–1999*. Toronto: The Commission. Available at http://www.health.gov.on.ca/hsrc/bettere/home.html.

Ontario Medical Association Subcommittee on the Antenatal Record. (2000). A guide to the revised antenatal record of Ontario. *Ontario Medical Review*, March 1–6. Available at http://www.oma.org/pcomm/omr/mar00.htm.

Ontario Ministry of Health and Long-term Care. (2000). *Antenatal Record 2*. Available at http://www.forms.ssb.gov.on.ca/mbs/ssb/forms/formsrepository.nsf/Forms/MOH-014-0375-64/$File/0375-64_.PDF

Pettinari, C. J. (1988). Task, talk and text in the operating room: A study in medical discourse. In R. O. Freedle (Ed.), *Advances in Discourse Processes*, 23. Norwood, NJ: Ablex.

Reddy, M., Pratt, W., Dourish, P., & Shabot, M. M. (2002). Asking questions: I information needs in a surgical intensive care unit. *American Medical Informatics Association Fall Symposium (AMIA'02)*, 647–651. San Antonio, TX, November 9–13, 2002. Available at http://www.ischool.washington.edu/wpratt/Publications/AMIA-mreddy-pratt-infoneeds-final.pdf.

Sharpe, M. (2004). Exploring legislated midwifery: Texts and ruling relations. In I. L. Bourgeault, C. Benoit & R. Davis-Floyd (Eds.), *Reconceiving Midwifery*, 150–166. Montreal: McGill-Queen's University Press.

Smith, D. E. (1990). *Texts, Facts and Femininity: Exploring the Relations of Ruling*. New York: Routledge.

Spink, A., & Cole, C. (2004). Introduction to the special issue. *Journal of the American Society for Information Science and Technology*, 55, 657–659.

Star, S. L., & Griesemer, J. R. (1989). Institutional ecology, 'translations' and boundary objects: Amateurs and professionals in Berkeley's museum of vertebrate zoology, 1907–1939. *Social Studies of Science*, 19, 387–420.

Stooke, R. K. (2004). *Healthy, Wealthy and Ready for School: Supporting Young Children's Education and Development in the Era of the National Children's Agenda*. Unpublished doctoral dissertation. London, Ontario: The University of Western Ontario.

Thomas, H. (1992). Time and the cervix. In R. Frankenberg (Ed.), *Time, Health, and Medicine*, 56–67. London: Sage.

Wilson, T. D. (1999). Models in information behavior research. *Journal of Documentation*, 55(3), 249–270.

Yakel, E. (2001). The social construction of accountability: Radiologists and their record-keeping practices. *Information Society*, 17, 233–245.

Chapter 6

Information Grounds: Theoretical Basis and Empirical Findings on Information Flow in Social Settings[1]

Karen E. Fisher and Charles M. Naumer
The Information School
University of Washington

1. INTRODUCTION

Do you go to a place for a particular reason but wind up sharing information just because other people are there and you start talking? If so, then you are likely participating in an information ground. In this chapter, we discuss how the social atmosphere of such venues as health clinics, beauty and tattoo parlors, bike shops, and sport events can foster information sharing in spontaneous, serendipitous, and planned ways. Moreover, we explain how information ground is a novel and timely framework for studying information behavior in rich and holistic ways, along with results up-to-date from current research.

At face value, the notion of information grounds may appear intuitive and obvious; however, its formal identification as a theoretical notion in the late 1990s fit with other developments in the field of information behavior. Historically, research on information behavior primarily focused on individuals' use of information sources and their socio-demographic characteristics—examinations which Zweizig and Dervin (1977) explained as "use and user studies". These studies, which addressed such questions as "how often is the X system used and by whom?" explained little about the reasons that people engage in information seeking and to what, if any, effect. Research in the early 1980s signaled a breakthrough. Marking the user-centered paradigm (Dervin & Nilan, 1986), several frameworks emerged, such as Dervin's Sense-Making (1992) and Belkin's Anomalous States of Knowledge (Belkin, 2005; Belkin, Oddy, & Brooks, 1982), that focused primarily on the how and why of uses that people make of information systems and cast users in the forefront with emphasis on understanding contextual aspects of the user's situation (Dervin, 1992).

In the 1990s, this research direction was cemented with the biannual, European "Information Seeking in Context" (ISIC) conference series, which pushed researchers to fully consider the holistic impact of context on information behavior. Indeed, two of the most cogent articulations on the nature of context were presented at ISIC by Dervin (1997) and later Kuhlthau (1999). It was this move, together with the proliferation of ethnographic or qualitative methodologies (with its own inherent focus on holistic examination), the

[1]This chapter expands greatly on an overview of information grounds by Fisher (2005).

A. Spink and C. Cole (eds), New Directions in Human Information Behavior, 93–111.
© 2006 *Springer.*

advent of using a social constructionist approach (Tuominen & Savolainen, 1997), and a renewed focus on information behavior and everyday life[2] that led to the identification of information grounds.

Before launching our discussion of information grounds research, we wish to acknowledge that the notion of "place" as a research phenomenon is hardly new to scholars in such fields as sociology, anthropology, and geography—especially human geography. For his history dissertation, for example, Relph (1976) explored the nature of place from varied perspectives and highlighted the 1960s work of geographer Fred Lukermann, who characterized "place" as where:

1. Location is fundamental.
2. Nature and culture are involved.
3. Spaces are unique but interconnected and part of a framework of circulation.
4. Spaces are localized.
5. Spaces are emerging or becoming, and have a historical component.
6. Have meaning.

More recently, the monograph *Senses of Place* edited by Feld and Basso (1996) contains ethnographies of what "place" means to such different populations as the Apache of Arizona and the Kaluli people of New Guinea in terms of expressing and knowing. Lippard (1997) in *Lure of the Local: Senses of Place in a Multicentered Society* similarly discusses "place" by blending history, geography, cultural/social studies, and contemporary art. One of the most recent treatises on "place" was published in 2004 by Creswell, a professor of social and cultural geography at the University of Wales. Penned *Place: A Short Introduction*, Creswell colorfully discusses the many dimensions of "place" and explains the difficulties with trying to establish any one universal definition as he explores numerous examples using varied contexts.

The most significant work on place, however, is likely the widely popularized book by Oldenburg (1999, originally published in 1989) entitled *The Great Good Place: Cafes, Coffee Shops, Bookstores, Bars, Hair Salons, and Other Hangouts at the Heart of a Community* that launched the term "The third place" and the respective names of many community-oriented businesses, including "Third Place Books" in downtown Seattle. As its title suggests, Oldenburg asserts that some public places such as coffee shops and hair salons operate as our "third place", meaning it is where one can be found when one is not at home or at work. A veritable social good (and necessity), Oldenburg provides numerous examples of these third places (which he continues as a series of case studies in his edited 2002 book) and conceptualizes on their nature. To be successful and attract people, he argues, as a neighborhood locale a third place must exhibit eight characteristics:

---

[2]Historically, most studies of information behavior have focused on such elite populations as scientists and engineers, especially as it was these populations for whom the majority of information systems were designed. In the 1960s and 1970s, several landmark studies were conducted on how people seek everyday information. Their approaches, however, involved large-scale surveys that were problematic for several reasons, including expense (Fisher et al., 2005). After a long hiatus during the late 1970 and 1980s, researchers again began focusing on everyday folks but also began drawing upon qualitative methods.

1. Occur on neutral ground where "individuals may come and go as they please, in which none are required to play host, and in which all feel at home and comfortable" (Oldenburg, 1999, p. 22);
2. Be a leveler, meaning it is an inclusive place that is "accessible to the general public and does not set formal criteria of membership and exclusion" and therefore promotes the broadening of social networks where people interact with others who do no comprise their nearest and dearest (p. 24);
3. Have conversation as the main activity—as Oldenburg explains, "nothing more clearly indicates a third place than that the talk is good; that it is lively, scintillating, colorful, and engaging" (p. 26), moreover, "it is more spirited than elsewhere, less inhibited, and more eagerly pursued" (p. 29);
4. Be accessible and accommodating: the best third places are those to which one may go alone at most anytime and be assured of finding an acquaintance;
5. Have "regulars" or "fellow customers" as it is these, not the "seating capacity, variety of beverages served, availability of parking, prices, or other features" that draw people in, "who feel at home in a place and set the tone of conviviality" while nurturing trust with newcomers (pp. 33–35);
6. Keeps a low profile as a physical structure, meaning it is "typically plain", unimpressive looking from the outside and not elegant, which "serves to discourage pretension among those gather there" and meld into its customers' daily routine (p. 37);
7. Has a persistent playful, playground sort of mood: As Oldenburg explains, "those who would keep a conversation serious for more than a minute are almost certainly doomed to failure. Every topic and speaker is a potential trapeze for the exercise and display of wit" (p. 37);
8. Is a home away from home, the place where people can be likely found when not at home or at work, "though a radically different kind of setting from home, the third place is remarkably similar to a good home in the psychological comfort and support that it extends" (p. 42).

In the remainder of his 1999 edition, Oldenburg describes other aspects of third places such as their personal benefits, which include novelty, perspective, spiritual tonic, and friendship; societal good in terms of their political role, habit of association, role as an agency for control and force for good, recreational spirit, and importance "in securing the public domain for the use and enjoyment of decent people" (p. 83). After exploring the nature of several third place examples in-depth, Oldenburg addresses the negative or downside of third places such as segregation, isolation, and hostility.

The notion of "place" also has not been ignored within the field of library and information science (LIS). While researchers such as Leckie and Hopkins (2002)—who drew upon Oldenburg's third place framework to study public libraries in Toronto and Vancouver, Shill and Tonner (2003) and Wiegand (2003) recently addressed the notion of "library as place", a continuing extensive examination is culminating as a special issue of the journal *The Library Quarterly* in 2006. But perhaps the most significantly-related work from LIS was conducted by Elfreda Chatman, who borrowed the concept of "small worlds" throughout many of her renowned ethnographic studies involving everyday life and marginalized populations.

While Chatman tended to analytically leave the physical setting in the background and focus more on the people present, she nonetheless always considered "place" as an intrinsic part of context and discussed its impact on her population's information behavior. For Chatman (2000), who borrows largely from Shutz and Luckmann (1974) and Kochen (1989), a small world is a "world in which everyday happenings occur with some predictability" and "allows for the presence of 'legitimized others'" by this meaning "people who share physical and/or conceptual space within a common landscape of cultural meaning." As Chatman (2000) further explains:

> Within the conceptualized understanding of information behaviours, the legitimized others place narrow boundaries around the possibilities of these behaviors. In other words, legitimized others shape, change, or modify the information that enters a small world in light of a world view. In this instance, a world view is that collective sense that one has a reasonable hold on everyday reality" (p. 3)

Four concepts that Chatman considers central to understanding small worlds are social norms, world view, social types and, of course, information behavior (Chatman, 2000; Pendleton and Chatman, 1998)—all of course which might be fruitfully observed while studying information grounds.

In the remainder of this chapter, we explore the nature of information grounds by discussing the results from several studies, starting with the initial exploration at foot clinics in Canada.

2. A DAY AT THE CLINIC

Information grounds arose unexpectedly from Pettigrew's (1998, 1999, 2000) field-work at community foot clinics on how nurses, the elderly, and other individuals share human services or everyday information. Using Granovetter's (1973, 1982) strength of weak ties framework, she hypothesized that the nurses provided the seniors with everyday information that the seniors could not obtain from other network members but that they would not use the nurses' information until first conferring with strong ties. This stance was investigated by observing 108 seniors as they received foot care from 24 nurses for incidents of everyday information sharing, and then conducting separate, follow-up interviews with 24 nurse-senior pairs or dyads. Consistent with the ethnographic approach—as described by Chatman (1992)—Pettigrew kept extensive field notes of all forms of information sharing at the clinic.

While she initially expected everyday information to flow in the direction of nurse → senior, she quickly learned that seniors were ripe sources of everyday information for the nurses themselves, that multiple persons participated in exchanges (e.g., several seniors and nurses), and that seniors shared information while waiting for treatment and afterwards. These observations led to new research questions about the role of the clinic itself as a physical and social setting that promoted information exchange. Moreover, she observed that information needs were rarely stated as direct requests, but instead emerged subtly as people shared their situations with one another and chit-chatted.

Just as seniors were sometimes observed employing specific, indirect strategies to obtain information, the nurses used distinct techniques to identify information needs and to disseminate information—albeit sometimes unconsciously. In her field notes, Pettigrew also remarked on the significance of such physical factors as the availability of refreshments, comfortable furniture, treatment waiting times, and the illusion of privacy in some settings as affecting information flow. Further richness was contributed to the clinic setting by such social factors as the presence of different types of individuals, the special "caring, trusting" qualities that the seniors associated with the nurses, and the "event" nature of the clinic in that for many seniors the clinic was their only bi-monthly outing during the cold Canadian winter.

In her 1999 article, *Waiting for Chiropody*, Pettigrew thus argued that social settings contain varied sub-contexts, which can be viewed or studied from the perspectives of its different actors—in the foot clinic case being the nurses and the seniors—along with the nature of the physical environment itself and the event's inherent activities. Together, Pettigrew further asserted, these sub-contexts form a grand context and that it is through studying these elements both individually and collectively that one arrives at a deep understanding of the information-related phenomenon. Drawing upon Tuominen and Savolainen's (1997) social constructionist approach to studying information exchange which emphasizes the value of studying conversation as created events from different perspectives, she defined information grounds as synergistic "environment[s] temporarily created when people come together for a singular purpose but from whose behavior emerges a social atmosphere that fosters the spontaneous and serendipitous sharing of information" (1999, p. 811).

In the immediate years following her work on the foot clinics, Pettigrew turned her research focus to how people use the Internet to seek everyday information (Pettigrew, Durrance, & Unruh, 2002.). Information grounds, however, returned to the forefront, first due to attention it began receiving from other researchers and students. Little other work had paid deep attention to the nature and impact of social settings on information flow; instead, they were examined as a backdrop or another contextual factor to understanding the main actors as part of conducting egocentric research. Pettigrew had suggested that we move social settings to the forefront and study them holistically as an equal and motivating partner in the phenomenon of information exchange, that we study information flow as a by-product of social interaction.

To information professionals she challenged them to make social interaction a by-product of information flow and to turn information settings such as libraries into social scenes a la information grounds. As colleagues said that information grounds resonated with their professional and personal experiences, Pettigrew again began observing characteristics at a new research site—coping skills and literacy programs for new immigrants run by the Queens Borough Public Library (QBPL) in New York—that were similar to those recorded at the foot clinics. Further conceptual development was thus needed on the information ground concept.

3. SOME PROPOSITIONS FROM QUEENS, NEW YORK

While there are many different definitions of "theory", a commonly accepted version in the social sciences is "a statement or group of statements about how some part of the world works—frequently explaining relations among phenomena" (Vogt, 1993,

- Context rich
- Temporal setting
- Instrumental purpose
- Social types
- Social interaction
- Informal & formal info flow
- Alternative forms of info use

Figure 1. Information grounds.

p. 232). In this sense, the purpose of theory is to orient the researcher towards a research problem by helping to phrase research questions and isolate key concepts, to help him/her know how to approach a problem methodologically, and to assist in interpreting results (Pettigrew & McKechnie, 2001).

Moreover, it is a researcher's responsibility to contribute to theory building by testing emergent concepts across different populations or studies and to use those results to build propositions that explain the theory in nuts and bolts for others—perhaps the most illustrative information behavior example of this exercise being Chatman (2000), who traced with exceedingly strong detail how her different theories of information behavior were both grounded in empirical fieldwork and other conceptual frames such that they emerged naturally as part of theory development.[3]

Drawing upon findings from the foot clinic, Fisher (formerly "Pettigrew") described information grounds in Fisher, Durrance, and Hinton (2004) as comprising seven key concepts—as seen in Figure 1—and they derived the following propositional statements:

Proposition 1: Information grounds can occur anywhere, in any type of temporal setting and are predicated on the presence of individuals.

Proposition 2: People gather at information grounds for a primary, instrumental purpose other than information sharing.

Proposition 3: Information grounds are attended by different social types, most if not all of whom play expected and important, albeit different roles in information flow.

Proposition 4: Social interaction is a primary activity at information grounds such that information flow is a by-product.

---

[3] The monograph *Theories of Information Behavior* edited by Karen E. Fisher and colleagues (2005) was inspired by and thus dedicated to the late Elfreda Chatman. It contains overviews of 75 theories written by 85 authors worldwide, and its introductory chapters were written by Marcia J. Bates, Brenda Dervin, and T. D. Wilson.

Proposition 5: People engage in formal and informal information sharing, and information flow occurs in many directions.

Proposition 6: People use information obtained at information grounds in alternative ways, and benefit along physical, social, affective, and cognitive dimensions.

Proposition 7: Many sub-contexts exist within an information ground and are based on people's perspectives and physical factors; together these sub-contexts form a grand context.

These propositions were tested in a field study of how new immigrants in Queens, New York, use coping skills and literacy programs run by QBPL at different non-library building locales in Queens, New York. From interviews and observations with 45 program users, staff, and other stakeholders at two different field sites, they derived a grand context (in Pettigrew's (1999) terms) woven from three sub-contexts: the immigrants of Queens, NY; the QBPL, its service model and activities for immigrants; and professional contributions of QBPL staff. Similar to Pettigrew's findings regarding foot clinics, they concluded that the QBPL sites were information grounds and that they supported the derived propositions. For example, the information grounds occurred wherever the QBPL held its programming regardless of type of building or whether the QBPL was featured predominantly.

People gathered at the locales for the express purpose of increasing their literacy or coping skills; not primarily information sharing although the latter was indeed a by-product. They learned that the different actors—from the frontline and behind-the-scenes QBPL staff to the range of users, from the newly immigrated to the more established—played different roles in the information-sharing process, where QBPL staff acted in roles of subject or cognitive authority similar to Pettigrew's (1999, 2000) nurses but also were recipients of everyday information gleaned from the program participants themselves. Because of the hodgepodge of people present and the pressing needs of the clientele for everyday information in general, as they adjusted to life in a new country and spoke in a new language in which they held varied levels of fluency, it quickly became obvious that people shared information in multiple directions often as part of social interaction and that topics of information could arise both quite serendipitously as well as through framing via the programs' subjects.

Fisher, Durrance, and Hinton (2004) further learned that QBPL staff engaged considerable effort in nurturing these information grounds for their immigrant clients by heavily promoting the programs outside the QBPL confines and connecting with local community-based organizations and opinion leaders, making special effort to ensure that people felt welcome, comfortable, and safe (i.e., no one was going to report anyone for anything, such as to Immigration Services) including through employing multilingual staff and preparing materials in varied languages, and hosting frequent ethnic programs that celebrated cultures from around the world.

The extent to which the QBPL customers benefited along multiple dimensions from the literacy and coping skills programs was well illustrated by the repeated finding that users had learned of QBPL prior to ever reaching the shores of the U.S.: in their home countries as they prepared to leave, future customers learned by word of mouth that they should go to the QBPL for help once they arrived in New York. In addition to learning to speak and read English, they would learn valuable information about getting by in their new country and all in a relaxed atmosphere surrounded by people who understood their situation if not experiencing something similar and who could likely speak their language.

Thus, in terms of outcomes or benefits to the immigrant users, Fisher, Durrance, and Hinton (2004) reported that the information grounds facilitated two types, which they labeled (1) building blocks towards information literacy and (2) personal gains achieved by immigrants for themselves and their families. We further summarized that "successful introduction to the QBPL—as per its mission, programming, and staff— can lead immigrants to a synergistic information ground that can help in meeting broad psychological, social, and practical needs" (Fisher, Durrance, & Hinton, 2004, p. 754). Commenting on the settings' multiplier effect, we noted that the immigrants benefit in broad, unexpected ways from participating in the coping skills and literacy programs, and that the programs' social and physical setting along with the QBPL staff play major contributing roles.

4. EMPIRICAL TESTING FALL 2003

The results from the two in-depth qualitative studies of foot clinic and QBPL programs prompted the need for further empirical testing of the information ground framework but this time with a large population. Research was needed using an open-ended approach that solicited data specifically about people's information grounds and what made them viable.

Two studies were deployed during fall 2003 and were guided by the same three research questions:

1. What are people's information grounds?
2. What characteristics make an information ground opportune for acquiring information?
3. What types of information do people obtain at information grounds?

The first study (Fisher et al., 2005) was conducted in partnership with the United Way of King County, a large non-profit organization that receives public funding and allocates it to different community organizations. As part of its operations, the United Way conducts periodic assessments of the public's needs for health and human services. In return for assisting with designing the survey instrument, Fisher and colleagues were permitted to include a set of questions about residents' information grounds.

As explained in-depth in Fisher et al. (2005), this study used sample clustering by zip code to survey 612 residents of East King County in Washington State (a large urban/rural area) by telephone. calls lasted on average 32 min. The 612 respondents, who were largely female (63%), white (84%), well-educated, and earning above the poverty line, were asked the following questions:

1. Sometimes people go to a place for a particular reason such as to eat, get a haircut, to worship, for child care, get something repaired, make crafts, see a health provider or get exercise, but end up sharing information just because other

people are there and you start talking. Does such a place come to mind for you? What is it?
2. What are some examples of information that you might pick up there?
3. What makes this a good place for obtaining information, either accidentally or on purpose?

For each of these open questions, the United Way contracted callers were instructed to record the respondents' answers using the respondents' own words.

The second study used the same questions but employed a slightly different methodology; instead of contacting people by telephone, 38 distance masters students at the University of Washington approached 276 individuals in varied public settings in the Northwest, Utah, California, and Washington, DC. These public settings ranged from urban streetscapes to coffee houses to public transport. The findings from both studies were remarkably similar.

While a main theme was that people were looking for "mingeable" places—in the words of one respondent, Fisher et al. (2005) reported that the two most popular information grounds were places of worship and the workplace, followed by activity groups (e.g., clubs, teams, playgrounds, fitness clubs), personal services (e.g., hair salons, tattoo parlors, barber shops), and restaurants/bars. More unusual information grounds included a needle exchange program, the local dump where people forage on weekends, military training venues and Oprah.com. A key distinction emerged regarding one's motivation for being at an information ground, meaning Fisher and colleagues classified settings in which one has little choice but to be present as "hostage phenomena", these sites included waiting rooms at auto repair shops; medical and dental offices; grocery store queues; laundromats; ferries, buses, and trains; and luggage carousels at airports.

In answer to Question #2 "What are some examples of information that you might pick up there", both studies identified a broad range of topics ranging from news and current events to hobbies and travel, everyday advice, entertainment, goods and services, healthcare, work related, education, and spirituality to finances, government services, and what other people are doing. Responses to question #3 "What makes this a good place for obtaining information, either accidentally or on purpose?" revealed that information grounds facilitate "desirous mingling" because they focus on the people present, provide opportunity for people to bond and share common interests and needs, and you feel like other people understand you and you trust them. Information grounds were also valued because of their diversity (range of different people), and because one could receive encouragement in dealing with something and gain interpersonal skills. As Fisher and colleagues concluded, people value their information grounds because they emphasize the social nature of information exchange and go beyond direct fulfillment of an information need.

A third study was further conducted during fall 2003 and winter 2004 that employed the same set research questions and same instrument (that also comprised other questions). The population, however, was very different. Instead of asking members of the general public about their information grounds, Fisher et al. (2004) conducted in-person interviews with 51 migrant Hispanic farm workers and their families in Yakima Valley, Washington—a large agricultural capital. The combined transitory nature of their work along with low wages, education, healthcare, and other factors contributes to Hispanic farm workers' label as information poor: meaning they have little success in meeting substantial needs for information.

Fisher et al.'s (2004) study of farm workers and their families comprised interviews and observation with 60 individuals at community technology centers, one of which was held in an old community building that also housed the long-standing Hispanic radio station. This farm working population was considered special because of their "at risk" nature (suspicion, illegal aliens, etc.), and four of the researchers were fluent in Spanish, one was Mexican-born and one was from the Yakima area—all coached in matters of cultural awareness and sensitivity.

The 51 participants were male (57%) and female (43%), young (mostly between the age of 17 and 30), and from large households (up to 11 people). The most popular information grounds were church, school, and the workplace; other sites included the farm workers' medical clinic, hair salons, garages, and the Hispanic radiostation premises. Food-oriented locales were noticeably absent. Participants valued information grounds because they interacted face-to-face with people whom they regarded as trustworthy and reliable. Information topics ranged from family issues, employment, and legal help to gossip and current events.

Information grounds also facilitated the phenomenon of interpersonal berrypicking. A spin-off of Bates' (2005) berrypicking theory that typically involves how users conduct online searches a bit at a time such that they evolve iteratively, interpersonal berrypicking implies that a person, in this case a Hispanic farm worker, uses information grounds to meet new social contacts or nurture existing ones in the aim of bettering his/her access to new information.

While the three field studies conducted in fall 2003 yielded valuable insights into the nature of information grounds, many new questions arose for study. As Fisher et al. (2005) wrote:

> The notion of IGs may be only newly proposed in the literature, but the phenomenon itself is not new, only its identification. Linked strongly with people's natural inclination of constructing and sharing information interpersonally and thus socially, IGs have been around since time immemorial and yet, little research—at least from an IB perspective—has explored their nature http://InformationR.net/ir/10-2/paper223.html.

More insights were needed into the people at information grounds, how these people are connected, what they do when visit their information grounds, and what they like about them.

5. EMPIRICAL TESTING FALL 2004—THE COLLEGE STUDENTS

In fall 2004, Fisher and Naumer began a field study that focused on deriving an information ground typology that captured such nuances as:

- focal activities;
- actor/social type roles;

- effects of information type (trivial vs. big decision information; insider vs. outsider);
- motivation (voluntary vs. forced or hostage, example, choir groups vs. waiting rooms);
- membership size and type ("open" vs. "closed").

By far the most exhaustive and interesting information ground study-to-date, this study examined college students at the University of Washington. Located on a large campus in the north-central area of Seattle, the University of Washington's 45,000 undergraduates and graduate student base are primarily Caucasian. Regarding the 30,000 undergraduates just half of whom are female (52%), 87% are state residents, and 68% are Caucasian followed by Asian American (24%); Latino (4%), African American (3%) and Native American (1%).

The survey, which comprised 27 primarily open questions, was conducted in late October 2004, a few weeks after the fall quarter had begun. Of the 729 students surveyed, 55% were female and 45% were male. Approximately 72% were undergraduates, 21% were graduate students, and 7% were non-degree seeking students. The mean age was 23.6 years old and the mean period of time as a University of Washington student was approximately 2 years.

The most common information ground identified was coded as *"campus"*. Expressed by half the respondents, "campus" was defined as classroom spaces, in the hallways before and after class, study centers, studios (as in the Art and Architecture schools), rehearsal area (for the Band and Drama departments), Red Square—one of the main large outdoor gathering areas, and student lounges. Note, "campus" did not include the Huskey Union Building, known as the "HUB", which contains varied restaurants, recreational venues, and other services. Instead, HUB-type responses were coded in terms of the specific internal, HUB place that a respondent described. Thus, if someone said a hair salon at the HUB was his/her information ground, then the response was coded as "hair salon".

After "campus", the most common information grounds identified were restaurants and coffee shops, workplaces, and social gatherings. Approximately 33% of respondents identified these as one of their information grounds. However, when asked at which information ground they encounter the *best information*, roughly 42% of respondents indicated a restaurant or coffee shop whereas only 14% indicated campus. Social gatherings and the workplace were each considered to be the best place by approximately 30% and 23% of the respondents, respectively. In contrast to the information ground studies discussed earlier, "church" as a primary information ground was noticeably absent.

Moreover and surprisingly for the college student population, only about 3% considered online sources to be an information ground, which was startling since 63% earlier told us that they invariably turn to online source as their first choice when seeking everyday information and only 26.5% indicated a preference for seeking information from strong or close interpersonal ties (under the research heading of "information habits", the United Way telephone study and in-person survey in fall 2003 revealed that 39.9% prefer getting their information from strong interpersonal ties while 39.2% turn to the Internet). Considering that the college population surveyed is most likely to be relatively technically savvy and have access to the technology that would allow them to access online sources, this finding suggests that places that include opportunities for face-to-face interaction may be more desirable for some populations.

In answer to "why the places they choose were the most important or best place to encounter information", respondents' replies were coded along three main categories: information-related, people-related, and place-related. In terms of being information-related, almost 50% of the respondents talked about the quality of information encountered at these places. The most common characteristic mentioned was the relevance, meaningfulness, or usefulness of the information encountered. Another common characteristic mentioned was the quality or comprehensiveness of the information.

Other answers referred to the interesting nature of information, the reliability of information, unanticipated information, and the abundance and accessibility of the information. About 25% of college students indicated a particular information grounds was best because of a reason that involved interaction people. Common reasons included both the presence of people representing diversity of opinion as well as the other extreme in which people held the same beliefs and opinions as the respondent. Other people qualities were helpfulness, trustworthiness, and shared interests. Finally, over 25% of respondents indicated that a characteristic of the place visited was what made their information grounds important. The most common reasons had to do with a place being familiar or comfortable. Many respondents indicated that the convenience of the place was also an important factor.

In terms of the people in attendance, almost half of the respondents said that they knew most of the people at their information ground well and over 40% indicated that they either recognized them but did not know their names or knew their first names. Only about 10% indicated that they would not recognize the people at their information ground. When asked if they interact with any of these same people in other settings over 75% of indicated that they did indeed, indicating that that the information grounds of college students comprise fairly strong, multiplex ties. When asked how often they frequented the information ground at which they receive the most important or best information, 50% indicated they visit it daily and 40% answered weekly—meaning 90% are frequent, regular visitors of their information grounds.

Over 70% of respondents also indicated that they had been going to their place for over a year. This finding may support the theory that people follow habitual patterns in seeking information and that information grounds may be an important aspect to people's information seeking habits. This finding would support principles of everyday information seeking proposed by Harris and Dewdney (1994) in their book "Barriers to Information: How Formal Help Systems Fail Battered Women", specifically their sixth principle (p. 27), that "people follow habitual patterns in seeking information"—meaning people tend to adhere to deeply engrained patterns or habits when seeking information much the same as they do when carrying out other routine tasks, such as driving to work.

College students' responses when asked what they have in common with the people at their information grounds were divided into four categories: activity, background, characteristic, and interests. The activity category indicated that the respondent shared a common activity with the other people in a way that involved interaction such as rock climbing or taking the bus. Many people identified a common employer or the fact that they all attended school as the element that created a background commonality. This type of response was coded as the respondent speaking to a common background which could entail a common employer, school, neighborhood, education level, or income level.

Therefore, background represented identity based on shared circumstances rather than direct interaction and shared experiences. The third category of response focused on characteristics that could be physical, mental, or emotional. For example, many respondents indicated that they were all of the same gender, same age, or that they were all "stressed out". Finally, the most common response accounting for over 50% of respondents were common interests such as sports or Chinese cooking.

In contrast to the earlier question about what factors made a particular information ground the best for encountering important everyday information, we later asked the college students what they liked about their information grounds in general. Instead of focusing on information-related attributes, responses here dwelt around such place attributes as atmosphere and ambience: over 50% of respondents mentioned this as an important consideration. Other reasons—which were all mentioned by 11% or less of the respondents—included making connections with people, amenities, convenience, and resources. When the answers to this question were categorized according to whether they related to the information, people, or place Fisher and Naumer found that about 75% related to the physical location, whereas approximately 14% focused on people and only 6% addressed information. This suggests that physical, place-related factors play an extremely important role in the effectiveness of an information ground, at least in the case of college students.

Significantly we sought to identify what kinds of topics are encountered at students' information grounds. Several broad categories emerged from coding the open response data, including: events, information, knowledge, issues, opinion, and people. Most responses indicated that students encountered multiple types of information at their information grounds and could seldom be labeled exclusively under one category. The category of event information encompassed anything "about local or campus happenings like concerts and cultural events". Responses categorized as information referred to factual information such as "new technologies" or "computers". This category was different than the category of knowledge which referred to information that was interpreted. Responses coded as knowledge included "deeper philosophical knowledge" or "life lessons, advice."

There were also many responses directed at specific issues such as "presidential election" or "world events and issues." Another area included a desire for information that included the same or differing perspectives on information such as "personal experiences of others: foreign students in the United States, fresh perspectives" and "People's thoughts and opinions". Finally, numerous responses were concerned with information regarding people and were often concerned with the social aspects of information exchange. These responses often dealt with friends and family and included responses such as "How friends are doing today. How are friends' classes" and "Learning new things about what family members are doing".

When asked what percentage of the everyday information that they encountered at the information grounds occurred by chance, college students' responses were fairly uniform across quartiles (i.e., 25%, 50%, 75%, 100%). Slightly more respondents answering that 50–75% of the information encountered were by accident or chance. Respondents indicated that information about events, opinions, and people was the types of information most likely to be encountered by accident or chance.

6. DISCUSSION

The above studies reveal that information grounds are an emergent and significant area for future study. While there are several parallels with research undertaken in cognate fields, especially examinations of "place" in fields such as human geography, and Oldenburg's third place, as well as within LIS—most notably in terms of Chatman's work on small worlds—much research remains to be undertaken. Regarding Oldenburg's third places, work is needed on how information grounds are similar and dissimilar as there are many: some information grounds—for example—are hostage settings while others fail to meet several of the eight propositions that Oldenburg outlines. Regarding small worlds, as Chatman discusses them, we need to explore how particular information grounds are an element of the small world phenomenon and under which circumstances.

Research is also needed on how information needs are expressed and recognized at information grounds, and how information is socially constructed among different actors—phenomena for which the *New Yorker's* financial page writer Surowiecki's (2004) work *The Wisdom of Crowds* and his colleague Gladwell, author of the *Tipping Point* (2002) and most recently *Blink* (2005) may provide light in addition to the findings from basic research undertaken by academics such as Savolainen's (1995) everyday life information seeking model. Yet research also needs to address how people's perceptions and participation in information grounds change over time, the life cycles of information grounds (how they are created and sustained; what causes them to disappear or transform), and how they can be used to facilitate information flow.

How, for example, can employers alleviate the stressors of unemployment by helping laid-off employees establish or identify "replacement" information grounds that can facilitate the availability of information required during times of transition? How can healthcare providers utilize information grounds to help people and their caregivers as they progress through stages of illness or grief? In sum and pragmatically speaking, information grounds yield local and global impact because they occur across all levels of all societies, especially as people create and utilize them to perform tasks in the course of daily life. The better we understand where information grounds are situated for different populations as well as how they emerge and function, the better we can design ways of facilitating information flow therein.

As we continue analyzing the College Student data to flesh out the information ground typology and explore further the notion of information ground as place and its fit with small world theory and other frameworks, several other information ground studies are underway, which are summarized as follows. Readers interested in tracking our research on information grounds, collaborating on future studies or contributing an anecdotal information ground page to our Information Behavior in Everyday Contexts (IBEC) Website are invited to visit us at http://ibec.ischool.washington.edu.

Information Grounds during Baby Story Time (E. F. (Lynne) McKechnie, Associate Professor, and Pam McKenzie, Assistant Professor, Faculty of Information and Media

Studies, University of Western Ontario): Ethnographic observation and interviewing was conducted by McKechnie and McKenzie (2004) at eleven, 30 min sessions of public library baby/adult caregiver story times to discover what actually happens at these sessions. One of the surprising results was that the adult caregivers engage in everyday life information sharing about topics such as parenting, health, child development, travel, and daycare. These findings suggest that story time programs, in addition to being important literacy events for the children participating, also act as information grounds or informal sites where information is shared. This study was funded by ALA's Carroll Preston Baber Research Grant award.

Information Grounds of Seattle's Polish Community (Tom Dobrowolsky, MLIS Student, The Information School, University of Washington): Seattle contains a small, though active, Polish-American community. Transcending any one neighborhood, this network comprises several social hubs, events, and gathering places in order to actively promote Polish culture and to connect Polish-Americans with their ethnic roots. In this ethnographic study, 15 members were interviewed and participant observation was conducted in three popular gathering places. Observations involved detailed descriptions of the events taking place, the places themselves, the people, and groups present, and the social phenomena which occurred in them. Findings revealed the participants' information grounds and how they were used to disseminate everyday information. Additionally, findings addressed how the social nature of information exchange, via information grounds, functioned to establish a sense of community and to maintain Polish ethnic identity within this geographically disparate social network.

The Virtual Jaamati: Technology to Facilitate Information Grounds at Coffee Shops (C.A. Burrell and Dev Nambi, Undergraduate Students, The Information School, University of Washington): The Virtual Jaamati project uses location-specific computing at such places as bars, libraries, and cafes to facilitate information sharing. The software enables patrons (using optional aliases) to connect to a wireless network using a personal computing device to gain access to services such as profiles, forums, announcement archives, photo galleries, and intra-grounds Instant Messaging. We are evaluating the information behavior people at coffee shop as they use the Virtual Jaamati software. Findings will reveal ways in which the software facilitates communication and interaction among users.

Seattle's Pike Place Market Study (Steve Lappenbusch, PhD Student, Department of Technical Communication, and University of Washington): Considered the soul of Seattle, the Pike Place Market by the waterfront has been continuously operating for nearly a century. The Market's traditions, products, and people make it a unique shopping destination and a thriving community. Open 7 days a week, the vendors at this covered, 9-acre, multiplex market range from sellers of fish, fruits, and vegetables to specialty items and clothing. With nine million visitors each year, the Market also engages local farmers, craftspeople, businesspeople, and performers in addition to providing a home to 500 residents, most of whom are low-income seniors, as well as a variety of services for the needy.

The research questions guiding the study of Pike Place include: (1) What kinds of information grounds emerge in the daily interactions of Market workers and customers? (2) What benefits do people report or anticipate from participating in these information grounds at the Pike Place Market? and (3) What roles do different people play in the flow of information in the Pike Place Market? Data are being collected through unobtrusive observation and in-depth interviews with different stakeholders, including Market staff, vendors, regular shoppers, and tourists.

Verbena: Overcoming Poverty as Part of the Information Ground Life Cycle (Kris Unsworth, PhD Student, The Information School, University of Washington): Verbena is a Seattle-based, non-profit health services, and advocacy organization that serves lesbian, bisexual and queer women, and transgendered individuals. This research focuses on the creation and staying power of an information ground, and addresses three key questions: How are information grounds created? How does an information ground change over time? and How is an information ground maintained? Implicit in these questions will be how the information ground, from initial creation through its maintenance and various transitions, provides a space for addressing the needs of its inhabitants or actors.

The provision of health services developed from the organization's initial purpose, which was to provide a support network for lesbian cancer survivors. This research will examine the development of this organization or information ground via its history and current services, including outreach. Stakeholders of interest include Verbena's organizers, board of directors, frontline staff, and clients. Since sexual minorities may face unique barriers to healthcare and may also be at a higher risk for health-related problems, it is reasonable to refer to some members of the population served by Verbena as the "information poor". Thus Chatman's (2000) information poverty framework for understanding the social life of specific groups will be used to add context to the needs of lesbian, bisexual and queer women, and transgendered individuals.

Information Grounds of Tweens (Karen Fisher, Associate Professor, and Colleagues, The Information School, University of Washington): Adolescents between the ages of 9 and 13, known as Tweens, may be considered "placeless" because society discourages them from hanging out in public venues and because they do not own their own space; moreover, they are considered information poor because their needs for everyday information that accompany their burgeoning psychological, social, and physical development are largely negotiated and translated by adults. In this National Science Foundation funded study, Fisher and colleagues are conducting focus groups and follow-up independent interviews with tweens from different socio-demographic areas in Seattle to learn about tweens' information grounds and what makes them unique from those places favored by adults. Emphasis is also placed on understanding the role of interpersonal communication among tweens.

Information Grounds of Stay-at-Home Mothers (Karen Fisher, Associate Professor, and Colleagues, The Information School, University of Washington): Stay-at-home moms played multifaceted roles such as caregiver, shopper, chauffeur, money manager, etc., that require a broad range of everyday information. Virtually nothing is known, at least from an information behavior perspective, about this population. In a National Science Foundation funded study, Karen Fisher and colleagues are conducting unobtrusive and participant observations of mothers as they interact with one another during parent–child activity and exercise programs. Additionally, they are asking mothers to keep diaries of their information-sharing incidents which are then discussed during periodic interviews with the researchers. In addition to exploring the nature of the information grounds of stay-at-home mothers, this study is focusing on the role of interpersonal communication.

References

Bates, M. J. (2005). Berrypicking. In K. E. Fisher, S. Erdelez, & E. F. McKechnie (Eds.), *Theories of Information Behavior*. Medford, NJ: Information Today.

Belkin, N. (2005). Anomalous state of knowledge. In K. E. Fisher, S. Erdelez, & E. F. McKechnie (Eds.), *Theories of Information Behavior*. Medford, N.J: Information Today.

Belkin, N. J., Oddy, R. N., & Brooks, H. M. (1982). ASK for information retrieval. part I: Background and theory. *Journal of Documentation,* 38(2), 61–71.

Chatman, E. A. (1992). *Information World of Retired Women.* New York, NY: Greenwood Press.

Chatman, E. A. (2000). Framing social life in theory and research. *New Review of Information Behaviour Research: Studies of Information Seeking in Context,* 1, 3–17.

Creswell, T. (2004). *Place: A Short Introduction.* Malden, MA: Blackwell.

Dervin, B. (1997). Given a context by any other name: Methodological tools for taming the unruly beast. In P. Vakkari, R. Savolainen, & B. Dervin (Eds.), *Information Seeking in Context: Proceedings of an International Conference on Research in Information Needs, Seeking and Use in Different Contexts* (August 14–16, 1996, Tampere, Finland, 13–38. London: Graham Taylor.

Dervin, B., & Nilan, M. (1986). Information needs and uses. In M. E. Williams (Ed.), Annual Review of Information Science and Technology, 21, 3–33.

Feld S., & Basso K. H. (Eds.) (1996). *Senses of Place.* Santa Fe, New Mexico: School of American Research Press.

Fisher, K. E. (2005). Information grounds. In K. E. Fisher, S. Erdelez, & E. F. McKechnie (Eds.), *Theories of Information Behavior*. Medford, NJ: Information Today.

Fisher, K. E., Durrance, J. C., & Hinton, M. B. (2004). Information grounds and the use of need-based services by immigrants in Queens, NY: A context-based, outcome evaluation approach. *Journal of the American Society for Information Science and Technology*, 55(8), 754–766.

Fisher, K. E., Marcoux, E., Miller, L. S., Sanchez, A., &.Cunningham, E. R. (2004). Information behavior of migrant hispanic farm workers and their families in the Pacific Northwest. *Information Research*, 10(1), paper [Available at http://InformationR.net/ir/10-1/paper199.html].

Fisher, K. E., Naumer, C. M., Durrance, J. C., Stromski, L., & Christiansen, T. (2005). Something old, something new: Preliminary findings from an exploratory study about people's information habits and information grounds. *Information Research*, 10(2) Paper 223 [Available at http://InformationR.net/ir/10-2/paper223.html].

Gladwell, M. (2002). *The Tipping Point: How Little Things Can Make a Big Difference.* NY: Little, Brown.

Gladwell, M. (2005). *Blink: The Power of Thinking Without Thinking.* NY: Little, Brown.

Harris, R. M., & Dewdney, P. (1994). *Barriers to Information: How Formal Help Systems Fail Battered Women.* Westport, CN: Greenwood.

IBEC (2004). *Information Grounds.* Available at: ibec.ischool.washington.edu.

Kochen, M. (Ed.) (1989). *The Small World.* Norwood, NJ: Ablex.

Kuhlthau, C. C. (1999). Investigating patterns in information seeking: Concepts in context. Proceedings of the Second International Conference on Research in Information Needs, Seeking and Use in Different Contexts, 13–15 August, 1998; Sheffield, UK. Edited by T. D. Wilson & D. K. Allen. London: Taylor Graham, 10–20.

Leckie, G. J., & Hopkins, J. (2002). The public place of central libraries: Findings from Toronto and Vancouver. *Library Quarterly*, 72, 326–372.

Lippard, L. (1997). *Lure of the Local: Senses of Place in a Multi-Centered Society*. NY: New Press.

McKechnie, L., & McKenzie, P. (2004). The young child/adult caregiver story time program as information ground. *Library Research Seminar III*, Kansas City, KA, October 15, 2004.

Oldenburg, R. (1999). *The Great Good Place: Cafes, Coffee Shops, Bookstores, Bars, Hair Salons, and Other Hangouts at the Heart of a Community*. NY: Marlowe.

Oldenburg, R. (2002). *Celebrating the Third Place: Inspiring Stories About the "Great Good Places" at the Heart of Our Communities*. NY: Marlowe.

Pettigrew, K. E. (1998). *The Role of Community Health Nurses in Providing Information and Referral to the Elderly: A Study Based on Social Network Theory*. Unpublished doctoral dissertation. London, ON: The University of Western Ontario. [www.ischool.washington.edu/fisher/dissertation].

Pettigrew, K. E. (1999). Waiting for chiropody: Contextual results from an ethnographic study of the information behavior among attendees at community clinics. *Information Processing and Management*, 35(6), 801–817.

Pettigrew, K. E. (2000). Lay information provision in community settings: How community health nurses disseminate human services information to the elderly. *Library Quarterly*, 70(1), 47–85.

Pettigrew, K. E., Durrance, J. C., & Unruh, K. T. (2002). Facilitating community information-seeking using the internet: Findings from three public library-community network systems. *Journal of the American Society for Information Science and Technology*, 53(11), 894–903.

Pettigrew, K. E., & McKechnie, L. M. (2001). The use of theory in information science research. *Journal of the American Society for Information Science and Technology*, 52(1), 62–73.

Relph, E. (1976). *Place and Placelessness*. London: Pion.

Savolainen, R. (1995). Everyday life information seeking: Approaching information seeking in the context of "way of life." *Library and Information Science Research*, 17(3), 259–294.

Shill, H. B., & Tonner, S. (2003). Creating a better place: Physical improvements in academic libraries, 1995–2002. *College and Research Libraries*, 64, 431–466.

Shutz, A., & Luckmann, T. (1974). *The Structures of the Life-World*. London: Heinmann.

Surowiecki, J. (2004). *The Wisdom of Crowds: Why the Many are Smarter Than the Few and How Collective Wisdom Shapes Business, Economics, Societies and Nations*. NY: Doubleday.

Tuominen, K., & Savolainen, R. (1997). A social constructionist approach to the study of information use as discursive action. In P. Vakkari, R. Savolainen, & B. Dervin (Eds.), *Information Seeking in Context: Proceedings of an International Conference on Research in Information Needs, Seeking and Use in Different Contexts, 14–16 August 1996, Tampere, Finland*, 81–96. London: Graham Taylor.

Vogt, W. P. (1993). *Dictionary of Statistics and Methodology: A Non-Technical Guide for the Social Sciences*. Newbury Park: Sage.

Wiegand, W. A. (2003). To reposition a research agenda: What American studies can't teach the LIS community about the library in the life of the user. *Library Quarterly*, 73, 369–382.

Zweizig, D., & Dervin, B. (1977). Public library use, users, uses: Advances in knowledge of the characteristics and needs of the adult clientele of American public libraries. In M. Voigt & M. H. Harris (Eds.), Advances in Librarianship (Vol. 7, pp. 231–255). New York: Academic Press.

Chapter 7

Information Sharing

Sanna Talja
Department of Information Studies

Preben Hansen
Swedish Institute of Computer Science University of Tampere

1. INTRODUCTION

The traditional humanistic concept of individuals is as the originators of knowledge and of the growth of knowledge and human mental powers as processes initiating from the innovative capabilities of single individuals. This view has influenced both the conceptualizations used in information seeking research, and the research and development of systems for supporting information access and knowledge creation. Research and theories of information seeking have traditionally focused on the "information man", on the individual as a seeker, and user of information (Talja, 1997).

This has also, to a large extent, been the case for IR and seeking research (Hansen & Järvelin, 2000, 2004). The collective aspects of human information behavior (HIB) have only been conceptualized as consulting, information seeking, use of personal sources, and peer influence. Such conceptualizations suggest a one-way process in which an individual consults another individual. Group seeking, the more or less systematic collaboration in information acquisition, has received less attention.

Romano et al. (1999) have aptly coined the term "the IR paradox" to describe the discrepancy between the inherently social nature of work and information practices,[1] and the design of IR systems and interfaces to support individuals working independently. Most interfaces to information tools and systems (databases, library catalogs, and IR applications) reflect single user stereotypes. They have mainly been designed to support people as individual actors as they engage in information activities.

Recent studies undertaken in the areas of both work and everyday life information seeking (ELIS) show that collaborative information seeking is as common and natural as individual seeking (Hansen & Järvelin, 2000, 2004; McKenzie, 2003; Talja, 2002). These studies show that information acquisition and filtering tasks are commonly distributed among several individuals, and purposefully planned and undertaken as collective and collaborative efforts. Distributed collaboration is increasingly built into work practices, as a structural component of work.

---

[1] By information practices we refer to practices of information seeking, retrieval, filtering, and synthesis.

A. Spink and C. Cole (eds), New Directions in Human Information Behavior, 113–134.
© 2006 *Springer.*

Information technologies that support collaboration such as e-mail, intranets, desktop videoconferencing, and collaborative data mining have stimulated the proliferation of alliances between organizations and between disciplinary communities (Kanfer et al., 2000). People commonly work in groups and solve information problems in interaction with other people (Hansen & Järvelin, 2004). Given this background, collaborative information behavior (CIB) is emerging as a new direction and central research area within HIB. The purpose of this chapter is to address this new direction for HIB research and the need for a clear formulation of the issues and questions belonging to CIB research, to describe the main dimensions of CIB, and to provide theoretical grounding for CIB research.

Classic information seeking models such as Kuhlthau's (1993) ISP model, Ellis' (1993) model, and Wilson's (1999) model, enabled the systematic study of information seeking behavior. CIB is a new topic within HIB research that cannot be tackled by leaning on earlier models of information seeking. Taking collaborative information practices as the focus of research mandates some reformulations in conceptualizations of users, technologies, and information seeking. We contribute by outlining a social practice approach to CIB research.

The chapter proceeds by first defining CIB and its research questions. Section 2 summarizes earlier research efforts and findings in this field, and points out gaps in the existing body of research. Section 3 selectively draws upon the insights emerging from the body of research reviewed, and proceeds to outline the social practice approach.

2. DEFINITIONAL ISSUES IN CIB

CIB can be broadly defined as an activity where two or more actors communicate to identify information for accomplishing a task or solving a problem. CIB includes processes of problem identification, analysis of information need, query formulation, retrieval interactions, evaluation, presentation of results, and applying results to resolve an information problem, as shown in Figure 1.

CIB ranges from sharing accidentally encountered information to collaborative query formulation, database searching, information filtering, interpretation, and synthesis. The systematicity of CIB thus varies from *ad hoc* sharing of information between team members to a planned division of labor where some members work together to find information for a specific task whereas others focus on other issues.

We may define *collaborative information seeking and retrieval* (CIS&R) as active and explicit seeking and retrieval of information for solving a specific task (Hansen & Järvelin, 2005). *Information sharing* incorporates both active and explicit and less goal oriented and implicit information exchanges. Information sharing is about sharing *already* acquired information, while CIS&R deals with cooperative searching *for* information (Hansen & Järvelin, 2004). These may often coincide in practice, however. Fidel et al. (2004) similarly distinguish information sharing from CIS&R. In their view, information sharing denotes direct information exchanges among those involved in solving a problem; such information exchanges qualify as CIS&R only if actors collaborate to acquire information they *did not already have*.

Collaborative information activities may be classified into *document-based* and *human-related* (Hansen & Järvelin, 2004). Document-based collaborative information

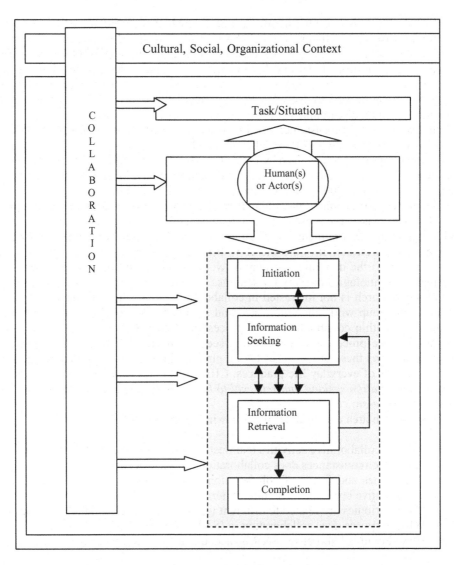

Figure 1. Collaboration and information behavior.

activities involve the creation and use of documents (electronic and paper-based). In human-related CIS&R, people use the knowledge and expertise possessed by other humans directly. Examples are asking colleagues for advice and judgments. From an IR systems design perspective this is an important distinction. It shows that there is a need for supporting collaborative document seeking, retrieval, reuse of already found documents and already conducted searches, and for systems that support the human–human sharing of advice and judgments.

Fidel et al. (2004) raise the important question whether all situations where people look for information together represent CIS&R. A librarian may help a user in the library, for instance, and a user may look at Frequently Asked Questions (FAQ) files for a direct answer to her question. Fidel and her colleagues conclude that information seeking and retrieval is collaborative only when the actors involved are colleagues or otherwise engaged in the same work or everyday life activities. A librarian helping a user belongs to the field of mediated searching (Spink et al., 1999), whereas cases where two librarians search together to help a customer, or cases where two customers together look at FAQs for an answer, represent CIS&R (Fidel et al., 2004).

Another important issue raised by Fidel et al. (2004) is that CIB is tightly interwoven with work and other mundane practices, and cannot be studied separately from them. Hansen and Järvelin (2005) stressed that de-contextualized approaches to information seeking and retrieval cannot but yield narrow findings that do not capture real-life practices. It would make little sense to study CIB independently of the work domains, tasks, and everyday life environments in which needs for information are embedded. Collaborative information activities are therefore best captured by naturalistic research that pays attention to the dynamic interplay of work practices, information practices, and information technologies in everyday settings.

CIS&R research is not interested in collaboration *per se*. It is not interested in the dynamics of group work, the emergence and sustenance of collaborations, or human relationships within collaborative work processes. Rather, CIB research looks at collaboration in the processes of information seeking, retrieval, filtering, and synthesis. However, it views these processes as taking place and being deeply embedded in work and other kinds of everyday life practices. CIB investigates *manifestations of collaboration in information seeking and retrieval to better understand and support work and knowledge processes*.

This research area encapsulates the following questions and problems:

- How do collaborative activities manifest themselves in IS&R? When and in what kinds of circumstances does collaboration in IS&R occur?
- What types and forms of collaborations can be observed and identified (e.g., collaborative browsing, searching, filtering)?
- What attributes are related to different types and forms of collaborative IS&R?
- What purposes does collaboration in IS&R serve?
- How should collaborative IS&R be accounted for in IR systems design?

Considering the support for collaboration in the design of information systems, the following motivations form the basis for research:

- From research and development of tools that supported and enhanced individual use of text-based information systems (system-oriented approaches), there is now an increasing interest in supporting groups and collaborative work, also in IS&R processes.
- From the assumption that IR is a need of specific categories of users, the goal has shifted to a refinement or enhancement of tools or systems that take into account work and knowledge sharing practices, that are necessities in organizations in the

conduct of their business; and that involve their users and user communities as co-designers.

- In both professional and private environments, people are moving increasingly in digital information spaces, involving communication with distributed people and groups.

The scientific and practical aims of CIB studies are to:

- Observe collaborative activities in authentic settings; focusing on what people actually do;
- Apply naturalistic and work practice-driven data collection methods and analysis in order to inform the design of systems for supporting knowledge sharing and collaborative information seeking and retrieval.

3. CIB STUDIES

Before 2000, studies on CIB were scarce. The body of CIB research has increased in recent years, albeit slowly. As Case (2002) notes, information seeking research evolved from library user and use studies. Some elements of the former systems-oriented viewpoint lingered as the interest broadened to HIB in any work or leisure context. The persistence of what may be called the *sources and channels approach* to information seeking explains why collaborative information seeking, retrieval, browsing, and filtering have rarely been taken as objects of study in their own right.

The next section investigates CIB studies conducted in different settings (Library, Academic, Other Professional, and Everyday Life Contexts), and points out gaps in existing research. The purpose of the review is to identify and collect together specific dimensions of collaborative information practices for the purposes of creating a theoretical framework for CIB studies. We do not intend to be exhaustive. Rather we give some relevant and informative examples across research areas. In comparison to information seeking research, a richer area of potential studies is the field of Computer Supported Cooperative Work (CSCW),[2] which contains a larger body of research on collaborative information seeking, retrieval, and filtering.[3]

---

[2]CSCW studies the ways people work collaboratively with the enabling technologies of computer networking, and associated hardware, software, services, and techniques. It is concerned with designing shared information spaces and supporting heterogeneous, open information environments that extend existing single-user applications (Schmidt & Bannon, 1991). In this field, also much innovative technology to support collaborative information seeking and retrieval have been developed. We will not discuss these technologies in detail here (for an early review, see Twidale and Nichols, 1998a).

[3]Also the field of Knowledge Management (KM) has considerable overlap with both HIB research and CSCW. Knowledge management describes the means by which an organization efficiently plans, collects, organizes, uses, controls, disseminates, and disposes of its information, and through which it ensures that the value of that information and human expertise is identified and exploited to the fullest extent. This field takes as its fundamental research interest the enhancement of knowledge sharing in organizations. Davenport (2002) reviews this research in detail; therefore, it will not be discussed here.

3.1 CIB in the Library Context

Some important early CIB studies were conducted in the library context (Crabtree et al., 1997; Procter et al., 1998; Twidale, Nichols, & Paice, 1997). These studies observed collaboration taking place in physical and digital libraries between users, and between users and intermediaries. Twidale, Nichols, and Paice (1997) found by observing online public access catalogs (OPAC) users in a university library that users often assisted each other and worked together even though OPACs lack designed-in technological support for cooperative work. For instance, a group of students could be using a single terminal to perform coordinated joint searches, and individual users often leaned over and asked the users of adjacent terminals for help (ibid). These studies indicated that CIB not only takes place in formally designated collaborations and teams. Users informally train and assist each other in the use of IR interfaces and in solving IR problems.

To date, empirical studies of collaborative information *searching* among end-users have remained scarce. Through studying user–user interactions and collaborative searching in physical and digital libraries a better understanding may be gained of not only of information seeking and searching behaviors in general, but also of the design of both physical and digital library spaces that ideally allow for collaborative working and help-giving.

Collaborative activities have been studied and observed also among search intermediaries (Crabtree et al., 1997; O'Day & Jeffries, 1993). O'Day and Jeffries (1993) observed and identified the following forms of CIB among search intermediaries: Sharing search results with other members of a team; self-initiated broadcasting of interesting information; acting as a consultant and handling search requests made by others; and archiving potentially useful information into group repositories.

3.2 CIB in Academic Settings

Few empirical studies have directly focused on scholars' collaboration during the IS&R process, or on the design of tools and techniques for supporting CIS&R within research groups. It is common for studies such as Palmer's (1999, 2001) in-depth studies of the knowledge processes of interdisciplinary scholars to show the meaning and importance of collaboration for scholars. However, most studies, including Palmer's, take individual scholars as the unit of analysis, rather than "collaboratories" (Finholt, 2002), or "information-exchange groups" (Swanson, 1966).

Already in 1966, Swanson concluded on the basis of earlier user studies that "the process of retrieving information, or finding literature relevant to some topic", seems to be "more a matter of interpersonal communication than of indexing and classification" (Swanson, 1966, p. 85). Studies of scholarly communication conducted in the 1960s and 1970s established that scholars' social ties and networks profoundly affect their information gathering, reading, awareness, and interpretation of documents and literatures (Crane, 1972; Menzel, 1959; Parker & Paisley, 1967). Even when scholars seemingly conduct their research and writing alone, scholars' social networks are truly the *place* where information is sought, interpreted, used, and created (Talja, 2002).

For example, in 1999, 94% of philosophy articles explicitly recognized the contributions of colleagues to the work reported (Cronin, 2004). This lead Cronin (2004) to remark that:

> to be sure, the highly articulated collaboration associated with, say, a massive clinical trial is very different from the kinds of low-key, personal communications that take place between individual philosophers, but both disciplinary tribes nonetheless exhibit collaborative behaviors (p. 558).

Talja (2002) studied variation in the criteria for document selection and corresponding variation in collaborative document seeking, retrieval, and filtering practices in research teams and projects. Based on a comparative qualitative study across four fields, she identified four different types of CIS&R practices: Strategic, paradigmatic, directive, and social. Talja (2003) concluded that different kinds of functionalities within existing systems, and different types of IR systems are needed to support different types of CIS&R.

Blake and Pratt (2002) observed two groups of scientists in the medical and public health domains conducting systematic literature reviews for the Cochrane database, studying the methods the groups used to identify, extract, analyze, and aggregate information. The study findings were used to develop a tool called METIS for supporting the collaborative, iterative, interactive information synthesis process of public health, and medical scientists who have a need to perform comprehensive searches and to collaboratively synthesize and verify the accuracy of the information.

In a study that looked at the formation of collaboration within a newly established distributed multidisciplinary research center, Hara et al. (2003) classified forms of collaboration that emerged within the center into complementary and integrative. They found that personal compatibility, research work connections, external and internal incentives, and socio-technical infrastructure impacted the type of collaboration that emerged between groups.

Though scientific work and collaborations may have some important similarities across domains, it is vital to also understand their specificities (Karasti, Baker, & Bowker, 2003). More empirical studies of information practices within scientific collaborations are needed to better support collaborative work in science. CSCW has mainly studied other forms of work than scientific collaboration (Karasti, Baker, & Bowker, 2003) and, while important studies on scientific work and collaboration practices have been conducted for a long time in *science and technology studies*, these studies have not been conducted from the viewpoint of document retrieval, or addressed the issue of how to bridge technology development with what we know about scholarly work.

3.3 CIB in Other Professional Settings

Within information behavior research, collaborative dimensions of information seeking have been studied in professional contexts such as command and control (C2) (Prekop, 2002; Sonnenwald & Pierce, 2000), engineering and software design (Bruce et al., 2003; Fidel et al., 2000; Fidel et al., 2004; Poltrock et al., 2003; Sonnenwald, 1995;

120   S. Talja and P. Hansen

Sonnenwald & Lievrouw, 1997), and the patent domain (Hansen & Järvelin, 2002, 2004, 2005). Studies such as these show how other people often not only play a role as potential *sources* of information but can be viewed as a more integral and ingrained part of IS&R.

Kuhlthau (1993) and Marchionini (1995) proposed that collaborative activities may occur in earlier stages of IS&R processes. Hansen and Järvelin's (2004) empirical study of CIB of engineers in the patent domain showed, however, that work task performance may involve highly collaborative aspects throughout the task initiation stage, the task planning and preparation stage, and task completion stage (information use and creation stage). Patent engineers were involved in diverse collaborative activities; for instance, collaboration could be related to internal or external activities, or to individual or group related activities (Hansen & Järvelin, 2005).

Hertzum (2000) and Hertzum and Pejtersen (2000) investigated the role of people as information sources in the work of software engineers engaged in a systems design task. They found that engineers interacted socially to acquire information without engaging in any explicit search activity. Engineers were looking for practical experience rather than hard facts, and they were also looking for commitments rather than information. Engineers had a need to consult people with specific competencies and experiences. Information seeking was thus tightly interwoven with co-operative work: Engineers searched for documents to find people and searched for people to obtain documents. Consequently, Hertzum and Pejtersen (2000) stressed the importance of providing support for searching for people when searching information systems.

Sonnenwald (1995) studied diverse system design situations involving users, developers, and designers. She introduced the concept "contested collaboration" highlighting the fact that although communication and collaboration are often of paramount importance to work task outcomes, collaboration is affected by complex systems of social relationships and work organization. Groups may have different specialized languages, different goals and priorities, differences in their perceptions of quality and success, and different histories and work practices (Sonnenwald, 1995; Sonnenwald & Pierce, 2000).

In a study of information behavior in military command and control teams, Sonnenwald and Pierce (2000) studied collaboration in dynamic situations with rapidly changing information and a need for continuous information exchange. They showed the importance of dense social networks and "interwoven situational awareness", defined as individual, intragroup, and intergroup awareness. Sonnenwald, McLaughlin, and Whitton (2004) discussed how contextual, task and process, and socio-emotional situation awareness can be supported when collaborating virtually across distances. Even though these studies do not explicitly discuss information searching, the findings provide insights into basic intra- and intergroup communication that are relevant for any study of collaborative work.

Prekop (2002) studied CIB by observing a command and control capability study group in the military, focusing on the contexts, roles, and patterns of collaborative information seeking. He distinguished different information seeking roles: Information referrers, gatherers, verifiers, information seeking instigators, information indexers, group administrators, and managers. Related to these roles, he observed three types of CIB: Information seeking by recommendation, direct questioning, and advertising information paths.

Fidel et al. (2004), Bruce et al. (2003), and Poltrock et al. (2003) studied manifestations of CIB in design teams. They found the actors' situation (e.g., lack of knowledge about organizational practices), the specific work task, the nature of information sources, the nature of information needed, the way work was organized in teams, and organizational culture, to explain motivation and engagement in CIB activities.

Ehrlich and Cash (1994) studied CIB in a customer support organization. Their study showed that customer support personnel relied on the skills and insights of their colleagues to use the organization's document database and to make sense of the information found. The personnel "turned information into knowledge" through joint problem-solving, re-registration of problems, data interpretation, and sifting of information through collaborative indexing. Ehrlich and Cash argued that easy information access does not primarily depend on usability of digital library interfaces, because the ability to frame questions correctly is crucial for finding the information needed. This enterprise often relies on social interaction, drawing on the expertise and interpretive resources of the work community.

The study by Harper (1998) and Harper and Sellen (1995) in the International Monetary Fund (IMF), supports Ehrlich and Cash's insight that there is a trade-off between the suitability of asynchronous communication and groupware for supporting knowledge work, and the amount of professional judgment needed in work tasks. Collaborative sharing is thus often not as important to the sharing of objective "facts" as it is to the interpretation of existing information.

In recent years, studies focusing on collaborative information activities within organizational settings have increased in number. Within information behavior research, studies looking at how work organization (both social and physical), the nature of work tasks, organizational history, culture and memory practices, nature of information needed, and dimensions of the information space/universe surrounding work, affect information practices, are still relatively scarce, however. Studies that have looked at how individuals' social networks, perspectives, motivations, and work styles affect the emergence and outcomes of collaboration practices have thus far been slightly more common.

3.4 CIB in Everyday Life Contexts

In everyday life, people routinely assist each other in solving information problems (McKenzie, 2003). Pettigrew (1999), in a study of the flow of human services information at community foot clinics, developed the concept of information grounds, environments temporarily created by people who have come together to perform a given task, and which foster both the purposeful and spontaneous sharing of information.

Erdelez and Rioux (2000) examined the less purposeful and goal-oriented process of sharing encountered information with others. They suggested that sharing enthusiasm with content, and good feelings associated with helping others, among other factors, motivate people to engage in this behavior. Within ELIS studies, McKenzie (2003) identified a variety of information practices such as actively seeking out a known source, being contacted by a previously unknown source, and being given unasked-for advice. Her findings suggest that information-seeking theories have offered limited insight into "how information comes or is given through the initiative or actions of another agent" (McKenzie, 2003, p. 25).

Sharing interests and concerns with others enables people together to formulate meanings and practices that they pursue in their free time as hobbies or "serious leisure" (Hartel, 2003) activities. However, direct user–user collaboration in information seeking and retrieval is an under covered area also in studies of everyday life and hobby-related information seeking.

3.5 Summary

From the review of a selected set of literature, we can identify a set of main dimensions according to which CIBs can be classified and analyzed:

- *asynchronous and synchronous* activities,
- *co-located and remote* collaborations,
- *loosely and tightly coupled* activities,
- *planned and unplanned* collaboration,
- *intragroup or intergroup* collaboration,
- *direct and indirect* collaboration,
- *coordinated and differentiated* activities.

Collaboration and communication may be asynchronous or synchronous— asynchronous communication through, for example, ordinary mail and book or journal reading; or synchronous through human face-to-face real-time communication. Computer-mediated communication may also be asynchronous through e-mail, searching the Internet and log viewing, or synchronous through video conferencing (Ehrlich & Cash, 1994; Haake, Wiil, & Nürnberg, 1999). Collaboration may be co-located or remote, carried out virtually through computer networks.

Indirect collaboration can mean consulting human experts through systems and services such as Answer Gardens (Ackerman & Malone, 1990) or FAQ. Another form of indirect collaboration are recommender systems, systems taking advantage of recommendations from other people through observations of their information seeking behavior such as search paths and annotations; and recommendations based on usage rates. Loosely coupled activities include explicitly stated recommendations, and sharing of accidentally encountered information between people not otherwise working together.

Another example of indirect collaboration is social browsing. For instance, people may post queries to a discussion list, and people may help each other in information searching even when not directly involved with each others' projects. Tightly coupled activities in the context of IS&R include for instance sharing queries and strategies for their refinement, and executing information filtering and judgment in direct active collaboration with others. Tightly coupled collaborations can extend to include work on interpretations and reviews.

Collaboration may be related to individuals' or groups' activities and concerns, and it may involve two or more people within the same organization (intragroup), or work groups from different organizations (intergroup) (Hansen & Järvelin, 2004, 2005). CIS&R may be coordinated—two or more people share a common aim or task and work on it together. Differentiated group searching means that members of a group are working in the same area but the performance of the task is divided between them so that their specific searching aims are different (Twidale, Nichols, & Paice, 1997). CIS&R may occur in *ad hoc*, in social interaction and joint computer use, or it may be more or less systematically planned in advance.

In addition to the dimensions outlined above, collaborative activities vary according to the dimension of *awareness* (Sonnenwald, McLaughlin, & Whitton, 2004). Awareness is usually understood as knowledge and understanding of the activities of others, groups or individuals, which are important in providing a context for one's own activity (Dourish & Bellotti, 1992). Actors' awareness of people, activities, and information objects may vary. Awareness of information can be investigated by focusing on, for example, topics, types of sources, and information types (Hansen & Järvelin, 2005). Awareness is to a high extent unexplored issue in cooperation in CIS&R.

Finally, collaboration related to information seeking and retrieval may include:

- sharing the same need for information,
- sharing search strategies,
- sharing search results,
- sharing retrieved information objects,
- further processing of the retrieved information objects: Interpretation, filtering, synthesis,
- archiving potentially useful information into group repositories.

Table 1 relates the main dimensions of CIB to the studies reviewed above. Again, the treatment is not exhaustive but relies on a sample of relevant studies.

As shown by Table 1, the dimension that has been investigated most is direct, synchronous collaboration. There is less research on distributed collaboration and indirect collaboration. More research exists on intragroup than intergroup collaboration. Again, it must be borne in mind that this conclusion is based on a selection of articles seeking to probe deeper into collaboration in the retrieval, filtering, interpretation, and information synthesis stages of the IS&R process. There exists more work on the emergence and sustenance of collaborations than the way information is shared, sought, retrieved, and used within organizational and social activities and interactions.

4. A SOCIAL PRACTICE APPROACH TO CIB STUDIES

In this section, we outline a *social practice approach* for CIB studies. We combine empirically grounded observations of CIB from the studies reviewed above with theories of situated action and learning (Chaiklin & Lave, 1993; Lave & Wenger, 1991; Suchman, 1987), and workplace studies (Heath, Knoblauch, & Luff, 2000). Workplace studies and CIB both take an interest in how people naturally act and interact to discover solutions and interpret information in authentic collaborative work and everyday life settings.

CIB Dimension	O'Day and Jeffries (1993)	Erlich and Cash (1994)	Twidale et al. (1997)	Haake et al. (1999)	Sonnenwald and Pierce (2000)	Hertzum and Pejtersen (2000)	Talja (2002)	Poltrok et al. (2003)	Hansn and Järveln (2004, 2005)
Asynchronously	X	X		X				X	X
Synchronously	X	X		X		X		X	X
Co-located	X					X		X	
Distributed								X	
Loosely coupled				X			X		X
Tightly coupled				X			X		X
Intragroup	X				X	X		X	X
Intergroup					X				X
Direct	X	X	X	X	X	X	X	X	X
Indirect	X								X

Table 1. Dimensions of CIB in Articles Reviewed

4.1 The Embeddedness of CIB in Social Practices

As noted earlier, the processes of information seeking, retrieval, filtering, and synthesis take place within and are deeply embedded in work and other kinds of social practices. Information seeking and retrieval are *dimensions of social practices*. They are instances and dimensions of our participation in the social world in diverse roles, and in diverse "communities of sharing". Receiving, interpreting, and indexing information—giving names to pieces of information for the purposes of retrieval and re-use—are part of the routine accomplishment of work tasks and everyday life.

Järvelin and Ingwersen (2005) emphasized that if we look at the broader context of work *per se*, and not only information seeking or receiving processes, information seeking rarely constitutes "an independent system, or meaningful system, of activities as a focus of attention". Indeed, many of the studies reviewed in the previous section extend beyond the seeking and searching stages to information filtering, evaluation, and synthesis stages (Blake & Pratt, 2002; Harper & Sellen, 1995). It seems that in CIB studies, the extension comes naturally, because in real life, information seeking is not an isolated incident. For example, looking at scholarly work "in the wild", we find that researchers seek documents to produce new documents.[4]

While information use is included in most theories of HIB, empirical studies have commonly focused more on information needs and the seeking process (its stages, actors, access strategies, and sources) (Järvelin & Ingwersen, 2005). Less attention has been devoted to how people manage and reprocess the information they find (Bishop, 1999; Bruce, Jones, & Dumais, 2004). Bishop (1999) succinctly described the continuum between seeking and finding information in documents and using them to create new documents in the following manner:

> A journal article provides the starting point for a researcher's own contribution to scientific knowledge. Ideas and information from that source document are selected, compiled with elements from other documents and eventually integrated into a document representing the researcher's own work and ideas (p. 257).

Hence, scholars seeking documents often simultaneously retrieve them, access them, evaluate them, and extract information from them. The use of information is a behavior embedded in work practice, and the structure of documents created and used at work "reflects the structure of work" (Bishop, 1999, p. 257). The structure of documents, in turn, influences how people "structure their work and writing" (Bishop, 1999, p. 257). This observation applies not only to academic work. Workplace studies have similarly taken an interest in how documents are assembled, read, and exchanged within the developing course of practical activities, and how documents organize interaction and cooperation in work environments (Heath, Knoblauch, & Luff, 2000).[5]

---

[4]Throughout this section, we draw insights from our empirical studies. The first author is conducting a study focusing on information and collaboration practices within a research group, the other on the work of patent engineers.

[5]Davenport and Cronin (1998, p. 270) underlined the need to study "texts at work". They argued that information seeking research has, to a large extent, "uncoupled texts from workflow", alienating

Studies from medical care settings (Gorman et al., 2001; Reddy, Dourish, & Pratt, 2001), for example, in the same way as the studies by Ehrlich and Cash (1994) and Harper and Sellen (1995) described above, relate shared information/documents and information repositories to the work activities that are conducted over and through them. These studies have shown how information itself often does not tell a complete story (Reddy, Dourish, & Pratt, 2001). Developing and sharing understandings of the information is as important as the availability of the information itself, and integrating pieces of information into the context of work often requires active collaboration.

Järvelin and Ingwersen (2005), proposing a task augmentation view for information behavior research, noted the shortage of studies attempting to relate system features to characteristics of work practices. They stated that "supporting information management and information systems design may be the weakest contribution of information seeking [research] so far" (Järvelin & Ingwersen, 2005).

Studies on CIB within work contexts show how information is used, managed, and integrated into the work of those who share it, shedding light onto how collaborative seeking and searching, filtering, and analysis, can be supported. The works of Blake and Pratt (2002), Twidale and Nichols (1998b), and Crabtree et al. (1997) exemplify how CIB studies help in supporting the design of "collaborative information spaces".[6]

4.2 Studying Humans and Information Technologies as Intertwined and Mutually Shaping

In the social practice approach, the focus is on the joint accomplishment of work and other tasks at hand through the organization of interaction and the use of supporting technologies and artifacts (information objects, information repositories). The social practice approach sees a mutually shaping relationship to exist between information and collaboration practices and the tools developed for the purposes of communication and knowledge sharing. Work practice is organized in every case in relation to some material base of technologies (Suchman & Trigg, 1991). Thus, work and collaboration practices, and information and communication technologies (ICTs) are co-constituted.

Kling, McKim, and King (2003) introduced the concept of socio-technical interaction networks (STINs) to highlight the relationships between social actors, technologies, and artifacts. The STIN model is not an information seeking model, it is a model for developing and maintaining communication forums such as electronic journals, and therefore not directly applicable in HIB research. However, the STIN model is useful for understanding the co-constitution of work practices and technologies-in-use.

The STIN was originally developed to avoid shortcomings of what Kling, McKim, and King (2003, p. 55) call "standard models" of scholarly communication. Standard

professionals at work "from the texts that constitute that work". Hence, work practice is equally constituted by texts/documents/information objects, interactions, and technologies.
[6]This term originates from the work of Schmidt and Bannon (1992), and is used here for a lack of a better term. Research groups, for instance, need and create—through artfully integrating various technologies due to the lack of a single good system—shared workspaces incorporating searches made, documents found, and subsequent work on those documents (Talja, 2003).

models, according to Kling and colleagues (2003), are limited on their outlook because their interest lies in an individuals' use or non-use of specific information channels or communication forums. Kling and colleagues argued that when the focus in on the individual actor as a user of technology, the ecology of the communications in which that actor is embedded, as well as potentially different ways of configuring technologies in practice,[7] are lost from view.

The STIN model seeks to account for the specifics of the work settings in which people try to use technologies. Also, it seeks to account for the *features* of the technologies in the studied settings (not only their use or non-use), assuming that features and characteristics of technologies are likely to vary across settings. The STIN model thus attempts to form a non-generalized, contextualized account of the relationships between people and people, and between people and technologies, and between technologies (Kling, McKim, & King, 2003).

Understanding the mutually shaping relationship between work practices and technologies not only yields better insight into information and collaboration practices than models that do not account for technologies-in-use, it also enables a better understanding of how to develop systems for supporting those practices. Often, the development of IR systems relies heavily on tests within experimental settings sometimes neglecting the social, interactive side of work, and other practices.

4.3 Communities of Practice

The social practice approach works from the basic assumption that all information seeking is social, because all human practices are fundamentally social. This is based on an understanding that

1. A common sense of what constitutes competent practice originates not from the "heads of individual actors" but "among members of a community of practitioners"; and that
2. Practices are always organized in relation to some others (Cronin, 2004) who may be co-workers, co-producers, recipients, or customers. In this sense, all work is collaborative, and the accomplishment of work tasks requires some form of collaborative interaction (Suchman, 1987; Suchman & Trigg, 1991).

When information seeking is conceived as part of work practice or other social practices, the actors who search for and interpret information, whether individuals or teams, are *participants in a practice*. This implies that even the most seemingly solitary act of using IR systems always rests upon a heterogeneous system of social relationships,

---

[7] An important aspect of work and other social practices that we can not elaborate at length here is the way work groups co-design and re-design technologies to adjust them to the task at hand. Nardi and Miller (1991) studied spreadsheet users in organizational settings. In the same way as library OPACs, spreadsheets are usually presupposed to be single-user applications, and lack designed-in technological support for cooperative work. Nardi and Miller found, however, that spreadsheets function as de facto *cooperative work environments*. Spreadsheet work flows across different users in fluid, informal ways, and users, or domain experts, also have an important role as systems designers.

and involves tacit cultural knowledge (for instance, task knowledge, domain knowledge, and search knowledge). The actor brings into the act of searching a body of practice and procedures which have evolved historically and are shared and developed by a "community of practitioners".

Lave and Wenger (1991) developed the well-known "communities of practice" (CoP) concept to argue that all knowledge creation and learning is deeply *embedded* within concrete work tasks and interpersonal exchanges. Davenport (2001) suggested that the CoP concept is useful for exploring and understanding information practices and the emergence of knowledge both in corporate settings and less formal and loosely structured interest groups. The CoP concept is used here for conveying the idea of the fundamental socialness of information seeking and searching activities and the reliance of any social practice upon interactions of people interested in similar issues.

Originally, Lave and Wenger's CoP concept referred to the process of how newcomers learn their professions. They emphasized that learning takes place not by internalizing a "received" (abstract) body of knowledge and a set of procedures, but by taking part in the execution of concrete work tasks, through observing co-workers, seeing and learning how they do things, and by interacting with specific information objects, tools, and technologies.

Hara and Kling (2002) cogently argue that Lave and Wenger's theory does not account for how learning and sharing is a continuous activity also on the part of experienced workers. If a CoP is to perform its tasks in an optimum manner, also experts work as collaborators, deriving information from and developing their profession through interactions with colleagues. This emphasis in line with the results obtained by, for instance, Ehrlich and Cash (1994) and Harper and Sellen (1995) who argued that information often does not "speak for itself" but requires negotiation concerning its meaning and context.

CoP evolve in circumstances where people have common concerns, where they work together sharing a common space, and joint work tasks (Lave & Wenger, 1991). CoPs are groups of people sharing similar goals and interests; employing common practices; working with the same information objects, tools, and technologies; and expressing themselves in a common language. As shown by Sonnenwald (1995), a shared language is crucial for the joint accomplishment of work tasks, yet not necessarily easily achieved across groups and organizations.

4.4 Summary

Figure 2 shows the key assumptions of the social practice approach: (1) The embeddedness of information practices in work and other social practices; and (2) the reliance of any work and social practice upon a community of practitioners, a socio-technical infrastructure, and a common language.

Figure 2 shows the full "cycle" of information practices as a continuum. The social practice approach does not assume that information activities always take place in a linear fashion, however. In many cases, the process does not involve all of the practices shown in the figure. For example, information may be given without being sought for, and in such cases, seeking is not involved. The retrieved or received information may not always require further processing such as archiving.

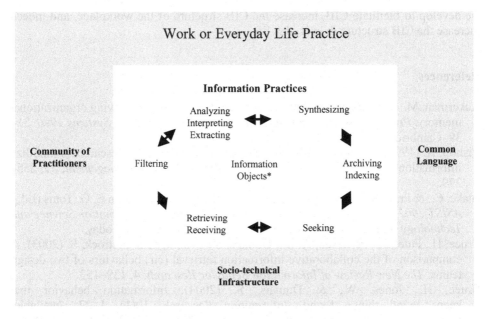

* human sources, documents, document parts, document bundles, document repositories

Figure 2. The social practice approach to CIB.

The social practice approach sees collaboration as an ingrained aspect of work and information practices. As it is based on both empirically grounded observations of the interplay between work practice and information activities, and situated learning theories, it is widely applicable as a starting point for exploring CIB in work and everyday life settings.

5. CONCLUSION

CIB is a new, emerging research area within HIB research. Research in this new field will extend our knowledge of how people access, retrieve, filter, and use information, and how this may be supported in IR systems design. This chapter has outlined key research themes to be addressed when CIB is investigated in different settings, and provided theoretical and empirical grounding for future CIB research.

The overview of the modes and dimensions of CIB, summarized in Table 1, set forth a frame for outlining research questions within CIB. Further research will uncover other important dimensions to be investigated. The social practice approach outlined in this chapter is applicable not only in CIB research; it may be seen as a new direction for the study of HIB in general. This CIB/HIB approach sees HIB as firmly embedded in work and other social practices, and views work practice, information objects, and information technologies as intertwined and mutually shaping. Importantly, the technologies we develop to facilitate CIB, increase the CIB structure of the workplace, and indeed increase the CIB structure in everyday life.

References

Ackerman, M., & Malone, T. (1990). Answer garden: A tool for growing organizational memory. *Proceedings of ACM Conference on Office Information Systems 1990,* 31–39. Cambridge, MA: ACM.

Bishop, A. (1999). Document structure and digital libraries: How researchers mobilize information in journal articles. *Information Processing and Management,* 35, 255–279.

Blake, C., & Pratt, W. (2002). Collaborative information synthesis. In E. G. Toms (Ed.), *ASIST 2002: Proceedings of the 65th American Society for Information Science and Technology Annual Meeting,* 44–56. Medford, NJ: Information Today.

Bruce, H., Fidel, R., Pejtersen, A. M., Dumais, S., Grudin, J., & Poltrock, S. (2003). A comparison of the collaborative information retrieval (cir) behaviors of two design teams. *The New Review of Information Behavior Research,* 4, 139–153.

Bruce, H., Jones, W., & Dumais, S. (2004). Information behavior that keeps found things found. *Information Research,* 10(1), 1–22. Available: http://www.informationr.net/ir/10-1/paper207.html. Retrieved 20 October 2004.

Case, D. O. (2002). *Looking for Information: A Survey of Research on Information Seeking, Needs, and Behavior.* Amsterdam: Academic Press.

Chaiklin, S., & Lave, J. (Eds.) (1993). *Understanding Practice: Perspectives on Activity and Context.* Cambridge: Cambridge University Press.

Crabtree, A., Twidale, M. B., O'Brien, J., & Nichols, D. M. (1997). Talking in the library: Implications for the design of digital libraries. In R. B. Allen & E. Rasmussen (Eds.), *Proceedings of the 2nd ACM International Conference on Digital Libraries,* 221–228. New York: ACM.

Crane, D. (1972). *Invisible Colleges: Diffusion of Knowledge in Scientific Communication.* Chicago, IL: University of Chicago Press.

Cronin, B. (2004). Bowling alone together: Academic writing as distributed cognition. *Journal of the American Society for Information Science and Technology,* 55(6), 557–560.

Davenport, E. (2001). Knowledge management issues for online organisations: "communities of practice" as an exploratory framework. *Journal of Documentation,* 57(1), 61–75.

Davenport, E. (2002). Organizational knowledge and communities of practice. In B. Cronin (Ed.), *Annual Review of Information Science and Technology,* 36:171–219. Medford, NJ: Information Today.

Davenport, E., & Cronin, B. (1998). Texts at work: Some thoughts on "just for you" service in the context of domain expertise. *Journal of Education for Library and Information Science,* 39(4), 264–274.

Dourish, P., & Bellotti, V. (1992). Awareness and coordination in shared workspaces. *Proceedings of the ACM Conference on Computer-Supported Cooperative Work,* 107–114. New York: ACM Press.

Ehrlich, K., & Cash, D. (1994). Turning information into knowledge: Information finding as a collaborative activity. In J. L. Schnase, J. Leggett, R. K. Furuta, & E. Metcalfce (Eds.), *Proceedings of Digital Libraries '94*, 119–125. Available: http://www.csdl.tamu.edu/DL94/paper/lotus.html. Retrieved 29 November 2001.

Ellis, D. (1993). Modelling the information-seeking patterns of academic researchers: A grounded theory approach. *Library Quarterly*, 63(4), 469–486.

Erdelez, S., & Rioux, K. (2000). Sharing information encountered for others on the web. *The New Review of Information Behavior Research*, 1, 219–233.

Fidel, R., Bruce, H., Pejtersen, A. M., Dumais, S., Grudin, J., & Poltrock, S. (2000). Collaborative information retrieval (CIR). *The New Review of Information Behavior Research*, 1, 235–247.

Fidel, R., Pejtersen, A. M., Cleal, B., & Bruce, H. (2004). A multidimensional approach to the study of human–information interaction: A case study of collaborative information retrieval. *Journal of the American Society of Information Science and Technology*, 55(11), 939–953.

Finholt, T. A. (2002). Collaboratories. In B. Cronin (Ed.), *Annual Review of Information Science and Technology*, 36, 73–107. Medford, NJ: Information Today.

Gorman, P., Ash, J., Lavelle, M., Lyman, J., Delcambre, L., Maier, D., Weaver, M., & Bowers, S. (2001). Bundles in the wild: Managing information to solve problems and maintain situation awareness. *Library Trends*, 49(2), 266–289.

Haake, J. M., Wiil, U. K., & Nürnberg, P. J. (1999). Openness in shared hypermedia workspaces: The case for collaborative open hypermedia systems. *SIGWEB Newsletter*, 8(3), 33–45.

Hansen, P., & Järvelin, K. (2000). The information seeking and retrieval process at the swedish patent- and registration office. Moving from lab-based to real life work-task environment. In N. Kando & L. Mun-Kew (Eds.), *Proceedings of the SIGIR 2000 Workshop on Patent Retrieval*, 43–53. Athens, Greece: ACM SIGIR.

Hansen, P., & Järvelin, K. (2004). Collaborative information searching in an information-intensive work domain: Preliminary results. *Journal of Digital Information Management*, 2(1), 26–30.

Hansen, P., & Järvelin, K. (2005). Collaborative information retrieval in an information-intensive domain. *Information Processing and Management*, 40.

Hara, N., & Kling, R. (2002). Communities of practice with and without information technology. In E. G. Toms (Ed.), *ASIST 2002: Proceedings of the 65th American Society for Information Science and Technology Annual Meeting*, 338–349. Medford, NJ: Information Today.

Harper, R. (1998). *Inside the IMF: An Ethnography of Documents, Technology and Organizational Action*. San Diego, CA: Academic Press.

Harper, R., & Sellen, A. (1995). Collaborative tools and the practicalities of professional work at the international monetary fund. In R. Katz, R. Mack, & L. Marks (Eds.), *Proceedings of the ACM CHI'95 Conference on Human Factors in Computing Systems*, 122–129. New York: ACM Press.

Hartel, J. (2003). The serious leisure frontier in library and information science: Hobby domains. *Knowledge Organization*, 30(3/4), 228–238.

Heath, C., Knoblauch, H., & Luff, P. (2000). Technology and social interaction: The emergence of "workplace studies". *British Journal of Sociology*, 51(2), 299–320.

Hertzum, M. (2000). People as carriers of experience and sources of commitment: Information seeking in a software design project. *The New Review of Information Behavior Research*, 1, 135–149.

Hertzum, M., & Pejtersen, A. M. (2000). The information-seeking practices of engineers: Searching for documents as well as for people. *Information Processing and Management*, 36(5), 761–778.

Järvelin, K., & Ingwersen, P. (2005). Information seeking research needs extension towards tasks and technology. *Information Research* 10(1), 1–17. Available: http://InformationR.net/ir/paper212.html. Retrieved 20 October 2004.

Jordan, B., & Henderson, A. (1994). *Interaction Analysis: Foundations and Practice.* Palo Alto, CA: Xerox Palo Alto Research Center and Institute for Research on Learning.

Kanfer, A., Haythornthwaite, C., Bruce, B., Bowker, G., Burbules, B., Porac, J., & Wade, J. (2000). Modeling distributed knowledge processes in next generation multidisciplinary alliances. *Information Systems Frontiers*, 2(3/4), 317–331.

Karasti, H., Baker, K., & Bowker, G. C. (2003). ECSCW 2003 computer supported scientific collaboration (CSSC) workshop report. *SIGGROUP Bulletin*, 24(2), 6–13.

Kling, R., McKim, G., & King, A. (2003). A bit more to it: Scholarly communication forums as socio-technical interaction networks. *Journal of the American Society for Information Science and Technology*, 54(1), 47–67.

Kuhlthau, C. (1993). *Seeking Meaning: A Process Approach to Library and Information Services.* New York: Ablex.

Lave, J. (1988). *Cognition in Practice: Mind, Mathematics and Culture in Everyday Life.* Cambridge: Cambridge University Press.

Lave, J., & Wenger, E. (1991). *Situated Learning: Legitimate Peripheral Participation.* New York: Cambridge University Press.

Marchionini, G. (1995). *Information Seeking in Electronic Environments.* Cambridge: Cambridge University Press.

McKenzie, P. (2003). A model of information practices in accounts of everyday-life information seeking. *Journal of Documentation*, 59(1), 19–40.

Menzel, H. (1959). Planned and unplanned scientific communication. *Proceedings of the International Conference on Scientific Information.* Washington, DC: National Academy of Sciences—National Research Council.

Nardi, B. A., & Miller, J. R. (1991). Twinkling lights and nested loops: Distributed problem solving and spreadsheet development. *International Journal of Man-Machine Studies*, 34(2), 161–184.

National Research Council. (1993). *National Collaboratories: Applying Information Technology for Scientific Research. Committee Toward a National Collaboratory: Establishing the User-Developer Partnership.* Washington, DC: The National Academy Press.

O'Day, V., & Jeffries, R. (1993). Information artisans: Patterns of result sharing by information searchers. *Proceedings of the ACM Conference on Organizational Computing Systems, COOCS'93*, 98–107. New York: ACM Press.

Palmer, C. L. (1999). Structures and strategies of interdisciplinary science. *Journal of the American Society for Information Science*, 50(3), 242–253.

Palmer, C. L. (2001). *Work at the Boundaries of Science: Information and the Interdisciplinary Research Process.* Dordrecht: Kluwer.

Parker, E. W., & Paisley, W. J. (1967). *Scientific Information Exchange at an Inter-disciplinary Behavioral Science Convention.* Stanford, CA: Stanford Institute for Communication Research.

Pettigrew, K. (1999). Waiting for chiropody: Contextual results from an ethnographic study of information behavior among attended at community clinics. *Information Processing and Management*, 35, 801–817.

Poltrock, S., Grudin, J., Dumais, S., Fidel, R., Bruce, H., & Pejtersen, A. M. (2003). Information seeking and sharing in design teams. *Proceedings of the 2003 International ACM SIGGROUP Conference on Supporting Group Work*, 239–247. New York: ACM.

Prekop, P. (2002). A qualitative study of collaborative information seeking. *Journal of Documentation*, 58(5), 533–562.

Procter, R., Goldenberg, A., Davenport, E., & McKinlay, A. (1998). Genres in support of collaborative information retrieval in the virtual library. *Interacting with Computers*, 10, 157–175.

Reddy, M., Dourish, P., & Pratt, W. (2001). Coordinating heterogeneous work: Information and representation in medical care. In W. Printz, M. Jarke, Y. Rogers, K. Schmidt, & V. Wulf (Eds.), *Proceedings of the Seventh European Conference on Computer-Supported Cooperative Work ECSCW 2001*, 239–258. Dordrecht: Kluwer.

Romano, N. C., Roussinov, D., Nunamaker, J. F., & Chen, H. (1999). Collaborative information retrieval environment: Integration of information retrieval with group support systems. *Proceedings of the 32nd Hawaii Conference on System Sciences.* Available: http://dlist.sir.arizona.edu/archive/00000435/.

Schmidt, K., & Bannon, L. (1991). CSCW: Four characters in search of a context. In J. Bowers & S. Benford (Eds.), *Studies in Computer Supported Cooperative Work: Theory, Practice and Design*, 3–16. Dordrecht: Kluwer.

Schmidt, K., & Bannon, L. (1992). Taking CSCW seriously: Supporting articulation work. *Computer-Supported Cooperative Work*, 1, 7–40.

Sonnenwald, D. H. (1995). Contested collaboration: A descriptive model of intergroup communication in information system design. *Information Processing and Management*, 31(6), 859–877.

Sonnenwald, D. H., & Lievrouw, L. A. (1997). Collaboration during the design process: A case study of communication, information behavior, and project performance. In P. Vakkari, R. Savolainen, & B. Dervin (Eds.), *Information Seeking in Context: Proceedings of an International Conference on Research in Information Needs, Seeking and Use in Different Contexts*, 179–204. London: Taylor Graham.

Sonnenwald, D. H., McLaughlin, K. L., & Whitton, M. (2004). Designing to support situation awareness across distance: An example from a scientific collaboratory. *Information Processing and Management*, 40(3), 989–1011.

Sonnenwald, D. H., & Pierce, L. G. (2000). Information behavior in dynamic group work contexts: Interwoven situational awareness, dense social networks and contested collaboration in command and control. *Information Processing and Management*, 36(3), 461–479.

Spink, A., Wilson, T. D., Ford, N., Foster, A., & Ellis, D. (1999). Information-seeking and mediated searching. Part 1. Theoretical framework and research design. *Journal of the American Society for Information Science and Technology*, 53(9), 695–703.

Suchman, L. (1987). *Plans and Situated Actions: The Problem of Human-Machine Com-munication*. Cambridge: Cambridge University Press.

Suchman, L., & Trigg, R. (1991). Understanding practice: Video as a medium for reflec-tion and design. In J. Greenbaum & M. Kyng (Eds.), *Design at Work: Cooperative Design of Computer Systems*. Hillsdale, NJ: Lawrence Erlbaum Associates.

Swanson, D. R. (1966). On improving communication among scientists. *Library Quar-terly*, 36(2), 113–125.

Talja, S. (1997). Constituting "Information" and "User" as research objects: A theory of knowledge formations as an alternative to the information man-theory. In P. Vakkari, R. Savolainen, & B. Dervin (Eds.), *Information Seeking in Context: Proceedings of an International Conference on Research in Information Needs, Seeking and Use in Different Contexts*, 67–80. London: Taylor Graham.

Talja, S. (2002). Information sharing in academic communities: Types and levels of col-laboration in information seeking and use. *The New Review of Information Behavior Research*, 3, 143–160.

Talja, S. (2003). Supporting scholars' collaboration in document seeking, retrieval and filtering. In H. Karasti, K. Baker, & G. Bowker (Eds.), *Proceedings of the Workshop on Computer Supported Scientific Collaboration*, 49–55. Eight European Conference on Computer Supported Cooperative Work, Helsinki, Finland, September 2003. Oulu: University of Oulu, Department of Information Processing Science, Research Papers, A34.

Twidale, M. B., & Nichols, D. (1998a). Computer supported co-operative work in infor-mation search and retrieval. In M. E. Williams (Ed.), *Annual Review of Information Science and Technology*, 33:259–319. Medford, NJ: Information Today.

Twidale, M. B., & Nichols, D. M. (1998b). Designing interfaces to support collaboration in information retrieval. *Interacting with Computers*, 10(2), 177–193.

Twidale, M. B., Nichols, D. M., & Paice, C. D. (1997). Browsing is a collaborative process. *Information Processing and Management*, 33(6), 761–783.

Wilson, T. D. (1999). Exploring models of information behavior: The "Uncertainty" project. *Information Processing and Management*, 35(6), 830–849.

SECTION 4
Multitasking, Non-linear, Organizing, and Digital Frameworks

Chapter 8

Multitasking and Co-ordinating Framework for Human Information Behavior

Amanda Spink and Minsoo Park
School of Information Sciences
University of Pittsburgh

Charles Cole
Graduate School of Library and Information Studies
McGill University

1. INTRODUCTION

Humans have for a millennium sought, organized and used information and evolved patterns of human information behavior (HIB) to resolve their human problems and survive (Spink & Currier, in press). However, despite the current focus on living in an "information age", holistic frameworks for conceptualizing HIB are still evolving. This chapter extends Spink and Cole's (in press) integrated HIB framework by proposing a more multitasking and co-ordinating framework for conceptualizing HIB.

Section 2 of this chapter conceptualizes HIB as an integrated process of information seeking/foraging/sense-making, information searching, information organizing, and information use on single or multiple topics. Section 3 of the chapter discusses what is meant by multitasking and then outlines an initial framework for HIB within a multitasking and co-ordination framework. Within this conceptualization, HIB is constructed as a series of tasks within a task-switching process. Multitasking is conceptualized as a binding process that works with human co-ordination behaviors to construct an information-behavior process. A case study is also provided that explores the interplay between information and non-information tasks. Multitasking information behavior also provides a framework for co-ordinating and integrating the different levels within HIB.

2. HUMAN INFORMATION BEHAVIOR

What is meant by the concept of HIB? The field of library and information science (LIS) has historically included the research area of HIB that seeks to study human behaviors related to information seeking, foraging, sense-making, searching, organizing, and use (Spink & Cole, 2004). In this chapter, we provide a new direction for the conceptualization of HIB that further enhances the integrated HIB framework proposed by Spink and Cole (in press).

A. Spink and C. Cole (eds), New Directions in Human Information Behavior, 137–154.
© 2006 *Springer.*

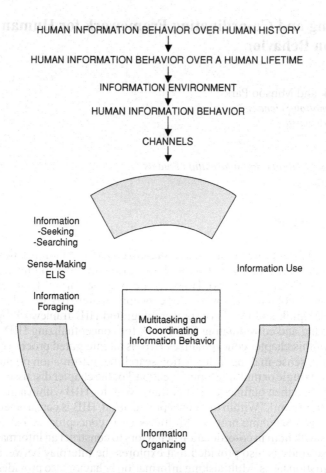

Figure 1. Integrated HIB framework.

Figure 1 provides the enhanced version of Spink and Cole's (in press) integrated HIB framework, including information seeking, foraging, sense-making, searching, organizing, and use.

In Figure 1, the constitutive HIB elements are divided into sections. The top section places the framework in the broad framework of HIB, both over human history and a human lifetime, which takes place inside some information environment with channels. The lower section of the framework is a first attempt to place the various HIB sub-processes in relation to each other and in relation to the totality of HIB at the top section of Figure 1.

2.1 Information Seeking/Problem-Solving Level

What do we currently know about information-seeking behavior? Spink and Cole (2004) define *information seeking* as, a sub-set of information behavior that includes the purposive seeking of information in relation to a goal. As shown in Figure 1, the *Information Seeking–Problem Solving* level exists in parallel with the other levels as people switch between seeking, foraging, and sense-making. The starting state of the information-seeking process is conceptualized as occurring as an information gap or anomalous state of knowledge or an information need (Wilson, 2000). The construction of an information-seeking process evolves in stages with key variables stated as relevance judgments and uncertainly.

The goal state is the resolution of the problem or cognitive state, and humans adopt different strategies and exhibit different information behaviors at different stages of their information-seeking process (Case, 2002; Kuhlthau, 1993; Marchionini, 1995) and related to social behavior (Brown, Ganesan, & Challagalla, 2001; Butler, 1993; Deutsch et al., 1988; Hildebrand-Saints & Weary, 1989; Morrison, 1993). However, there are limitations to the information-seeking level and models (Case, 2002; Spink & Cole, in press), and limited explanatory power underlying the concepts that underpin the information seeking/problem solving level.

2.2 Information-Searching Level

People often use information-retrieval technologies during an HIB process. In Figure 1, the information-searching level is a sub-set of the information-seeking level. During information seeking, humans may search for information via a computer system or the Web. A growing body of HIB studies show that people often have many tasks (or information problems/topics) at hand at the same time when interacting with an information retrieval (IR) system (Spink, Ozmutlu, & Ozmutlu, 2002; Spink, Park, & Jansen, in press). In these cases, a person may pool their topics together and interact with an IR system on more than one related or unrelated topics. Overall, a user's single session with an IR system or library may consist of seeking information on single or multiple topics and switching between topics.

2.3 Information Sense-Making/Everyday Life Information-Seeking Level

Alternatively, a body of HIB research focuses on the sense-making aspects of information seeking. A third level of HIB is the *Information Sense-making—Everyday Life Information-Seeking* level, which is a combination of non-purposive and purposive information behavior. Inputs are bits and pieces of data the individual gathers both consciously and unconsciously for the purpose of making sense of a problem situation. The problem situation can be very wide, such as the problem of human survival. The process starts only when the individual achieves a sense of comfort or coherence. This is knowledge-based output where the individual has made temporary sense or coherence from what Dervin (1992) suggests is the constant discontinuity of human existence.

The goal state is mastery of life. Within the everyday life information seeking/sense-making levels, the information user is conceptualized as constructing information based on the values and specific environment of the "small world" in which the user exists concurrently apart from and as a member of the larger society (Chatman, 1991; Savolainen, 1995). Some of the initial premises of ELIS/sense-making were begun by Dervin et al. (1976), especially Dervin's (1992) level to studying information needs, seeking, and use, called sense-making.

2.4 Information-Foraging Level

In addition to the information seeking and sense-making approaches, some studies view HIB from an information-foraging perspective. At the *Information-Foraging Level* in Figure 1, information searching is based on hard-wired strategies and tactics, and we assume input and output involve the same unchanging, hard-wired knowledge. Foraging is a concept used in evolutionary psychology (Kurland & Beckerman, 1985; Mithen, 1990) and information science (Sandstrom, 1994, 2001; Spink & Cole, in press). Pirolli and Card (1999) examine human interaction with IR and Web systems within an information-foraging level that is based on optimal foraging theory from evolutionary ecology.

The start state involves patches, clues, and internal and external decision states. The information-foraging process is an interaction between the person and their environment that includes the concepts of cues and diet enrichment. The goal state is a stable state that maximizes gains of valuable information per unit cost. The objective of Pirolli and Card (1999) is to relate information foraging to the design of information searching IR environments for diverse groups of users.

2.5 Information-Use Level

What do we currently know about information-use behaviors? The *Information Use/Modular Thinking Level* involves information use beginning with pre-conscious data pick-up from the environment while the individual is attending to other information-foraging activities. Dervin (1992) states that information use is a process condition where the user tries to make sense of discontinuous reality in a series of information-use behaviors. There are internal use behaviors (comparings, categorizings, polarizings, etc.) and external use behaviors (listenings, agreeings, disagreeings, etc.).

A problem-solving definition of information use is the incorporation of found information into their pre-existing knowledge base, by thinking, by taking notes, or in some way cognitively processing/acquiring the information (Ford, 2004; Todd, 1999).

According to this definition, studies of user cognition during user-IR system interaction should be labeled as information-use research (Cole, 2000; Ford, 2004). Incorporating found information into a human's pre-existing knowledge structure may provide a link into the wider notion of HIB because it describes the precise moment when the human information environment and human come together. Overall, limited studies have investigated information-use behavior in relation to other information behaviors.

2.6 Information-Organizing Level

What do we currently know about information-organizing behavior? *Human information-organizing behavior* (HIOB) is the process of analyzing and classifying materials into defined categories, for example, the Dewey Decimal Classification System (McIlwaine, 1997). Spink and Currier (in press) have defined HIOB as the process of analyzing and classifying materials into defined categories. They give as an example the Dewey Decimal Classification System (McIlwaine, 1997). While the example they give is a document organization system, their definition lends itself to creating a cognitive framework for HIOB. Few studies have examined human's information-organizing behavior in relation to other information behaviors.

The reason for this expanded purview is that, in our era of virtual information, LIS is beginning to think of document organization and human memory organization as one and the same thing, based on a theory of human information use and generation. In other words, IR systems on the Internet and elsewhere will increasingly devise so-called document organization systems—classification schemes, subject directories, and the like—that mimic how humans themselves think when interacting with information or data stimuli. Researchers are attempting to create one of these natural human information organization systems in a research project, the Information Need Identification for Information Retrieval System (INIIReye System) (Cole & Leide, 2005).

Section 3 of the chapter discusses the role of multitasking and co-ordination as conceptualizing and binding elements in the integrated HIB framework.

3. MULTITASKING BEHAVIOR

What is meant by the concept of multitasking? Multitasking is the ability of humans to simultaneously handle the demands of multiple tasks through task switching (Burgess, 2000; Carlson & Sohn, 2000; Just et al., 2000; Lee & Taatgen, 2002; Rubinstein, Meyer, & Evans, 2001). Owing to the increasing complexity of the global information, environment people are increasingly engaged in multitasking and information task-switching behaviors. Web search can also include information multitasking behaviors that occur when users juggle the challenge of seeking information on multiple topics. Multitasking continues to be an important research area for technology designers in general (Burgess, 2000). However, many interactive technologies do not provide effective support for managing multitasking behaviors (Wickens, 1992).

Cognitive psychologists have studied many aspects of multitasking or task switching (Carlson & Sohn, 2000; Miyata & Norman, 1986). Rubinstein, Meyer, and Evans (2001) found that multitasking between different types of tasks can reduce productivity. Rubinstein, Meyer, and Evans (2001) highlight the need for people to multitask in work environments, as they use the microprocessor while at the same time they talk on the telephone. People have many tasks at hand at the same time, including information-seeking tasks. In these cases, a person may pool their topics together and interact with the Web on more than one related or unrelated topics, resulting in users' Web search sessions ranging in duration from less than 1 min to a few hours.

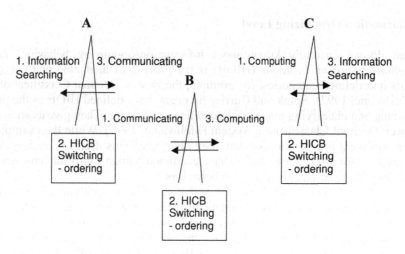

Figure 2. HICB—Switching between business consultant's three major task groups.

4. MULTITASKING INFORMATION BEHAVIOR

In this chapter, we propose that multitasking behavior is a key part of the integration of the various sub-sets in Figure 1 into the integrated HIB framework and a more holistic framework for HIB. Multitasking is a new direction for HIB research and thinking that expands the purview of what we should look for when studying HIB. Recent studies suggest that users' searches may have multiple goals or topics and occur within the broader context of their information-seeking behaviors (Spink, Ozmutlu, & Ozmutlu, 2002). Research studies also indicate that users' searches may have multiple goals or topics and occur within the broader context of their information-seeking behaviors (Spink, 2004; Spink, Ozmutlu, & Ozmutlu, 2002). This clearly places multitasking as a key ingredient in modeling the wider picture of information seeking in HIB.

In the realm of HIB research, the process of seeking information concurrently over time in relation to more than one, possibly evolving, set of information tasks (including changes or shifts in beliefs, cognitive, affective, and/or situational states), is called *multitasking information behavior* (Spink, Ozmutlu, & Ozmutlu, 2002). Understanding and modeling human information multitasking processes is a new and important research area for HIB research. We make a first attempt to model multitasking in HIB in Figure 2. We take a case study (in what follows) about multitasking and afterwards try to work it into the greater picture of HIB.

Recent studies of multitasking information behaviors have provided some initial insights into this important aspect of HIB. Multitasking information behavior so far has largely been within the information-seeking level. Spink (2004) reports results from a case study exploring the multitasking information behavior by an information seeker. The information seeker sought information on four unrelated personal information tasks. Findings include (1) a sequential flowchart of the information seeker's complex and iterative processes, including multitasking information behavior, electronic searches, physical searches, serendipitous browsing, and successive searches and (2) the information seeker engaged in a process of 17 information task switches over two information-seeking episodes. A model of information multitasking and information task switching was proposed.

New research on multitasking is beginning to expand our horizons from information seeking to the complexity of the human information condition and HIB. Spink and Park (in press) discuss multitasking information and non-information behaviors and propose a model of multitasking and task switching during HIB that includes cognitive, cognitive style, and individual difference variables. Spink, Park, and Jansen (in press) conceptualize HIB as a multitasking process, as people shift between different HIB tasks. For purposes of further exploring multitasking in HIB, Section 5 of the chapter discusses the construct of multitasking information behavior as larger than purposive information-seeking behavior, by putting it inside the larger HIB context of multitasking as a process of co-ordination within both an information—that is, information seeking—and a non-information—task interplay.

5. INFORMATION AND NON-INFORMATION TASK INTERPLAY

Current information seeking research, although focused on the task concept (Vakkari, 2003), has not touched on either multitasking or the interplay between tasks that require information behavior and those that do not. Research is needed to understand the co-ordination and interplay between information and non-information related behaviors. The case study is first attempt to explore the issue of multitasking information behavior, by examining the subject's tasks, his information behavior, and the interplay between information and non-information task-related behavior.

6. EXPLORATORY CASE STUDY

Section 7 of this chapter outlines results from a case study of the multitasking behavior of a business consultant, including information and non-information tasks. The goals of the exploratory case study were to:

1. examine how a business consultant conducts multitasking work task behaviors, including information and non-information tasks;
2. examine the patterns of multitasking work task behavior and task switching including information and non-information related tasks.

To explore multitasking behavior, we used a case study approach to understand how a business consultant with a set of real tasks constructed a multitasking process. Data were collected from a volunteer male business consultant who was working in the city of Pittsburgh in the office area of a client company. Previous researchers' studies have the information-seeking behaviors of business professionals (Choo, Detlor, & Turnbull, 2000; Kuhlthau, 1997; Leckie, Pettigrew, & Sylvain, 1996).

A case study approach allowed the researcher to focus on a holistic and intensive description and characterization of a single phenomenon (Merriam, 1988). The case study approach also allowed the researcher to use a mix of observational, diary, and interviews data-collection techniques to provide a baseline for further research using a larger sample of business consultants. This approach has been used by other information scientists to study the information behavior (Kuhlthau, 1997; Spink, 2004) and the relevance judgments (Tang & Solomon, 1998) of a single individual.

6.1 Study Participant

The volunteer business consultant, who agreed to participate in the study, was not an acquaintance of the first author, not a close friend, nor had the participant ever worked with or been employed by the researcher. He was a resident of Pittsburgh Pennsylvania with a graduate level education, a full time employee of a business consulting company and working for a client company in Pittsburgh. The volunteer was told that the researcher was studying work task patterns of professionals.

6.2 Data Collection

The researcher decided to use a combination of data-collection techniques during the case study, including a diary compiled by the business consultant, and on-site observation and interview. The business consultant was asked to keep a diary of work tasks for 1 day, including their thoughts and feelings during their work tasks. This data-collection technique was used successfully by Spink (2004) with library users. A major part of the data collection during the study was the diary of actions and thoughts compiled by the consultant during their work day. The researcher requested that the business consultant keep a diary of all his work tasks, including the time taken for each task, on blank lined paper during their work day. This qualitative data-collection technique allowed the researcher to gain a timeline and insights into the consultants' actions and thoughts as they worked.

In addition to the diary, the researcher decided to use on-site observation of the business consultant. The goal of the observation was to familiarize the researcher with the tasks and multitasking behaviors conducted by the business consultant. After completing the diary, the business consultant was interviewed for 30 min by the researchers about his multitasking behaviors. The goal of the open-ended interview technique was to discuss in detail the consultant's diary notes, tasks, and processes. The researcher created notes during the interview.

6.3 Data Analysis

The business consultant's diary, transcribed interview, and the interview notes were qualitatively analyzed to identify aspects of his multitasking behaviors. The goal of the analysis was to produce a taxonomy and flowchart of the business consultant's task switching during his work day. Data were also collected during the microanalysis on the task-switching occurrences and the sequences in which the task occurred. This type of sequential data, insufficiently large quantities, can be used as input for the statistical analysis of the patterns and transitions of sequences.

6.4 Types of Tasks

The types of information and non-information tasks, task frequency, task switching, and task interplay are discussed in what follows. Analysis of the business consultant's diary revealed 67 tasks (including repetitions) that could be reduced to 11 different tasks:

- *Dining task*—includes eating and drinking.
- *Personal communication task*—talking face-to-face with another person.
- *Email communication task*—emailing other people.
- *Voice mail communication task*—talking to other people via voice mail.
- *Email check task*—checking email.
- *Computer task*—using and modifying computer applications.
- *Information search task*—search the Web or other online information system for information.
- *Telephone communication task*—talking to other people on the telephone.
- *Reading task*—reading paper materials.
- *Teleconferencing task*—talking to other people via a teleconferencing system.
- *Writing task*—writing on paper.
- *Financial task*—writing checks and checking financial data.

For purposes of examining interplay between tasks, the 11 tasks were grouped into four broad types of major tasks—communication tasks, computing tasks, information searching tasks, and other tasks that are defined in what follows:

- *Communication tasks*—including interpersonal, telephone, voice mail, teleconferencing, and email tasks.
- *Computing tasks*—using computer applications to create documents or financial data.
- *Information-seeking tasks*—including searching Web and other IR systems for information.
- *Other tasks*—including writing, reading, social tasks, etc.

Section 6.5 of the chapter discusses the findings related to task frequency.

6.5 Task Frequency

A total of 67 tasks were conducted by the business consultant during a 1-day period. Table 1 shows the frequency of each task.

Computer tasks formed the largest task area, followed by sending emailing, information searching, and then personal and telephone communication tasks.

Table 2 shows the frequency of each major task.

Communication tasks formed the major part of the business consultant's work day, including interpersonal, email, telephone, voice mail, and teleconferencing tasks.

A. Spink and M. Park

Task	Frequency	Percentage
Computer task	23	34.4
Email communication task	14	21
Information search task	7	10.5
Personal communication task	6	8.9
Telephone communication task	5	7.4
Reading task	3	4.4
Dining task	3	4.4
Voice mail task	2	3
Writing task	2	3
Teleconferencing task	1	1.5
Financial task	1	1.5
Total	67	100

Table 1. Frequency of Tasks

Computing tasks formed the second largest set of the business consultants' work tasks, including creating and revising documents and databases.

Information-searching tasks were the third largest set of work tasks and occurred less often than other tasks. However, according to the business consultant's diary and

Major Tasks	Percentage of Total Tasks
Communication task	41.7
Computing task	34.4
Other task	13.4
Information searching task	10.5
Total	100.00

Table 2. Major Task Frequency

interview, their information-seeking tasks often occurred to support other tasks through a task-switching process.

Information-searching tasks were conducted to prepare for a computing or communication task, or results of another type of task. For example, a communication task may prompt a business consultant to seek information from the Web or a paper source (internal or external to the organization). Or a business consultant may seek information from the Web, electronic, or database source (internal or external to the organization), to prepare for a forthcoming meeting and communication task.

Section 6.6 of this chapter discusses the task switching and the interplay between different tasks.

6.6 Task Switching and Interplay Between Tasks

The multitasking behaviors by the business consultant consisted of task switching between different tasks, including information and non-information related tasks. A total of 66 task switches occurred during the 1-day period. Table 3 shows the pattern of switching between major tasks.

The patterns of multitasking and task switching consisted of interplay between different tasks. Most of the task switching occurred as an interplay between communication and computing tasks. The business consultant's day consisted of mainly communicating in person or via email or telephone and using computer applications. There were some 14 task switches to and from an information task and an interplay between information and non-information related tasks. However, information tasks occurred to support or respond to communication or computing tasks. For example, the business consultant sought information immediately before a meeting to support discussion in the meeting on a particular information task. Another example is the need to seek information to solve short-term or long-term computing and business problems.

Task/Task	Communication tasks	Computing tasks	Information searching tasks	Other tasks	Total
Communication tasks	13	12	2	3	30
Computing tasks	11	6	2	3	22
Information searching tasks	2	2	2	1	7
Other tasks	2	2	1	3	8
Total	28	22	7	10	67

Table 3. Number of Major Task Switches

Task switching occurred about every 15 min within a range of 2–30 min between the tasks switched. We are currently examining the issue of task interplay more carefully, including the sequences of task switching related to pre- and post-information-searching tasks. Section 6.7 of this chapter outlines the reasons for task switching by the business consultant.

6.7 Reasons for Information Task Switching

During the interview, the business consultant identified a number of reasons for their multitasking behavior, the ordering of the task switches, and the interplay between information and non-information related tasks:

- The business consultant experienced a shift of need when working one task and needed to proceed with another task.
- The business consultant first pursued communication tasks and spent most of their time conducting communication tasks. An outcome of a communication task was frequently the need to move to a computing task.
- The information tasks searched for were upgrade processes, how to cold start a database, network change, searching for a company URL on the Google Web search engine, and searching for financial information on the Web.
- Information tasks often occurred following a problem identified during a communication or computing task, or to support a communication or computing task.

6.8 Task Interplay and Switching

The business consultant's construction is a multitasking process consisting of four major tasks, including communication, computing, information searching, and other tasks. He co-ordinated a process of ordering, constructing, and switching between these tasks. During this complex process, the business consultant worked on information tasks and articulated the status of each task and the reasons for the ordering of his actions on each task.

This exploratory study begins the process of exploring the complex process of information task switching. The business consultant exhibited a complex process of task switching, including periods of concentration on specific tasks of varying familiarity and complexity. His reasons for task switching were related to the level of urgency for each task. Frequent task switching was an everyday process for the business consultant. The tasks observed in this study also varied in the length of time spent on each task. In this case, the business consultant was under time pressure to perform the tasks within a certain timeframe.

The findings from the case study suggest that information-searching tasks emerged from and supported his communication and computing tasks. A further key issue to be further explored relates to the planning and prioritizing of information and non-information-related tasks. Research shows that people reason over situations and actions in order to formulate a plan before taking action (Lee & Taatgen, 2002). The business consultant constructed a consciously reasoned and deliberate process. However, it was not obvious to the researcher that the business consultant had a detailed and explicitly devised plan to conduct multitasking activities—a finding that needs to be confirmed with a larger group of business consultants.

Many HIB models exist, but few have explicitly addressed multitasking information behaviors. The study reported in this chapter further identifies aspects of multitasking information and task-switching behavior. The study findings reported in this chapter also extend our previous research by providing a more in-depth understanding of multitasking information behaviors by a business consultant. The results from this exploratory case study provided insights into multitasking information behaviors and information task switching, and the interplay between information and non-information-related behaviors. The factors discussed in this study and the related studies show that multitasking information behaviors exist to allow people to cope with a complex world and set of demands in the workplace. From the findings over multiple studies in different information environments (Spink, 2004; Spink, Ozmutlu, & Ozmutlu, 2002), including the current study, multitasking behaviors are shown to specifically allow people to cope with a complex task laden and organized world.

7. MULTITASKING AND CO-ORDINATING INFORMATION BEHAVIOR

We would like to begin to model the co-ordinating and multitasking behavior found in the case study. Our starting premise is that during multitasking, humans cognitively and physically co-ordinate multiple tasks through task switching. We then propose that all HIB can be operationalized and contextualized as a multitasking behavior on the various levels of HIB shown in Figure 1.

We begin in Figure 2 by diagramming the switching behavior of the business consultant in the case study.

We show three of the four major task groups of the consultant, eliminating for now the catch-all group called "other tasks". From the findings in the case study, the three major task groups for the consultant are information searching, communication, and computing. This produces three separate switching activities in the consultant's business day, which we call A, B, and C in Figure 2. The switching or co-ordinating interface activity is defined as a co-ordinating HIB, which we label HICB (human information co-ordinating behavior). For three task groups, there are a total of six possible HICB permutations, indicated by the back-and-forth arrows.

We broaden or generalize the description of the HICB for the business consultant via co-ordination theory. Co-ordination theory is an emerging and interdisciplinary area of research. Malone and Crowston (1994) define co-ordination as managing dependences between activities and co-ordination theory, as the still-developing body of theories about how co-ordination can occur in diverse kinds of systems. Co-ordination theory provides a useful theoretical framework for analyzing the implications of HIB. Researchers in computer science, operations research, economics, and organizational theory have conducted research into co-ordination theory.

Co-ordination theorists have sought to understand the principles underlying how people collaborate and co-ordinate work effectively and productively in organizational contexts (Lewis et al., 2001; Olsen, Malone, and Smith, 2001). Co-ordination has been defined as the management of dependencies, or conflicts, between goals, tasks, and resources of various agents (Kling et al., 2001; Malone & Crowston, 1994; Rapoport & Fuller, 1998). Co-ordination theory offers an understanding of the nature of various kinds of dependencies among activities and how they can manage to avoid problems, such as unsatisfied pre-requisites for important tasks (Crowston, 1997).

Theoretically and practically, HICB can be conceptualized as a multitasking and co-ordinating process. Humans commonly face multiple and complex situations in organizing and seeking information that involves interplay of information and non-information tasks. Multitasking and co-ordinating information behavior is a relatively new and crucial area of HIB research. Further research is needed using a larger group of consultants to examine multitasking further. Studies are also needed to investigate how people co-ordinate their information and multitasking behaviors, the role of individual differences, and cognitive styles influence multitasking information behaviors and information task switching.

Section 8 of this chapter proposes a theoretical framework for the sustaining process of HICB.

8. THEORETICAL FRAMEWORK—SUSTAINING PROCESS OF HICB

Figure 1 shows that HIB focuses on many different processes that occur over time and need to be sustained. The processes of concern to HIB focus on the human construction of information during seeking, sense-making, foraging, searching, retrieving, and use processes, particularly human interaction with information systems including digital libraries and the Web. These processes include a human information problem that initiates HIB's related to a human problem state, cognitive state, and knowledge state (Ingwersen, 1996), and information-seeking behavior for the purpose of researching and completing an assignment (Kuhlthau, 1993) or for the purpose of defining and solving the user's problem (Popper, 1975; Spink & Cole, in press).

In particular, the concept of HICB is an important linking and sustaining process for a science of information that binds together the many HIB processes. The development of HIB necessitates a theoretical and empirical explication of the important nature and role of HIB's, including HICB. In HCIB, humans *co-ordinate* a number of elements, including their cognitive state, level of domain knowledge, and their understanding of their information problem, into a coherent series of activities that may include seeking, searching, interactive browsing, retrieving, and constructing information. A key process for HCIB is to sustain these activities toward completion of some information goal or object.

Information seekers perform *interdependent activities* to achieve *goals* or solve problems. These activities may also require or create *resources* of various types. In this view, information seekers *co-ordinate information tasks* arising from dependences that constrain how tasks can be performed. These dependences may be inherent in the structure of the problem (e.g., components of a system may interact with each other, constraining the kinds of changes that can be made to a single component) or they may result from decomposition of the goal into activities or the assignment of activities to other actors and resources.

9. CONCLUSION AND FURTHER RESEARCH

Humans construct their HIB processes as a series of tasks, including an embedded interplay of information topic, information behaviors, and related tasks. For example, embedded between telephoning and computing tasks, an information seeker co-ordinates many tasks when looking for medical information. Therefore, multitasking information-behavior research is a significant area of study. Despite the focus on tasks (Vakkari, 2003), current models of information behaviors do not consider multitasking behaviors. HIB is more complex than the consideration of information tasks in isolation from people's other tasks. Understanding and modeling multitasking information behaviors require an understanding of the co-ordination and interplay between information seeking/foraging/sense-making, organizing, and using tasks.

Conceptualizing information behavior as a multitasking process within a HICB framework embeds HIB models and studies such as feedback research and informatics research within the broader framework of multitasking research in the cognitive/behavioral sciences (Spink, Park, & Jansen, in press). However, in the HIB context, multitasking information behavior is still largely under-researched. In addition, current HIB models are based in a single information task paradigm. However, information behaviors are accomplished by people in much more complex ways. Conceptualizing multitasking and co-ordination behaviors is a relatively new and heuristic direction for HIB research. The authors are currently conducting further studies to extend our understanding of the nature, patterns, and impacts of HIB within a multitasking and co-ordinating framework.

References

Brown, S., Ganesan, S., & Challagalla, G. (2001). Self-efficacy as a moderator in information seeking effectiveness. *Journal of Applied Psychology*, 86, 1043–1051.

Burgess, P. W. (2000). Real-world multitasking from a cognitive neuroscience perspective. In S. Monsell & J. Driver (Eds.), *Control of Cognitive Processes: Attention and Performance XVIII*. Cambridge, MA: The MIT Press.

Butler, R. (1993). Effects of task- and ego-achievement goals on information-seeking during task engagement. *Journal of Personality and Social Psychology*, 65, 18–31.

Carlson, R. A., & Sohn, M.-Y. (2000). Cognitive control of multistep routines: Information processing and conscious intentions. In S. Monsell & J. Driver (Eds.),*Control of Cognitive Processes: Attention and Performance XVIII*. Cambridge, MA: The MIT Press.

Case, D. O. (2002). *Looking for Information: A Survey of Research on Information Seeking, Needs and Behavior*. Amsterdam: Academic Press.

Chatman, E. (1991). Life in a small world: Applicability of gratification theory to information seeking behavior. *Journal of the American Society for Information Science*, 42, 438–449.

Choo, C. W., Detlor, B., & Turnbull, D. (2000). *Web Work: Information-Seeking and Knowledge Work on the World Wide Web*. Amsterdam: Kluwer Academic Publishers.

Cole, C. (2000). Interaction with an enabling information retrieval system: Modeling the user's decoding and encoding operations. *Journal of the American Society for Information Science*, 51(5), 417–426.

Cole, C., & Leide, J. E. (2005). Human information organizing behavior. In A. Spink & C. Cole (Eds.), *New Directions in Human Information Behavior*. Berlin: Springer.

Crowston, K. (1997). A coordination theory approach to organizational process design. *Organizational Science*, 8(2), 157–176.

Dervin, B. (1992). From the mind's eye of the user: The sense-making qualitative–quantitative methodology. In J. Glazier & R. Powell (Eds.), *Qualitative Research in Information Management*, 61–84. Englewood, CO: Libraries Unlimited.

Dervin, B., Zweizig, D., Banister, M., Gabriel, M., Hall, E., & Kwan, C. (1976). *The Development of Strategies for Dealing with the Information Needs of Urban Residents. Phase 1: Citizen Study*. Washington, DC: U.S. Department of Health, Education and Welfare, Office of Education, Office of Libraries and Learning Resources.

Deutsch, F. M., Ruble, D. N., Fleming, A., Brooks-Gunn, J., & Stangor, C. (1988). Information-seeking and maternal self-definition during the transition to motherhood. *Journal of Personality and Social Psychology*, 55(3), 420–431.

Ford, N. (2004). Modeling cognitive processes in information seeking: From popper to pask. *Journal of the American Society for Information Science and Technology*, 55(9), 769–782.

Hildebrand-Saints, L., & Weary, G. (1989). Depression and social information gathering. *Personality and Social Psychology Bulletin*, 15, 150–160.

Ingwersen, P. (1996). Cognitive perspectives of information retrieval interaction: elements of a cognitive IR Theory. *Journal of Documentation*, 52(1), 3–50.

Just, M. A., Carpenter, P. A., Keller, T. A., Emery, L., Zajac, H., & Thulborn, K. R. (2000). Interdependence of non-overlapping cortical systems in dual cognitive tasks. *Neuroimage*, 14, 417–426.

Kling, R., Kraemer, K. L., Allen, J. P., Bakros, Y., Gurbaxani, V., & Elliott, M. (2001). Transforming coordination: The promise and problems of information technology in coordination. In G. M. Olsen, T. W. Malone, & J. B. Smith (Eds.), *Coordination Theory and Collaboration Technology*. Mahwah, NJ: Lawrence Erlbaum Associates.

Kuhlthau, C. C. (1993). *Seeking Meaning: A Process Level to Library and Information Services*. Norwood, NJ: Ablex.

Kuhlthau, C. C. (1997). The influence of uncertainty on the information-seeking behavior of a securities analyst. In P. Vakkari, R. Savolainen, & B. Dervin (Eds.), *Information-Seeking in Context*, 268–274. London: Taylor Graham.

Kurland, J. A., & Beckerman, S. J. (1985). Optimal foraging and homid evolution: Labor and reciprocity. *American Anthropologist*, 87, 73–93.

Leckie, G. J., Pettigrew, K. E., & Sylvain, C. (1996). Modeling the information-seeking of professionals: A general model derived from research on engineers, health care professionals, and lawyers. *Library Quarterly*, 66(2), 161–193.

Lee, F. J., & Taatgen, N. A. (2002). Multitasking as skill acquisition. *Proceedings of CogSci 2002: Annual Meeting of the Cognitive Science Society*, August 2002, Fairfax, VA.

Lewis, C., Reitsma, R., Wilson, E. V., & Zigurs, I. (2001). Extended coordination theory to deal with goal conflicts. In G. W. Olsen & T. W. Malone (Eds.), *Coordination Theory and Collaboration Technology*, 651–672. Mahwah, NJ: Lawrence Erlbaum Associates.

Malone, T. W., & Crowston, K. (1994). The interdisciplinary study of coordination. *ACM Computing Surveys*, 26, 87–119.

Marchionini, G. (1995). *Information Seeking in Electronic Environments*. New York: Cambridge University Press.

McIlwaine, I. C. (1997). The Universal Decimal Classification: Some factors concerning its origins, development, and influence. *Journal of the American Society for Information Science*, 48(4), 331–339.

Merriam, S. B. (1988). *Case Study Research in Education: A Qualitative Approach*. San Francisco: Jossey-Bass Publishers.

Mithen, S. (1990). *Thoughtful Foragers: A Study of Prehistoric Decision-Making*. New York: Cambridge University Press.

Miyata, Y., & Norman, D. (1986). Psychological issues in support of multiple activities. In D. A. Norman & S. W. Draper (Eds.), *User Centered Design*. NJ: Lawrence Erlbaum Associates.

Morrison, E. W. (1993). Longitudinal study of the effects of information seeking on newcomer socialization. *Journal of Applied Psychology*, 78, 173–183.

Olsen, G. M., Malone, T. W., & Smith, J. B. (Eds.) (2001). *Coordination Theory and Collaboration Technology*. Mahwah, NJ: Lawrence Erlbaum Associates.

Pirolli, P., & Card, S. K. (1999). Information foraging. *Psychological Review*, 106, 643–675.

Popper, K. (1975). *Objective Knowledge: An Evolutionary Approach*. Oxford: Clarendon Press.

Rapoport, A., & Fuller, M. A. (1998). Coordination in non-cooperative three-person games under different information infrastructures. *Group Decision and Negotiation*, 7(4), 363–382.

Rubinstein, J., Meyer, D., & Evans, J. (2001). Executive control of cognitive processes in task switching. *Journal of Experimental Psychology*, 27(4), 763–797.

Sandstrom, P. E. (1994). An optimal foraging approach to information seeking and use. *Library Quarterly*, 64(4), 414–443.

Sandstrom, P. E. (2001). Scholarly communication as a socio-ecological system. *Scientometrics*, 51(3), 573–605.

Savolainen, R. (1995). Everyday life information seeking: Leveling information seeking in the context of way of life. *Library and Information Science Research*, 17, 259–294.

Spink, A. (2004). Multitasking information behavior and information task switching: An exploratory study. *Journal of Documentation*, 60(4), 336–351.

Spink, A., & Cole, C. (2001). Everyday life information seeking research. *Library and Information Science Research*, 23(4), 301–304.

Spink, A., & Cole, C. (2004). Special topic issue: Information seeking research: Introduction: Part I. *Journal of the American Society for Information Science and Technology*, 55(8), 657–659.

Spink, A., & Cole, C. (in press). Human information behavior: Integrating diverse levels and information use. *Journal of the American Society for Information Science and Technology.*

Spink, A., & Currier, J. (in press). Towards an evolutionary perspective on human information behavior. *Journal of Documentation.*

Spink, A., Ozmutlu, H. C., & Ozmutlu, S. (2002). Multitasking information seeking and searching processes. *Journal of the American Society for Information Science and Technology*, 3(8), 639–652.

Spink, A., & Park, M. (in press). Multitasking interplay of information and non-information tasks. *Journal of Documentation.*

Spink, A., Park, M., & Jansen, B. J. (in press). Multitasking during web search sessions. *Information Processing and Management.*

Tang, R., & Solomon, P. (1998). Toward an understanding of the dynamics of relevance judgment: An analysis of one person's search behavior. *Information Processing and Management*, 34(2/3), 237–256.

Todd, R. J. (1999). Back to our beginnings: Information utilization, Bertram Brookes and the fundamental equation of information science. *Information Processing and Management*, 35, 851–870.

Vakkari, P. (2003). Task-based information searching. *Annual Review of Information Science and Technology*, 37, 413–464.

Wickens, C. D. (1992). *Engineering Psychology and Human Performance.* Harper Collins: New York.

Wilson, T. D. (2000). Human information behaviour. *Informing Science*, 3(2), 49–56.

Chapter 9

A Non-linear Perspective on Information Seeking

Allen Foster
Department of Information Studies
University of Wales Aberystwyth

1. INTRODUCTION

This chapter explores human information behavior (HIB) from within a non-linear perspective. The perspective offers a more fully developed framework for HIB in terms of non-linear, dynamic, and complex inter-relationships of behavior, activity, and context. Previously, the preserve of the sciences, the concept of non-linearity, or non-sequential behavior has existed in information science as a generality or passing comment for some years. It was not until recently that empirical research led to the development of a non-linear model of information-seeking behavior.

This chapter highlights the nature of non-linearity, discusses recent developments in the field, and suggests some of the implications that arise from this new perspective for the study of HIB.

2. THE CONCEPT OF NON-LINEARITY

The word "non-linear" is unusual in information science and is far more common in the pure and applied sciences. The focus of non-linear theories in the sciences is on understanding, and mathematically representing, the movement or transformation of one complex entity into another related one. In simple systems, a linear equation is sufficient to represent the relationship of concepts. The solution to a linear equation when plotted on a graph makes a straight line: a change to the variable of one axis leads to a change in the variable on the other axis. Change in the linear equation is smooth and continuous.

Non-linear equations produce a different graph shape: typically containing cloud shapes, rills, and whirlpools, but not usually lines. The relationship between variables is abrupt, paradoxical, and chaotic, and changes to one variable lead to apparently chaotic effects on other variables. Scientific groupings including physicists, mathematicians, economists, engineers, and geologists have accepted that for many models of the natural world, a linear equation produces an incomplete explanation (Gleick, 1987; Kauffman, 1991).

The explanations derived to model complex systems have the general label of "chaos theory" or "non-linear theory" (Gleick, 1987; Stewart, 1989; Waldrop, 1992). The

A. Spink and C. Cole (eds), New Directions in Human Information Behavior, 155–170.
© 2006 *Springer.*

new approach has enabled modeling of such systems as atmosphere, the solar system, turbulent fluids, plate tectonics, economies, and population growth. Such application has led to ways to recreate, study, and explain natural events of huge complexity be that the geophysics of mountain development, astronomic events such as the rings of Saturn, and the movement of atomic particles (Kellert, 1993).

The mathematics is incidental to the central concept of mapping the inter-relationship of complex variables. In the purest sense, non-linear theory is the representation of complex dynamical systems. It is here that the origin of the word non-linear in information science can be situated as we explore a new perspective that seeks a holistic understanding of the inter-relationship of multiple individually complex variables that form information behavior.

3. NON-LINEARITY AND INFORMATION SCIENCE

The development of non-linearity as a way to understand HIB within information science is at the beginning of exploration. This non-linear approach is represented in Foster's Nonlinear Model of Information Seeking Behavior (Foster, 2003, 2004a). Other contributions to a broader understanding of non-linearity are identifiable in the work of Erdelez (1997), Cheuk (1998), Spink, Ozmutlu, and Ozmutlu (2002), Spink (2004), and Spink, Park, and Cole (2005). This section of the chapter explores these contributions.

Foster's model of Nonlinear Information Seeking Behavior embodies the core principles of the non-linear perspective. Foster's model includes three-core processes, *opening, orientation, and consolidation*, and three levels of contextual interaction, *internal context, external context, and cognitive approach*, as shown in Figure 1 (Foster, 2004a, p. 232).

Each of the core processes, that is, opening, orientation, or consolidation continually interact internally with themselves, and with the information seeker's cognitive approach, internal context, and external context. These elements are considered wholly interactive and non-sequential. Each component of the model is composed of activities, events, and sub-processes. The following sections provide an overview of the core processes, contexts, and cognitive elements of Foster's Non-linear Model.

4. OPENING

Opening as a core process corresponds to activities connected with actively and passively seeking, exploring, and revealing information. Derived from in-viva coding, "opening" is an expression consistent with an information seeker's "opening up a topic" through a variety of activities. Opening activities include two complex processes, breadth exploration, and eclecticism. These involve combinations of other activities to form a larger process. Breadth exploration is a conscious expansion of searching to improve coverage of concepts and information sources and relies heavily upon the interplay orientation activities to generate keywords, sources, and to highlight further potential opening activities. Eclecticism merges passive and active approaches to accepting, gathering, and storing information.

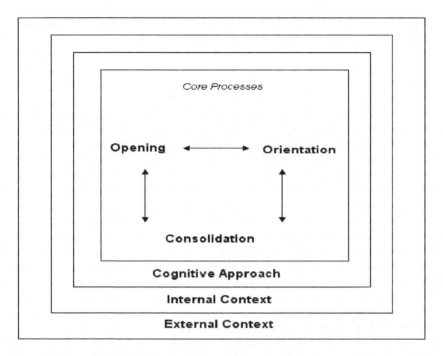

Figure 1. Nonlinear Model of Information Seeking Behavior (Foster, 2004a, b, p. 232).

Eclecticism follows the dictionary definition of the Oxford English Dictionary (OED) as "That which borrows or is borrowed from diverse sources . . . . Unfettered by a narrow system in matters of opinion or practice; broad, not exclusive, in matters of taste" (OED Online 2nd Ed., 1989). Eclecticism complements other aspects of information seeking, particularly networking and serendipity, and appears here as a strategy for accessing vast amounts of information, across disciplines and from many information sources, and not only accessing, but also storing and filtering information for future incorporation into further information-seeking activities.

The remaining activities of opening include networking through many channels, including conferences, social gatherings, colleagues, and departmental research groups. This was a way to increase access to information and sources and as a tool for exploring subjects, opening up new concepts, and areas not revealed through traditional searching. Keyword searching and browsing during opening were associated with many standard information retrieval tools. Monitoring via repeat visits to obtain updates has a similar meaning to that used by Ellis (1989), and highlighted in the data as part of the ongoing processes following identification of fruit-bearing sources of information.

The activity of chaining, identified by Ellis (1989), is present and adds an additional emphasis on the chaining of ideas from one source to another. Serendipity is a method for achieving breadth and identifying information or sources from unknown or partially unknown directions. Serendipity and activities that encourage the occurrence of serendipitous results frequently appear as a valued part of information seeking, as illustrated in more depth in Foster and Ford (2003).

5. ORIENTATION

The orientation process has a wide remit in information seeking and represents the activity involved in, as Foster (2003) suggested, "making sense" or "finding which way was up". The process involved in the identification is centered on picture building.

Picture building is a composite set of behavior associated with the activity participants described as mapping out, in their minds and on paper, the disciplines, and concepts relevant to achieving an overview of the topic. The process of picture building is interconnected with knowledge and previous experience and information gained through opening. Other orientation activities and particularly those grouped as identifying the shape of existing research supported this activity. Identifying the shape of existing research involved the sub-processes of identifying key names, identifying key articles, and identifying latest opinion in disciplines. Identifying and selecting sources and identifying disciplinary communities both deciding on the basis of information, past experience, topic, or general knowledge that disciplines or sources would be potentially useful places to look for information.

Picture building closely related to problem definition, which was present in the classic sense of defining the focus and boundaries of the information problem, but not fixed in time, and observed to be continually evolving throughout information seeking. Further activities included identifying keywords, which was readily identifiable as a key element of orientation, and reviewing which is identified as the use of existing knowledge in an area, reading or accessing a personal collection, and considering material already gathered. Determining "where I am now" through reviewing established a baseline of information from which ideas of "identifying the gaps that needed filling next" and "developing those seeds of information" to be followed.

6. CONSOLIDATION

The third core process, consolidation, contributes to every information-seeking interaction. The central theme of this process is judging and integrating the work in progress, and deciding whether further information seeking is necessary. Central to knowing enough is a continual questioning whether sufficient material to meet the present information need has been acquired? Two processes involve the creation and application of relevance criteria: refining and sifting. Refining involves setting boundaries for searches and narrowing or widening the search focus—that is, the creation of relevance.

Sifting is the application of relevance judgments to materials and sources. As information seekers identify information, sifting is assembled within their existing knowledge by the process of incorporation. In many cases, this appears as a combination of thinking, writing, and discussion. In addition, identifiable as part of consolidation are verifying of information, and finishing, which can be described as "sweeping up the loose ends" before closure.

7. CONTEXT

Foster's (2003) model states that information seeking is more than an interaction of activities, and is fully explored only where information-seeking core processes are placed within an interactive framework of contexts, and a cognitive approach. In this view, information seekers continually reconstruct their worldview, opportunities, and barriers to reflect the contexts, the cognition, and the activities represented by the core processes.

Major external influences are social and organizational, time, project, navigation issues, and access to sources. A source is entirely dependent upon the social and organizational context. Information seeking is framed by the resolution of specific information problems such as task complexity and by limits to time and financial resources, which Foster (2003) coded as time and the project. Navigation issues and access to sources refer specifically to the organization of information and to the problems incurred by researchers as they move from familiar territory outwards toward new information environments.

The impact of external context appears to vary with associated factors—that is, the strength of factors identified as part of internal context. The internal context is primarily the level of experience and prior knowledge held by the information seeker. Internal influences are factors unique to each information seeker's own profile. In Foster (2003), the influences were categorized as feelings and thoughts, coherence, knowledge, and understanding. Each represents complex concepts that are composed of many components, including internal feelings of uncertainty, self-perception, and self-efficacy, perception of topic, complexity, and distraction. Knowledge and understanding covers experience, information need, and knowledge level.

8. COGNITIVE APPROACH

Finally, the cognitive approach describes aspects of the mode of thinking observed in the participants, a willingness to identify and use information that might be relevant to an information problem. Foster (2003) identified four cognitive approaches:

1. *The Flexible and Adaptable approach* emphasizes the mental agility and willingness to adapt to the different information and disciplinary cultures encountered.
2. *Openness of approach* is an open-minded approach in which no prior framework for judging relevance exists. All sources, disciplines, and ideas are as viable until proven otherwise, and flexibility and adaptability are applied to identify how a new source might fit-in with their information needs.
3. *Nomadic Thought* appeared at first to be the same behavior as openness, but it goes further by embracing the process of thinking about a topic in many diverse ways to find the information needed in locations and ways remote from the original idea. Key elements include the idea of abandoning well-known and favored disciplines and sources in search of new material. This tends to contradict the traditional idea of staying within known disciplines and well-trodden resources.
4. *The Holistic approach* was highlighted as important to grasping and incorporating concepts from diverse areas and bringing them together either as an answer or to generate new questions and information-searching directions.

9. FOSTER'S NON-LINEAR MODEL AND BEYOND

As part of our growing understanding of HIB, Foster's (2003) Nonlinear Model of Information Seeking Behavior provides a detailed framework of behavior, connections, and inter-relationship of activities throughout information seeking. Together the core processes and the contextual aspects of Foster's model form a complex map of information-seeking behavior, described as follows:

> "With each information seeking experience, or contextual change, the opportunity and the need for information seeking change too. The relationship of core processes and developing context, interact freely to allow each core process to feed into any other and to be reiterative over time.... the concepts, represented in the interactivity of the core processes, and the absence of stages in the model, are analogous to an information seeker holding a palette of information behavior opportunities, with the whole palette available at any given moment. The interactivity and shifts described by the model show information seeking to be nonlinear, dynamic, holistic, and flowing" (Foster, 2004a, b, p. 235).

Interpreting information-seeking behavior using the non-linear model suggests that:

- The smallest action may lead to a significant information-seeking outcome.
- Each experiences contextual change and social interaction, and information-seeking activity affects an individual's further information-seeking behavior.
- Individuals continually construct and reconstruct their information problem.

Beyond Foster's (2003) Nonlinear Model of Information Seeking Behavior, the concept of non-linearity appears within the literature of information science in several places. Typically, these appearances have been in examples of work that have pushed at the boundaries of the explanations offered by the linear paradigm. Some elements of this literature are part of the non-linear perspective or highlight the possibility of non-linearity.

Two works highlighting non-linearity are Erdelez (1997) and Swain (1996). Erdelez, while writing on the concept of information encountering, emphasizes the value of innovative approaches in seeking to describe information behavior. It is particularly interesting in a discussion of non-linearity that information-seeking strategies were described by Erdelez as an opportunistic "haphazard, nonlinear movement from one source to another" (Erdelez, 1997, p. 418).

Elsewhere, research found exceptions and variations to the linear model exemplified by Kuhlthau's (1993) information search process (ISP) model. Swain's (1996) study found the stages of Kuhlthau's ISP to be present, but the stages are highly recursive and frequently combined steps or performed them in a different order from that suggested in Kuhlthau's model. Such observations offer a hint of the diversity in information-seeking behavior and again suggest that a simple linear interpretation may not sufficiently explain the complexity of information seeking.

Two earlier studies by Pappas and Tepe (1997) and Cheuk (1998) adopted the non-linear label to describe their work. The work of Pappas and Tepe (1997) described the pathway model based on six stages: appreciation, pre-search, search, interpretation, communication, and evaluation. The claim of non-linearity appears to arise from the continual nature of the evaluation process, rather than a complex inter-relationship of activities. As a model, it draws much of its substance and form from Kuhlthau's (1993) ISP model. Though claiming to be non-linear, it is actually a variation on linear theory.

Cheuk (1998) provides a more completely non-linear view. The Cheuk's (1998) information seeking and use model presents a set of critically different situations of information seeking and use in the workplaces: task initiation situation, focus formulating situation, ideas assuming situation, ideas confirming situation, ideas rejecting situation, ideas finalizing situation, and passing on ideas situation.

Cheuk's (1998) information-seeking situations were bypassing the widely accepted stage models of behavior and displacing these with a view of information seeking as one of dynamic situations not in a specified sequential order. The Cheuk approach contains some elements that suggest the beginnings of non-linearity, but focused upon task situations and therefore lacks a general view of information behavior fully linking situation, task, contextual, cognitive, and most importantly the individual activities of which information-seeking behavior is composed. The model is valuable in highlighting possible non-linear processes in behavior, and in offering a method of highlighting problem situations as a way to interpret that behavior.

A good example of studies tackling the complexities of placing information seeking within the holistic framework is the multitasking behavior study of Spink, Ozmutlu, and Ozmutlu (2002). Although earlier work on successive searching tended to assume a stage model as the basis of understanding (Spink, 1999), later developments of successive searching extend it into multitasking information seeking, which suggests another approach to the non-linear perspective (Spink, Ozmutlu, & Ozmutlu, 2002).

Multitasking information behavior is defined by Spink as "the process of seeking information concurrently over time in relation to more than one, possibly evolving, set of information tasks (including changes or shifts in beliefs, cognitive, affective, and/or situational states)" (Spink, 2004, p. 336). Tasks are said to be multiple, sequential, or concurrent. The framework offered for multitasking information behavior allows task switching and the elements of interest, planning, priorities, effectiveness, and serendipity into a wider understanding of information seeking.

These findings on multitasking information seeking are compatible with the work by Foster (2003, 2004a, b) on interdisciplinary information seekers that lead to the non-linear model of information-seeking behavior and related work on serendipity by Foster and Ford (2003). In Foster (2003), Nonlinear Model of Information Seeking Behavior is a long-term progression through life that forms a continuously evolving personal profile defined as the sum of previous knowledge and experience, including previous information seeking, their external context, and their developing and evolving cognitive dimensions. An information seeker's non-linear behavior interacts with elements such as prior knowledge, serendipity and leads us to a view compatible with successive searching and multitasking (Spink, 2004; Spink, Ozmutlu, & Ozmutlu, 2002) that information seeking is neither merely one search nor even a series of successive search episodes, but reflects the complexities of real-life information seeking.

Collectively, these studies relate a broader recognition and representation of non-linearity within two aspects: "situations" and "streams of successive information-seeking sessions". Retrospectively, they contribute a background to what at the time of writing is the most detailed behavioral study of information seeking within the non-linear perspective represented in Foster's (2004a, b) Non-linear Model of Information Seeking Behavior.

The non-linear perspective formed by these studies offers a first step in the evolution of information behavior studies from simple reductionist frameworks toward a complex dynamic explanatory framework. As a new conceptualization of information behavior, it offers an opportunity to build new explanations of complex phenomena, to test established theories of information behavior and expand our understanding of the many variations observable in information seeking. In exploring new boundaries to our understanding of information seeking and in offering new interpretations, non-linearity is at the forefront of information science development.

10. IMPLICATIONS AND AREAS FOR FURTHER RESEARCH

The advent of a new perspective derived from empirical and theoretical research offers some challenges not least by questioning core assumptions and revising our understanding of some of the most important behavioral processes identified in previous research. As Foster's model, Cheuk's model, and Spink's conceptualization of multitasking information seeking come together to form a core of a non-linear perspective, it becomes possible to consider the major implications of the perspective as relating to four aspects of non-linearity: (1) timing, (2) holism, (3) information skills training, and (4) methodology.

11. TIMING

Non-linearity states that events are no longer bound to problem-solving time, but belong to a wider perspective of "experiential cumulative information seeking" in which current information-seeking behavior may be said to be the product of all past experiences. This begins to offer a potential portrait of HIB through the whole life cycle. The non-linear perspective offers an alternative to previous linear models of information behavior. As a new perspective, it has the potential to displace existing theories, or to enhance research by offering a second position from which to interpret research findings: one area for such examination is the interpretation of problem solving.

The accepted norm for information-seeking research has been to understand the world as a movement from one point to another stage-by-stage, with various features allowing for the omission of stages, feedbacks, and iterations to allow a workable model to emerge. In a simplified model of human, problem-solving individuals work on one problem at a time, cumulatively building toward a solution to their information problem. The portrait of harmonious progression and development is disturbed when we recognize that HIB occurs as a complex dynamic interaction of core processes, contexts, and cognitive approach.

The revision of concepts begins with problem definition, which in the classic sense, was a process of defining the focus and boundaries of an information problem. In Foster's (2003) study, the process of problem definition is not within a timeframe. Instead, it occurs continuously through to closure. This contrasts with linear models in which problem definition is a stage at the beginning of information seeking (Kuhlthau, 1993; Wilson, 1999). Revising problem definition also raises questions about problem solving and the concepts built around it.

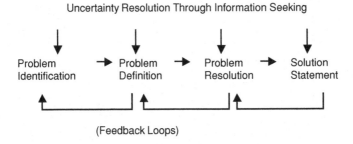

Figure 2. Wilson's problem-solving model (Wilson et al., 2002).

Within the non-linear model of information-seeking behavior, the goal of achieving problem solution and uncertainty takes on new dimensions. Instead of a progression through stages heading toward a solution, a problem may be thought of as multiple problem elements providing a problem situation which may be longitudinal or short term and may be either a single task or part of multiple tasks as proposed by Spink, Ozmutlu, and Ozmutlu (2002) with regard to multitasking information seeking. The new picture becomes one of multiple individually non-linear information-seeking tasks interwoven and interacting over time.

In the Wilson's et al. (2002) model of uncertainty, resolution through successive feedback loops leading in stages from problem identification to solution statement (Figure 2). Uncertainty reduced and a problem statement or solution achieved (Wilson et al., 2002). The uncertainty resolution framework assumes that as stages are experienced that problem solving moves forward toward a solution.

Using the non-linear perspective, the concept of uncertainty is a variation of uncertainty resolution proposed. For the purposes of this initial exploration, an information problem interpreted from within the non-linear perspective may be taken to include the components of Foster's core process of orientation. The level of certainty for each problem element is the product of an interaction between orientation, and context, opening, and consolidation. Previous theory accepts that increases and decreases in overall uncertainty will occur in information seeking, but usually associates this with problem stage rather than problem element (Kuhlthau, 1993; Wilson et al., 2002).

In Figure 3, these problem elements are represented by the X-axis. The level of certainty rather than uncertainty is indicated in Figure 3 by the Y-axis, labeled "level of certainty".

In Figure 3, using this conceptualization, information-seeking results affect individual problem elements. For example, finding a new information source would increase the level of certainty related to source selection.

Similarly, some events could reduce the level of certainty for one or more aspects, or as in the case of serendipitous information seeking bypass many elements to produce a large change in certainty in some problem elements (Foster & Ford, 2003). Over time previous knowledge, previous information seeking, and other contextual elements contribute to the level of certainty related to different problem elements.

The outcome of problem solving within this non-linear view suggests that information seekers will cease information seeking once they have achieved what they consider an

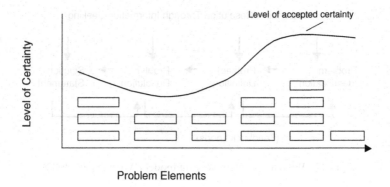

Figure 3. A variation on uncertainty resolution.

appropriate level of certainty for each of the problem elements for which they establish a personal threshold: for a particular scenario, an information seeker is making the judgment that they have enough information. In Figure 3, the level judged as an acceptable certainty level is represented by the curved horizontal line. For each problem element, different levels of certainty are accepted by the information seeker. This interpretation of problem solving and the concept of enough fully integrates contextual and cognitive elements. In connection with other theories, such as March's (1994) satisficing, this may offer the beginnings of an explanation of why information seeking in different task situations, disciplines, and by different individuals, presents differences in the level of certainty found to be acceptable.

Beyond the immediate view of non-linear information seeking and the focus on timing, the alternative model has an interesting potential to stimulate a revision of concepts and models, which hitherto accepted the linear framework to represent the passage of time in information seeking. In developing the non-linear perspective, there is considerable scope for further research looking at the interaction between different information problems, and tracking how the behavior stimulated by one information problem feeds into work on others.

Foster's research (2003) found some evidence of the interaction between tasks and this, in combination with Spink, Ozmultu, and Ozmultu's (2002) concept of multitasking information seeking, will be of value in developing a more detailed understanding of information behavior. Further questions arising from these initial explorations suggest a need to ask what role cognitive styles, individual differences, level of experience, and task complexity contribute to the non-linear view of timing, problem solving, and level of certainty considered acceptable: the level at which an information seeker says they have enough information.

12. HOLISM

The paradigm presented here is perhaps best thought of as the first step in the evolution of a new generation of models that begin to explore information seeking fully from an holistic viewpoint. This is compatible with the holistic view expressed in Dervin and

Nilan (1986). As the non-linear perspective embraces dynamic flowing relationship of core processes, information seeking, context, time, and tasks, the unit of observation expands from the study of individual tasks, individual search sessions, and the study of activities in relative isolation, and becomes the study of activities within a mesh of complex interactions. Indeed as noted previously, other non-linear studies within the science non-linear systems composed of multiple sub-units cannot be understood by analyzing the components individually. The very fact of interaction within the system and the coupled nature of the components defeat such component level study (Bosanac & Bogunovic, 2002).

The implication for the study of information-seeking behavior is that if we are to understand information seeking, then we must be conscious of how each individual information-seeking behavior relates to all other behaviors. To understand inter-related behavior implies tracing the interactions and multiple pathways between core processes and their associated activities, contextual and cognitive levels.

Further research will need to examine information activities and particularly their inter-relationships. In some cases, this is a simple mapping of connections, in others a significant change of interpretation. Initial research by Foster (2003) suggests that non-linear interactions have great similarities between the activities identified in previous information-seeking behavior research and work on non-linearity (Foster, 2003, 2004a, b). The differences may be subtle, as for example, the variations on Ellis's (1989) chaining and monitoring, or more substantial such as breadth exploration, eclecticism, and serendipity (Foster & Ford, 2003).

The challenge for future research comes not in accepting holism as a radically different approach, but in incorporating and revising our understanding of already well-researched concepts, and identifying the variations that may only come into view once the behavior is considered fully within the non-linear holistic framework.

13. INFORMATION SKILLS TRAINING

Beyond pure research, non-linearity has an implication for the teaching of information skills: it offers a substantially different view that specifies a non-linear and holistic approach to understand information seeking. That different approach may be used as a framework and rationale for teaching information skills. There is a considerable literature in existence putting forward complex interpretations of how to teach information skills using various linear models. Traditional approaches have worked with the assumption that teaching should involve breaking information seeking down into stages, which must be completed before moving on to the next step. These approaches are a good tool to structure teaching in some contexts, perhaps to novice information seekers in particular (Swain, 1996).

In contrast to this, the non-linear perspective offers an alternative way to view the creation of an information literate individual. For the purposes of this chapter, information literacy is defined as being capable of successful information-seeking behavior and demonstrating a sufficient knowledge of the available information-seeking pallete to find information in any given context. In approaching the task of teaching with a non-linear perspective, the core processes and contexts, and cognitive approach become important. The core principle becomes the interaction between activities and the multiple ways to combine them. This raises some interesting questions for an educator, particularly in thinking about how you teach a non-linear approach. The beginnings of attempts at an answer to this problem have used Foster's (2004a, b) model to outline an approach to teaching.

The first problem of which skills, and when to introduce them, is a difficult obstacle to overcome. In Foster's model, three-core process represents the activities necessary to complete information seeking. An information literate person is able to successfully perform a version of the triumvirate of three-core processes. Learning the purpose and logic of each of the three-core processes is potentially the first conceptual element to teach.

The educator may demonstrate the existence of the full range of activities possible, but the number and range of skills taught will be determined by the learner's initial level of skill which may be readily explored with diagnostic assessments. In Foster's (2003) model, the concept of a skill level is defined by the contextual elements. In deciding how to approach the task of teaching a simple analogy has been useful to structure a curriculum. In this analogy, a simplified non-linear framework for a novice information seeker, analogous to a children's paint set, with a limited paint brush, provides a beginning level of information seeking representing the most basic aspects of opening, orientation, and consolidation, for example, browsing or keyword searching.

More advanced information seekers learn that complex mixtures of colors (activities) provide better results, and using different brushes (activities, sources, strategies) increases the scope for refined and complex outputs. Taking the analogy to its logical conclusion, expert searchers would choose from complete set of paints and a full set of broad and fine brushes, representing training in complex strategies, information sources, and approaches to problem solving. For a given context, it is necessary for the educator to determine the level of component activities required.

In a small scale initial trial (Foster, 2004a, b) of the technique involving the training of academics and Masters students for electronic information sources and refreshing information skills, the non-linear model offered a flexible tool with which to introduce strategies and activities which the learners could incorporate into their previous knowledge of searching. The result was the adoption of new methods, quick integration of previous experience with new ways of searching for information, and an increased level of reflective information-seeking practice.

The approach provides information seekers with a flexible framework that reflects the way people in real situations find it necessary to think about and to perform information seeking. This may be welcomed by the expert searchers and members of the information profession who have informally discussed the non-linear model and acknowledge that there is a fundamental variation between what they suggest to people (the stage approach), and what they do themselves (a complex non-linear approach).

As we debate how to put non-linearity into practice, questions arise about how different groups of learners will react to a non-linear framework and to answer this it is vital to examine cultural, educational, and contextual differences. Research is necessary to determine which activities are important to teach different user groups, and on which aspect much may be learned from previous work on tasks, disciplines, and everyday life information seeking. In terms of the learning outcome, it will be of interest to examine the effect of the training model on the speed and success of learners becoming information literate.

Similarly, questions of whether non-linear training require more or less involvement by the educator/learning facilitator, and whether the resources required different from those involved in traditional training arise. This in turn raises the possibility of developing resources to support non-linear training. Finally, there is potential to use the non-linear perspective as a way to package information skills in a manner that reflects practical behavior and real-world solutions rather than the artificial conceptualization of stages, and this may be acceptable to a diverse groups for whom traditional information skills training is unsuitable.

Information skills training using the non-linear perspective offers substantial scope for innovative approaches and also raises many practical questions of interest to theorists and practitioners.

14. METHODOLOGY

The focus of the non-linear perspective suggests that researchers must focus on the dynamic interplay of all variables in order to fully appreciate and explain information behavior. If we use Foster's (2003) Nonlinear Model as a guide, then research must record information-seeking activities described as interactions within the core processes, contextual and cognitive aspects. Identifying and recording these variables and their multiple links is a formidable task, and one which when translated into the study of information seeking in everyday life must be driven by robust methodologies.

Studies are usually conducted by in-depth interviewing and analysis mainly from the naturalistic approach favored by exploratory social science researchers. The potential for extending our understanding using these naturalistic methods is large and offers interesting possibilities for future research. However, as we move toward what must necessarily be a complex mapping of behavior, we will increasingly need to draw upon innovative combinations of human cognition, ethnographics, simulations, and mathematics to record, map, and explore. Researchers may be able to move in the direction of non-linear mathematical modeling in the manner proposed by Snyder (1992) to model human communication, and used by Ganzach (2001) to model clinical decision making in the psychological sciences.

Collecting considerable amounts of complex data on concurrent tasks and behavior will highlight the ways to analyze and present that data. The cliché is that a picture speaks a 1000 words, and for non-linear information seeking creating a graphical representation of data that is accessible and enables research analysis is a significant challenge. Software such as Atlas.ti by Scientific Software offers valuable features. However, there is a need to develop techniques to enhance the ways in which variables and interactions are represented and explored. Recent advances in data visualization techniques, 3D graphics, and the availability of powerful desktop computers begin to offer a potential for mapping the events and interactions of the non-linear model in a complex multilayered four-dimensional simulation of real-time information seeking.

15. CONCLUSION AND FURTHER RESEARCH

The models, studies, and implications presented in this chapter offer the outline of a non-linear perspective that suggests that HIB is dynamic, non-linear, and complexly interactive, and therefore best understood from a holistic approach. The combination of

A. Foster

studies contributing to the non-linear perspective suggests a way to place HIB clearly within the life cycle of an information seeker. People will potentially experience difference immediate situations, and work on multiple problems simultaneously, while moving through information seeking not in the linear patterns originally envisaged by theorists, but in complex dynamic patterns representing the complex reality of information seeking.

As a new direction for HIB research, the non-linear perspective is at the beginning of its development. Its future development is likely to produce models that are:

1. More highly detailed.
2. Seek to fully identify and represent a complex mapping of interactions and behavior.
3. Will be derived from multiple methods drawn from a wide disciplinary base; and more speculatively.
4. That the analysis and visual representation of the dynamics of non-linear models may require mathematics and computer simulations.

This chapter raises some implications and areas for further research. However, there are many questions about how non-linearity works for different individuals and contexts. Key questions for research will include how common non-linear information behavior is, and particularly are some disciplines, or tasks, more linear than others, is non-linear information seeking more common amongst experienced information seekers. Focusing on the individual level, we should ask: are some information seekers more adept at non-linear information seeking than others; what role individual differences and cognitive styles play as part of context have in non-linear behavior; this may include examining hypotheses related to the presence of dominant information-behavior patterns (Foster, 2004a, b; Spink & Park, in press).

In developing these questions, we may look beyond a single perspective to consider if HIB consists of a scale of linearity incorporating both linear and non-linear behavior. Beyond information science, we may raise some interesting interdisciplinary questions if we consider HIB not at the individual, or even multiple tasks, but as part of the largest context of human experience, the human life cycle.

Further implications and questions will arise from this approach as researchers think about what non-linearity conceptualizations mean when applied to different parts of information behavior. The exploration of non-linearity as a perspective requires a further development, but it contains a framework of great potential as we explore new directions in HIB.

References

Bosanac, G., & Bogunovic, N. (2002). Nonlinear information processing in extracting predictive attributes of an ECG signal. In *Proceedings of the 6th Multi-conference on Systematics, Cybernetics and Informatics*, Vol. II, July 14–18, 2002, Orlando, FL, USA, 275–279.

Cheuk, W.-Y. B. (1998). An information seeking and using process model in the workplace: A constructivist approach. *Asian Libraries*, 7(12), 375–390.

Dervin, B., & Nilan, M. (1986). Information needs and uses. *Annual Review of Information Science and Technology*, 21, 3–33.

Ellis, D. (1989). A behavioural approach to information retrieval design. *Journal of Documentation*, 45, 171–212.

Erdelez, S. (1997). Information encountering: A conceptual framework for accidental information discovery. In P. Vakkari, R. Savolainen, & B. Dervin (Eds.), *Information Seeking in Context: Proceedings of an International Conference on Research in Information Needs, Seeking, and Context*. Los Angeles: Taylor Graham.

Foster, A. E. (2003). *Interdisciplinary Information Seeking Behavior: A Naturalistic Inquiry*. Unpublished Ph.D. Thesis, University of Sheffield, UK.

Foster A. E. (2004a). A nonlinear model of information seeking behavior. *Journal of the American Society for Information Science and Technology*, 55(3), 228–237.

Foster, A. E. (2004b). A nonlinear model of information seeking behavior. *Paper presented at the Information Seeking in Context Conference (ISIC 2004)*, Dublin, Ireland.

Foster, A. E., & Ford, N. J. (2003). Serendipity and information seeking: An empirical study. *Journal of Documentation*, 59(3), 321–340.

Ganzach, Y. (2001). Nonlinear models of clinical judgment: Communical nonlinearity and nonlinear accuracy. *Psychological Science*, 12(5), 403–407.

Gleick, J. 1987. *Chaos: Making a New Science*. London: Heinemann.

Kauffman, S. A. (1991). Antichaos and adaptation. *Scientific American*, 265(2), 64–70.

Kellert, S. H. (1993). *In the wake of chaos: Unpredictable order in dynamical systems*. Chicago: University of Chicago Press.

Kuhlthau, C. C. (1993). *Seeking Meaning: A Process Approach to Library and Information Services*. Norwood, NJ: Ablex.

March, J. G. (1994). *A Primer on Decision Making: How Decisions Happen*. New York: The Free Press.

Oxford English Dictionary (2nd Edn.) (1989). [Online]. Available from http://dictionary.oed.com/cgi/entry/00065211 (accessed 13 December 2001).

Pappas, M. L., & Tepe, A. E. (1997). *Pathways to Knowledge: Follet's Information Skills Model* (3rd Edn.). McHenry, IL: Follet Software.

Snyder, H. (1992). An examination of the utility of nonlinear dynamics techniques for analyzing human information behaviors. *Proceedings of the 55th Annual Meeting of the American Society for Information Science*, 29, 98–100.

Spink, A. (1999). Towards a theoretical framework for information retrieval in an information seeking context. In T. D. Wilson & D. K. Allen (Eds.), *Exploring the Contexts of Information Behaviour: Proceedings of the Second International Conference on Research in Information Needs, Seeking and Use in Different Contexts, 13–15 August 1998, Sheffield, UK*, 21–34. London: Taylor Graham.

Spink, A. (2004). Multitasking information behavior and information task switching: An exploratory study. *Journal of Documentation*, 60(4), 336–351.

Spink, A., Ozmutlu, H. C., & Ozmutlu, S. (2002). Multitasking information seeking and searching process. *Journal of the American Society for Information Science and Technology*, 53(9), 695–703.

Spink, A., & Park, M. (in press). Information and non-information task interplay: An exploratory study. *Journal of Documentation*.

Spink, A., Park, M., & Cole, C. (2005). Multitasking framework for human information behavior. In A. Spink & C. Cole (Eds.), *New Directions in Human Information Behavior*. Springer: Berlin.

Stewart, I. (1989). *Does God Play Dice? The Mathematics of Chaos*. Harmondsworth, Middlesex: Penguin Books Ltd.

Swain, D. E. (1996). Information search process model: How freshmen begin research. In S. Hardin (Ed.), *Global Complexity: Information, Chaos, and Control: ASIS '96 Volume 33: Proceedings of the 59th American Society for Information Science Annual Meeting*, 95–99. Medford, NJ: Information Today.

Waldrop, M. M. (1992). *Complexity: The Emerging Science at the Edge of Order and Chaos*. London: Penguin Books.

Wilson, T. D. (1999). Exploring models of information behavior: The 'Uncertainty' Project. In T. D. Wilson & D. K. Allen (Eds.), *Exploring the Contexts of Information Behavior*. (In *Proceedings of the Second International Conference on Research in Information Needs, Seeking and Use in Different Contexts*, 13/15 August 1998, Sheffield, UK), 55–66. London: Taylor Graham.

Wilson, T. D., Ford, N., Foster, A., Ellis, D., & Spink, A. (2002). Information seeking and mediated searching. Part 2: Uncertainty. *Journal of the American Society for Information Science and Technology*, 53(9), 704–715.

Chapter 10

A Cognitive Framework for Human Information Behavior: The Place of Metaphor in Human Information Organizing Behavior

Charles Cole and John E. Leide
Graduate School of Library and Information Studies
McGill University

1. INTRODUCTION

Human information behavior (HIB) is a way of broadening the perspective when looking at the nexus between the information user and the information he or she is purposively or non-purposively seeking, for both conscious and unconscious reasons, wherever it may be found (for other HIB definitions, cf. also Case, 2002; Wilson, 2000). HIB includes several sub-sections, divisions, or facets, which we will only list here (the HIB sub-sections are fully discussed elsewhere in this volume, Spink, Park, & Cole, 2005; cf. also, Spink & Cole, in press), including:

- information foraging,
- everyday life information seeking,
- information seeking,
- information search,
- information use,
- information organizing behavior.

Briefly, HIB includes all facets of the human information condition, including *information foraging*, which takes an evolutionary perspective, and *everyday life information seeking* (ELIS), which delves deeply into the small world of the user, and this effects what information is; *information seeking*, the traditional interest of Library and Information Science (LIS), focuses on purposive information behavior; *information search* describes user–IR system interaction, and *information use* is when an environmental stimulus—which includes stimuli obtained from human reading, viewing, and listening activities—modifies the user's knowledge structure. We are just beginning to explore HIB and all its facets and these definitions are not set in stone. There will no doubt be other facets added to the list in the future. This chapter explores the additional facet or sub-section of HIB called *human information organizing behavior* (HIOB).

Spink and Currier (in press) have defined HIOB as the process of analyzing and classifying materials into defined categories. They give as an example the Dewey Decimal Classification System (McIlwaine, 1997). While the Dewey example is a document organization system, their definition lends itself to creating a cognitive framework

A. Spink and C. Cole (eds), New Directions in Human Information Behavior, 171–202.
© 2006 *Springer.*

for HIOB as well. We would like to expand the purview of HIOB to include such a cognitive framework—that is, how human perceptual and cognitive resources are organized to receive, analyze, and classify newly received information into defined categories.

In this chapter, after discussing various models, theories, and principles of cognitive HIOB, we focus in on only one part of cognitive HIOB: metaphor instantiation. Metaphor instantiation is an HIOB device for jump-starting human memory organization when an individual finds new and unfamiliar information in the environment. In three case studies, we then examine the application of metaphor instantiation as a memory device for facilitating unfamiliar information processing. This chapter is conceived as a first step to building, piece by piece, a full cognitive framework for HIOB.

2. COGNITIVE HIBO: A LINK WITH THE PAST AND THE FUTURE

There is sound support in LIS history and development for the extension of HIBO to include a cognitive framework. At the end of the 19th century, when the great subject catalog and classification schemes were being developed, the objective of these systems was to represent information sources to the user in a way that was faithful to the structure of the document or information store—a pre-coordinate conception of information organization determined by experts. But in the construction of these catalog and classification schemes, there was consideration for the user's own process of identifying needed information (e.g., Cutter's (1876/1904) famous second Object).

Now, with the advent of interactive technologies and the metaphor of information processing derived from the computer, and with advances in psychology and our understanding of how the mind works when receiving messages (Barsalou, 1992), in LIS there is increasing emphasis on how the user constructs and organizes information when interacting with information objects in the user's environment (Dervin & Nilan, 1986). Part of the construction process involves the user organizing new information into new or existing memory structures—an interactive, Internet-age, post-coordinate conception of information organization determined by the user's selection of keywords and the algorithms of the IR system at the time of search (Foskett, 1996; Jacob, 2004; Lancaster, 1998; Mills, 2004).

In this regard, an important marking point is Vannevar Bush's (1945) famous conceptualization of the Memex machine that is now seen as a precursor to the Internet, described in his Atlantic Monthly article "As We May Think". Bush's Memex was an attempt to create a machine that seamlessly—that is, naturally—brought together human associative thinking and instantaneous informational support, according to the natural organizational framework of the human mind when it is interacting with information: "With one item in its grasp, it snaps instantly to the next that is suggested by the association of thoughts, in accordance with some intricate web of trails carried by the cells of the brain" (Bush, 1945, p. 106).

In our era of virtual information storage and retrieval, LIS is beginning to think of document organization and human memory organization as interconnected and increasingly mutually operational. In other words, if LIS has some say in the matter, IR systems on the Internet and elsewhere will increasingly devise document organization

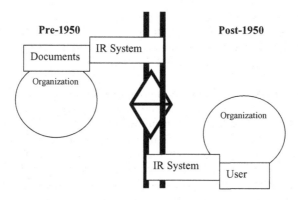

Figure 1. Toward a cognitive framework: Evolution of LIS interest in HIOB.

systems—classification schemes, subject directories and the like—that mimic how humans themselves think when interacting with information.

Figure 1 graphically represents the changing focus of IR system information organization schemes pre-1950s and post-1950s. The left-hand side of Figure 1 represents the document organization focus of HIOB as it was until the 1940s–1950s when developments in electronic technology began to occur (e.g., Bush, 1945; Shannon, 1949); the right-hand side represents the changing IR research focus as research into HIOB becomes more and more interested in representing how humans are informed when interacting with the information environment. If these two sides of the information organization coin are juxtaposed, one object of HIOB research is to create a transducer linking how humans conceptualize documents to create document organization systems and how humans naturally categorize, process, and store information in memory.

3. THE GENERAL PROBLEM

The general problem addressed in this chapter is the domain novice attempting to formulate his information need into an effective query to an IR system. Currently, the user of an IR system must either click on concept terms in the system's subject directory or type concept terms representing his information need into the system query box. For domain novice users, these concepts are taken from what little they know about the domain—concepts users think they know a little about but primarily want to find out more about. The concept terms in the query, representing the user's information need, are the user's own, fluctuating conceptualizations of categories of objects, events or subject topics, found in his/her own memory (Barsalou, 1992). However, "the user's initial statement of need is not an accurate description of relevant documents [in the database], because it is a different category of object" (Oddy, 2004; cf. also, Belkin, Oddy, & Brooks, 1982). Popper (1975) describes it as two different worlds.

In effect, the general problem of this chapter can be thought of as what a transducer would be like between the separate and distinct information organization schemes of the system and the user:

- The system's knowledge-by-description concept-based information organization scheme of traditional subject directories and classification schemes and
- The user's knowledge-by-observation category-based organization of information in the user's memory (Novak, 1998; Russell, 1961).

This transducer is sketched in as the diamond symbol in the middle of Figure 1.

A transducer serves to allow conversion of input energy of one form into output of a second, different form, such as converting an analog signal into compressed digital format. To enable a domain novice user to understand and effectively use an IR system's document or information organizing scheme, the transducer must be able to carryout the decoding/encoding operations required to render a signal compatible with the organization structure of the other. If the signal comes from the IR system's organization scheme, the transducer converts this signal so that it can be understood by the user; for a signal coming from the user, the transducer converts the signal for the IR system.

Let us consider the user's point of view for a signal coming from the IR system's document organizing scheme. A domain expert user is equipped with the vocabulary of the domain, and can situate and identify her information need inside the structure of the scheme. For a domain novice, the information organizing structure is not present. Part of the domain novice's problem situation is to overcome this absence and allow new information in. Evolutionary psychology looks at this same problem from the widest possible perspective: form the perspective of human adaptation for long term survival in a constantly changing, often hostile environment. Overcoming the absence of the cognitive/memory structures needed to process new, environmental stimuli is essential to the ability of humans to adapt to and survive in a changing environment.

In an article on evolutionary psychology and HIB, Spink and Cole (in press) discuss one possible view of how humans overcome this paradox, based on a notion from evolutionary psychology that human cognition has a modular architecture. According to the modular architecture view, a dramatic adaptation occurred 35,000–70,000 years ago (Mithen, 1996, 1998): the formerly strictly modular human cognitive architecture, containing firmly defined and task-specialized human intelligence modules. Then suddenly transformed, developing gateway mechanisms between the separate intelligence modules. So that data from the specialized module databases could flow the one into the other. When the flow occurred, the human could see their environment from a different perspective. This allowed *Homo sapiens* hunter-gatherers to survive while other human species did not—hunter-gatherers became more efficient at exploiting their environment, more able to cope with environmental extremes, and more flexible in their social behavior (Mithen, 1998).

The effect of modular architecture is what has been termed a fundamental sort of metaphorical thinking, where we see something before us as "like" something else, because of the activation or instantiation of a perspective gained from another module (Gentner & Markman, 1997). Spink and Cole (in press) hypothesize that metaphor instantiation is similar to a form of super-ordinate category instantiation, like priming a pump, causing properties from one module to flow into the home module or topic module. Along with the metaphor, comes the structure of that metaphor as well (Markman & Moreau, 2001), thus creating a cognitive structure that can process the unfamiliar data from the changed environment.

In this chapter, we examine how a metaphor device can be inserted into the diamond in the middle of Figure 1, which we see as a transducer mechanism facilitating the HIOBs of categorization and metaphor instantiation while a user is using an IR system's document organizing scheme. We will discuss various theories and models of human memory mediation, categorization models, and models of metaphor instantiation. After analyzing these models, we report three case studies where we explore the application of metaphor instantiation in real-life information user situations.

4. THE COGNITIVE APPROACH IN LIS

The so-called cognitive school or cognitive approach in LIS is now solidly developed as the primary paradigm in information needs and uses research (Belkin, 1978; Brookes, 1980; Ingwersen, 1982; Neill, 1987; Saracevic & Kantor, 1997). An influential theory in the cognitive school is de Mey (1982), from which the cognitive school has adopted the notion that all human reality is mediated by categories stored in human memory.

Categorization "render[s] discriminably different things equivalent, to group the objects and events and people around us into classes, and to respond to them in terms of their class membership rather than their uniqueness" (Bruner, Goodnow, & Austin, 1956, p. 1). Bruner and colleagues distinguish five biological functions of categorization. Categorization:

- Reduces the complexity of the human animal's environment.
- Is the means by which objects in the environment are identified?
- Reduces the necessity of constant learning.
- Provides direction for instrumental activity (i.e., provides a goal for exploration).
- Provides an opportunity for ordering and relating classes of events (cited in Menzel, 1997).

Various theories have been postulated that use category organization as a basis for describing the chunks in memory we retrieve that serve as mediating devices between us—our genetic and experiential heritage—and the familiar and extraordinary external stimuli we come across everyday in our environment. In addition to so-called hard or simple categories—categories for horses, birds, what constitutes a home office, etc.— there are so-called soft categories that chunk information bits together into more complex conceptual networks of detail and behavior.

5. AD HOC CATEGORIES

An example of complex conceptual network category is what Lakoff (1987), citing Barsalou (1983), calls an ad hoc category—a category we make on the run—such as: "Things to take from one's home during a fire" (Lakoff, 1987, p. 46), "Possible costumes to wear to a Halloween party", and "places to look for antique furniture" (Barsalou, 1983, p. 211). Another type of ad hoc category is when a doctor makes a medical diagnosis (Custers, Regehr, & Norman, 1996). Soft or ad hoc categories are more subjective and context dependent than hard categories, requiring perspective facilitator features, for example, to be built into the thesaurus or other document organizing scheme (Svenonius, 2004).

Ad hoc categories are perspective or context dependent, they therefore may change significantly for the same observer over time—that is they are verb-like, not noun-like. When IR system users conceptualize information categories for their goal or assignment (e.g., writing a undergraduate term paper assignment), they use memory organization devices based on soft or ad hoc categories that shift, turn, and evolve over the course of doing the assignment.

Our research program is geared to the undergraduate seeking information for a course essay assignment (Cole et al., in press-a, b; Leide et al., 2003). The ad hoc essay category, if it is structurally defined, "refers to a mental representation of relations among components of an object that specifies its global form and structure ... " (Schacter, Cooper, & Delaney, 1990, p. 9). We define the person's mental organization of their ad hoc category for their essay topic as just such a structure, made up of components and relations between these components, all of which constitutes a memory organization structure for that essay topic.

5.1 Ad Hoc Category Formation: Human Information Organizing Behavior

The conceptual notion of information organization in ad hoc categories in memory category is, as we have said, based on de Mey's notion that we view the world in a mediated fashion, mediated by memory structures we call categories (or some variation of categories like frame theory (Minsky, 1975), scripts (Schank & Abelson, 1977), schemata (Graesser, 1981) or macrostructures in reading (Kintsch & van Dijk, 1978; but for a dissenting view, Anderson, 1985; Bower & Clapper, 1989)). How is an ad hoc category such as an essay topic category formed? A key part of the perception and cognition activities that occur when a user seeks, finds and uses unfamiliar information, is the user's own HIOB, which includes the user's organization and/or reorganization of stored or old information into a memory category capable of processing the new or unfamiliar information.

In this section of the chapter, we would like to be more specific about ad hoc category formation and reformation in response to unfamiliar environmental stimuli in a book or on a Web page diagramming the IR system's document organization scheme. Elsewhere (Cole, 2000), we have broken down these formation/reformation processes as human decoding and encoding processes that are automatically launched by the human organism when an unfamiliar environmental stimulus enters the human perceptual/cognitive system. In the specific case, we are concerned with here—domain novice users using an IR system to explore a new essay topic—the incoming stimulus is an information organization scheme presented to the user by the IR system to help him/her effectively access needed information from the system's database.

Mediated perception/cognition through ad hoc category formation and reformation assumes the centrality of top-down information processing, with, however, a bottom-up component that initiates the operation of the perceptual/cognitive system. We will divide these bottom-up and top-down processes into decoding, category activation or instantiation, and encoding parts of the perceptual/cognitive system of the user (Cole, 2000).

- *Decoding*: A chair, for example, is first of all perceived in bottom-up fashion as a set of primitive properties in vision (lines, planes, solids), which may have specific use electrodes or neurons for each located in the visual cortex. These properties assume a structural formation indicating a relationship network between the properties (Barsalou, 1992, p. 24).
- *Category Activation or Instantiation*: The cognitive system forms a structural description, then retrieves the appropriate category for chair from the user's memory by a process of matching the input stimuli to prototypes (best example of category) or exemplars (category invested with an amalgam of specific instances of category from our experience, like robin (good exemplar) and ostrich (bad exemplar)) of the category for "bird" stored in memory (Barsalou, 1992). The category, or properties of the category, is then "instantiated"—that is activated (Glucksberg & McGlone, 1999).
- *Encoding*: "Information enters the cognitive system through encoding processes" (Barsalou, 1992, p. 117), organized by top-down memory organization operations directed by the retrieved category from memory. Barsalou (1983, p. 212) describes encoding as: "memory structures for these categories assimilat[ing] presented information".

The perceptual and/or cognitive operations necessary for decoding and encoding environmental stimuli may vary depending on whether the environmental stimulus is familiar, that is, having a previously constituted category stored in memory, or unfamiliar, when there is no matching category available in memory. The variance may be a question of degree: the amount of work for so-called bottom-up processes based in perception and top-down processing based in cognition depend on the degree of familiarity or unfamiliarity of the environmental stimulus, which is not black or white but rather more like a continuum.

Information organization by category in human memory for a familiar vs. unfamiliar environmental stimulus has been examined, notably by Palmer (1975). Palmer divided the perceptual/cognitive processing of environmental stimuli into bottom-up and top-down parts of an experiment. In the bottom-up part, two items at a time were shown to the subjects, for various time durations (20, 40, 60, or 120 ms). The more time the subject had to view the two items the more bottom-up or perceptual operations could take place. To study top-down cognitive processes, namely the effect of category information stored in the subject's memory, the two items shown to the subject were variously:

1. related-context pairs (kitchen-bread),
2. misleading-context pairs (kitchen-mailbox with same shape as loaf),
3. unrelated-context pairs (kitchen-bugle), and
4. no-context pairs (objects occurred without scenes).

For the related-context pair, the subject was shown a loaf of bread that was placed in a kitchen, the hypothesis being that the category "kitchen" would facilitate faster subject identification of the loaf. Figure 2 graphs the bottom-up operations in terms of time and activation for both unexpected and expected categorization.

As shown in Figure 2, unrelated and thus unexpected pairs interfered with categorization, requiring more bottom-up processing (Barsalou, 1992). Palmer (1975) and other

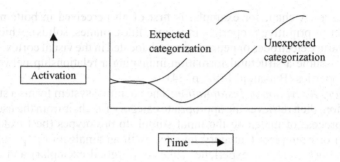

Figure 2. Effects of top-down processing on spreading activation: Expected and unexpected categorization (from Barsalou, 1992).

studies which examine categorization in the human information processing of familiar and unfamiliar stimuli indicate that more information processing is required of us when the stimulus cannot be matched immediately with the category of an object or event stored in memory.

5.2 A Type of Ad Hoc Category: Minsky's Frame Theory

Minsky's (1975) influential frame theory is a specific view of the ad hoc nature of category formation and reformation. Our memory stores a frame for a typical bird, allowing us to predict attributes of any bird we see before it is seen. But at the same time, frame theory builds in the capability for processing and using unfamiliar environmental stimuli. Features of a frame which are always true about the object or situation are anchored in essential upper-level nodes of the frame, while lower-level slots for non-essential attributes of a category are set on default (i.e., the most likely characteristic of the slot), that can quickly switch to less likely alternatives of an attribute (e.g., for a bird, its list of predators, with the default set on snakes).

A frame for Snake is shown in Figure 3, with round slots indicating the default setting for the Snake's eating function. Frames are interrelated with other frames, also indicated in Figure 3, with the Snake frame eating function connecting to a Bird frame via the latter frame's predators slot. The Snake–Bird example is taken from Wisniewski (1997). We further discuss the interconnectedness of memory frames in Leide et al. (2003).

Figure 3 shows how the mind, through interconnected slots, can quickly shift from one category frame to another—in this case from snake frame to bird frame. As well, frame categories that are interlinked via common features can be quickly retrieved, one after the other, based on their common node linkages (for spreading activation (Barsalou, 1983)). Also because of these linkages, unexpected environmental stimuli, leading to incorrect frame retrieval, can be correctly processed via frame theory, as suggested by Minsky:

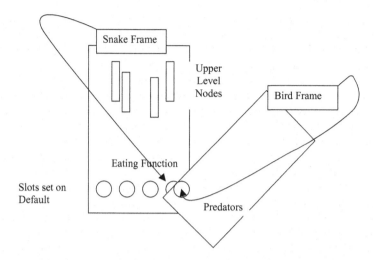

Figure 3. A frame representing snake category, connected through eating default slot to bird frame.

"Find a frame with as many terminals in common with [various attributes of the first retrieved frame] as possible, where we list high priority terminals already assigned in the old frame" (Minsky, 1975, pp. 249–250).

In fact, due to the interaction of different category frames and their intermingled attributes, the information processing of a person interacting with familiar and unfamiliar stimuli from the environment naturally and normally leads to an innate, automatic "seeing one thing as another". Bartlett's (1932) famous series of drawings changing slowly from a bird into a cat also illustrates this aspect of how we can change frames by, at the same time, retaining old node and slot attributes from the first retrieved frame.

In the abstract, one might deem this "seeing one thing as another" as fundamental to human information organization, rendering the organization of seeing, and thinking as fundamentally metaphorical. Elsewhere (Spink and Cole, in press), it has been conjectured that metaphorical thinking, seeing, and the memory organization that allows us to see and think this way is part of our inherent ability to adapt to and survive in a constantly shifting, often hostile environment.

6. RESEARCH HYPOTHESIS: METAPHORICAL THINKING, SEEING, AND MEMORY ORGANIZATION

In the three case studies that follow, we would like to develop a procedure to explore the hypothesis that metaphorical thinking, seeing, and memory organization, leading to metaphorically based HIOB, can be used to facilitate domain novice information need identification once it is built into the IR system (as suggested in the transducer diamond in Figure 1). The domain novice exploring a new topic area does not have an established category frame for the new topic area, but must somehow commence seeking, finding, and using information. In such cases, can metaphorical thinking supply a scaffolding structure from a known domain for a target unknown domain, providing a structuring vehicle until a more permanent one can be put in place?

We are just beginning our exploration of metaphor instantiation as the basis for designing interactive IR systems that could facilitate the user transducing an unfamiliar topic thesaurus by providing the user with a metaphorical frame to act as a temporary memory organization scaffold structure. Metaphor instantiation as an IR system design device may, however, be just a first stage of a multistage process. Caroll, Mack, and Kellog (1988), for example, claim that metaphor instantiation is the first stage of metaphor reasoning; the second stage is metaphor elaboration; and the third stage is metaphor consolidation. As well, there are intricacies in the appropriateness of the concept of metaphor over related terms like analogy. Gentner et al. (2001), for example, use the word "analogy" rather than metaphor to describe this same notion of temporary scaffolding.

In the three case studies that follow, we use the term metaphor in the broad sense of the word to include both similes, or narrow metaphors which contain the word "like" or "as", and analogies, which are frequently referred to as extended metaphors. To illustrate the differences between these three terms, we briefly refer to examples from Gentner et al. (2001):

1. A man is not necessarily intelligent because he has plenty of ideas, any more than he is a good general because he has plenty of soldiers (Chamfort).
2. My job is a jail.
3. His eyes were burning coals.
4. Tires are like shoes.
5. On a star of faith pure as the drifting bread/As the food and flames of the snow (Dylan Thomas).

Sentences (1) and (2) above are metaphors but can also be considered analogies because they form comparisons that share primarily relational information. But metaphors can also be based on common object attributes, as in sentence (3), or both, as in sentence (4) which is a narrow metaphor or simile. Most of the metaphors studied in the psychological literature are analogies—that is, they convey chiefly relational commonalities (Gentner et al., 2001).

Therefore, we are probably dealing here with extended metaphors (or analogies). In extended metaphors, the person maps the structure of the base domain to the target domain (Gentner et al., 2001), creating a new third metaphor category (Glucksberg & McGlone, 1999). For example, with the extended metaphor "My job is a jail", the metaphor involves the base domain "jail" and the target domain "job", creating a third category "confining space or situation", like a super-ordinate category uniting job and jail. The super-ordinate category includes conceptual nodes and relations between the categories (e.g., the prison guard has the relation of being the prisoner/employee's boss).

The metaphor may become its own category in the person's memory with extended use—that is, his job is a jail to indicate he is confined in his job like he would be if he were in a jail (Gentner et al., 2001). Another example of a metaphor becoming its own category, taken from Glucksberg and McGlone (1999), is "Cambodia has become Vietnam's Vietnam". (Metaphor as its own category represents a maximalist view (e.g., Lakoff, 1987). For a discussion of minimalist vs. maximalist view, see Glucksberg and McGlone (1999). For a dissenting view which is against linking the processes of categorization and analogy/metaphor see Ramscar and Pain (1996)).

7. THREE CASE STUDIES

The three case studies presented here attempt to incorporate the concept of metaphor instantiation IR system design. Such a design is intended to facilitate user identification of their information need by providing them with a known domain structure to the target or new subject domain. The known domain structure can be used as a temporary decoding device for domain novice users exploring a new topic area, until they find their rudder—that is until they can set up a structure specifically applicable to the target or new domain they are exploring.

We begin with the premise that the essence of the user–IR system interaction is the user's problem, information problem, or the current information seeking paradigm of the user's problem situation (Belkin, 1980; Case, 2002; Ingwersen, 1996; Wilson, 2000) (for a further discussion of problem situation, see Spink & Cole, in press). Our overall goal in these case studies, therefore, is to begin to understand how we can get the subject to transfer the structure of the metaphor into the problem situation of the subject.

In the three case studies that follow, our specific purposes are:

- to begin the task of finding the most effective way of getting at a definition of the user's problem situation that is most amenable to serve as the target for information need identification via metaphor instantiation and
- to find an effective methodology for invoking information need identification via metaphor instantiation that can be tested in subsequent research studies.

The reporting of the three case studies deliberately includes the hum and haw of normal human conversation, to show how difficult it is to get people to think in terms of metaphor, to diagram the metaphor, and then to apply the metaphor to their specific problem situations.

The first case study was exploratory; the second incorporated lessons learned from the first; and the third case study, we believe, was relatively successful at providing the basis of a methodology that can study and test hypotheses related to metaphor instantiation as an IR system design device or concept whose purpose is to facilitate information need identification for domain novice users exploring a new topic or subject area while concurrently accessing information from an IR system. Please note that while in the first case study there was written consent to use Professor Morton's name (as it is interesting in itself to see how a renowned domain expert carries out his research, their thinking process, etc.), the two Ph.D. students are referred to using the male pronoun to preserve their anonymity (as per their confidentiality agreements).

7.1 Case Study 1: Professor Desmond Morton

On November 11th, 25th, and December 4th, 2002, we conducted a series of interviews with one of the most renowned historians in Canada, Desmond Morton, the Hiram Mills Professor of History at McGill University. Professor Morton is a specialist in 20th century Canadian military, political, and industrial relations history. The subject of the interviews was Professor Morton's information "situation" for a book he was in the final stages of researching on the wives of World War I Canadian soldiers, subsequently published under the title "Fight or Pay: Soldiers' Families in the Great War" (Morton, 2004).

Case Study 1 formed part of a larger, ongoing project whose purpose is to design a complete, user-focused IR system called the INIIReye System (cf. Cole et al., in press-a, b; Leide et al., 2003). The purpose of the INIIReye System is to facilitate the IR system user's process of identifying his/her information need, if it is not known, during the online IR session, so that the user can better judge the IR system output for relevance to that information need. The intention of this case study was to test various features of the INIIReye System on a domain expert. Here, we focus on a secondary feature of the case study which was to explore the concept of metaphor instantiation as a device to facilitate the identification of the user's information need.

The initial 1 h interview with Professor Morton on November 11, 2002 was divided into two parts. The first part, lasting 40 min and centering on the INIIReye System, was conducted by the first author, while the second part, lasting 20 min, was a traditional reference interview intervention conducted by Kendall Wallis, acting head of the McLennan Library, McGill's humanities, and social science library. In the first part, Professor Morton was asked to list four research questions he wanted information sources to answer. He was then asked to diagram, with circles and lines connecting the circles, the concepts that made up the research question he considered would be the most important in the final version of his book.

In the traditional reference interview second part, Kendall Wallis conducted a traditional reference interview to establish a bench mark or gold standard search strategy. The McGill librarian then followed through with a search of the standard history databases to create a package of citations to books, journal articles, and documents the librarian considered relevant to Professor Morton's information need. The results of the two interventions were compared and evaluated by Professor Morton during the third interview (see below).

The second interview on November 25th, 2002 was conducted by the first author with Professor Morton in his history department office. For the purpose of getting Professor Morton to think of his information need in terms of a metaphor, the interviewer asked Professor Morton to write down four possible "descriptive" titles for the book he was researching at the time of the interview. Professor Morton was then given the following instructions:

> Now, we have a colon to the left of the title you have just written. Summarize the book title in a metaphor and write it to the left of the colon. This produces a metaphor + descriptive title as is the case with many books [especially in history].

Professor Morton wrote the following four metaphor + descriptive titles:

1. "Poor Angeline": Canadian soldiers' families in the First World War.
2. "Stick it to the Patriotic": The Patriotic Fund.
3. Pauperization or Progress: Social Engineering and Soldiers' Wives 1914–1919.
4. Supporting the Soldier: Military Family Policy in Canada 1914–1919.

Professor Morton was then asked to "Evaluate metaphor/titles by giving probability in percentage that you will select it as interesting". He overwhelming rated metaphor/title #1. "Poor Angeline", as most probable (90%). Because the metaphor titles Professor Morton had given were in fact not metaphors but rather "tags" (i.e., labeling devices, cf. www.dictionary.com), Professor Morton was then asked by e-mail to change the titles he had given so that they were more like metaphors, and to explain what he meant by the metaphor. On December 2nd, 2002, Professor Morton wrote the following in an e-mail:

7.1.1 Metaphors for a Book on Canadian Military Families, 1914–1919

1. Supporting the Soldier: Whose Hanging from Whom? (Supporting the soldier really meant supporting the wife or mother. Who really mattered most? (Hint: ask a feminist. Ask a CPF contributor.))
2. Pauperization or Progress: Bullying for Good Behavior. (Social workers believed that kindly advice combined with forceful power (the bully's self-image in all societies) would turn soldiers' wives into post-war poverty battlers. Or would it make them frightened dependents (the self-image of the bullied).)
3. "Stick it to the Patriotic": Cheers from the Fans. (Private Ernest Hamilton's advice to his wife was easy to give from England. Like hockey spectators, the blows are audible and exciting and unfelt. Taking on the arrogant folk who had the money didn't look easy to Mrs. H.)
4. Poor Angeline: Dreams and Realities in Financing Canadian Soldiers' Families in the First World War. (Organizers of the Patriotic Fund and their donors had an idealized vision of Canadian motherhood, sacrificing sons and husbands for the Empire. The requirement—that families be "in need"—included squalor, greed, disease, and selfishness.)

Note that title/sub-title #4. Poor Angeline, which was formerly listed first in the listing of four titles, is now listed fourth. Also note that #4. Poor Angeline was not rewritten as a metaphor, perhaps because Professor Morton thought that Poor Angeline, an old tale/song, was already sufficiently metaphorical and did not have to be rewritten.

At the third interview on December 4th, 2002, Professor Morton was asked to evaluate the citation lists supplied by the first author, based on the metaphor instantiation concept centered on "Poor Angeline", vs. the citation lists supplied by Kendall Wallis, based on a traditional reference interview and a follow up search of traditional history databases. The first author had conducted several different searches on:

- *Google*, using keywords: "Poor Angeline" (receiving 15 hits); "social engineering" patriotic fund (356 hits); "social engineering" pauperization (25 hits); pauperization or progress social engineering (146 hits); and "supporting the soldier" (78 hits);

- *America: History and Life*, using keyword: Angeline (20 hits);
- *Historical Abstracts*, using keyword: Angeline (15 hits); and
- McGill's *OPAC*, using keyword "Angeline" (15 hits).

All these searches were based on the metaphorical title and Professor Morton's explanation of "Poor Angeline: Dreams and Realities in Financing Canadian Soldiers' Families in the First World War".

Kendall Wallis conducted three searches on the database *America: History and Life*. These searches were:

- Canada AND charities in the Subject Term field, limited by Time Period 1910D or 1920D (receiving 9 hits);
- Canada AND Public Welfare in the Subject Term field, limited by Time Period 1910D or 1920D (38 hits); and
- World War I AND Canada AND Letters in the Subject Term field (9 hits).

Professor Morton evaluated the Kendall Wallis citations as more relevant than the metaphor-based citation lists of the first author, giving high marks to Wallis's search 1. Canada AND Charities. Professor Morton noted wryly that this search strategy had turned up, in first and second positions, two articles he himself had written about the Canadian Patriotic Fund.

The first author's metaphorical-based search strategy using *Google, America: History and Life, Historical Abstracts* and McGill's *OPAC* were almost completely irrelevant, roping in off the wall citations. For example, a dirty song with the title "Poor Angeline" produced the most hits using Google. The *Historical Abstracts* and *America: History and Life* databases, which had produced relevant hits for Kendall Wallis's traditional search strategy, produced, for the metaphor-based search strategy, irrelevant articles that happened to contain the word "Angeline" in the file record. The McGill *OPAC* list cited "Men Coping with Grief", which was only slightly relevant to Professor Morton's topic of a fund to provide support to Canadian soldiers' families during World War 1.

At the end of the final interview, the first author decided to further investigate possible metaphors for "Poor Angeline" Title/sub-title. In the written e-mail explanation for Poor Angeline dated December 2, 2002, Professor Morton had written that "Organizers of the Patriotic Fund and their donors had an idealized vision of Canadian motherhood, sacrificing sons and husbands for the Empire. The requirement—that families be "in need"—included squalor, greed, disease, and selfishness." The first author now asked him about this. Professor Morton explained that "it was like putting a round peg in a square hole." The first author immediately saw that this concrete metaphor was the way out of the dilemma of the tag line "Poor Angeline" which was not a metaphor, because the "peg in a hole" metaphor had an obvious structure of a round peg, a square hole, but it would also have to have a channel linking the two. Because the peg in a hole simile/metaphor seemed apt as a constructive metaphor, able to give a structure to the Poor Angeline section of Morton's book, the first author drew a diagram to represent this metaphor visually, labeling its parts with aspects of Professor Morton's actual problem situation. The diagram is reproduced in Figure 4. Although the visualized "peg in a hole" metaphor diagram did not evoke any comment from Professor Morton, it created a possible methodology for the metaphor instantiation concept that the first author wished to try out later on.

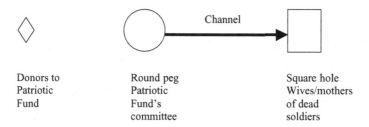

Figure 4. Metaphor of poor angeline title visually represented as "round peg in a square hole".

The authors felt this concrete metaphor when it was diagrammed out was worth studying using a different problem situation. Professor Morton's problem situation was that of a domain expert who, at the time of the intervention, was very near the end of researching a book. A more suitable problem situation, we decided, would be a domain novice at the beginning of some sort of research process.

7.2 Case Study 2: First Year Ph.D. Student

The second case study focused on the problem situation of a first year information science Ph.D. student at McGill University's Graduate School of Library and Information Studies. The one and only interview took place on November 24, 2004. At the time of the interview, the student was in the early stages of creating a research proposal for his Ph.D. thesis. The purpose of the second case study was to further explore and extend our experience with Professor Morton's "round peg in a square hole" metaphor diagram of his problem situation, shown in Figure 4, as a methodology for facilitating user identification of their information need while using an IR system.

We first asked the Ph.D. student to diagram out the topic terms derived from the statement of his Ph.D. topic. The 17 topic terms are listed here as the student wrote them (with equal signs, etc.):

1. information behavior;
2. information seeking;
3. health information seeking;
4. information search process (ISP);
5. information literacy;
6. health information literacy;
7. metacognition;
8. interventions;
9. mediation;
10. thinking;
11. problem solving;
12. finding information;
13. evaluating;
14. interpreting;

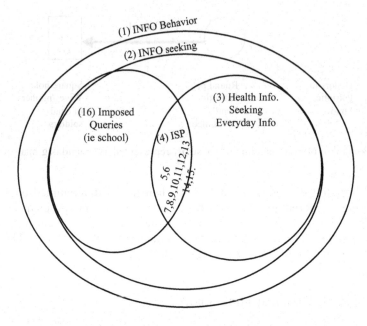

Figure 5. Subject's first sheet: Diagramming topic terms.

15. using information;
16. imposed queries;
17. everyday information seeking.

The Ph.D.'s diagram of the topic terms is shown in Figure 5. Figure 5 represents this student's broad topic outline, with a large circle labeled "(1) INFO. Behavior" encompassing all other terms. The numbers in parentheses correspond to the numbers in the above list of the student's topic terms. The intersection of two smaller circles, labeled "Imposed query" and "Health Info. Seeking and Everyday Info", contained in their intersection a whole host of concept terms under the general label "ISP" (referring to Kuhlthau's (1993) ISP model). We then asked the student to take only this intersection section of the diagram, and diagram for us the relationships of these concept terms in greater detail, shown in Figure 6.

In Figure 6, the Ph.D. student has drawn a "Problem Solving" arc from #12. Finding, through #14. Interpretations and #13. Evaluating, to #15. Using information, perhaps indicating some sort of process—that is the adolescents in the future study of this Ph.D. student are expected to find information, interpret, and evaluate its efficacy in fulfilling their need for information at the time, accepting, or rejecting it, before finally "using" the information in some way.

The important part of the case study came next when we asked the Ph.D. student to draw his topic as a metaphor. We include here the Questions (Q) and the Answers from the Ph.D. student (A).

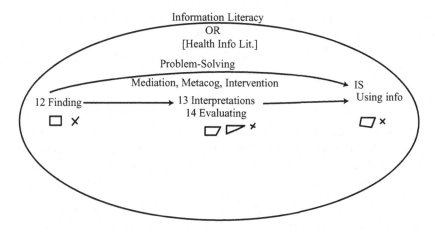

Figure 6. Subject's second sheet: Diagramming intersection of circles from Figure 5.

Q1: Can you think metacognitions, health information literacy and adolescence, those three concepts, in terms of metaphor, that can be drawn?
A1: This is my metaphor. [She begins drawing, cf. Figure 7.] It's a brick wall. O.K. let's pretend it's a brick wall. Why? Because this is part of, I didn't add it yet, the concept constructing knowledge, and people bring bricks together to construct the wall, they are constructing knowledge. Should I write that? Constructing brick wall, I guess I wasn't applying the information literacy, you know, I didn't say that . . .
Q2: Can you show the problems somehow visually, diagrammatically, show a problem in there of construction?

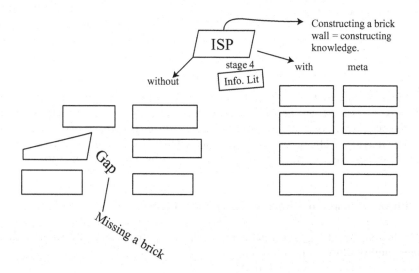

Figure 7. Subject's third sheet: Diagramming problem situation of adolescents.

A2: The problem: could be a good construction has reached the bottom, and the bad one, with poor metacognitive skills builds this brick wall with the gap, and there is a break [cf. "gap" in brick wall on left-hand side of Figure 7].
Q3: Now, we've just got a few more minutes. Can you think a metaphor again; I think really here what you've done from the adolescent's point of view, or inside adolescents' heads?
A3: Ya, because drawing that word cognition, we are talking about thinking.

In Figure 7, we would like to point out that the Ph.D. student is making a metaphor drawing from the problem situation of the subjects the Ph.D. student intends to study later on during his Ph.D. research (the Ph.D.'s intended study group is adolescents seeking health information). The ISP box above the two brick walls represents at this point in his research the problem situation of his intended study group, but may eventually evolve into part of the problem situation of the Ph.D. student himself. To get the student to draw a metaphor for his own problem situation, we ask the question again, as indicated in the following question–answer dialog:

Q: Now, step back a bit into your head as a problem, the problem you came as a metaphor, what would you think immediately?
A: My problem would be the process I am going through right now? Or defining?
Q: The process of finding or finding out . . .
A: We are not . . . the research problem, but my process is a problem. Is that what you are talking about?
Q: Yeah. The problem in your process, what is it? Can you think of that as a metaphor that you can draw? It is physical; I mean not like in the area flowing around or even that . . .
A: O.K., the problem I am facing in my research process right now is, "metaphorically speaking" . . . Too many doors. In other words I am making fateful choices. I have this, you know, like the research focus of metacognition, research focus of health info literacy, and there are other doors could be the ones people in our community are saying that I should also pursue. These are other doors that, I am getting bizarre, but these are choices that I have to make in the next two weeks. Anyhow, I don't know, is that what you are talking about?

In Figure 8, the metaphor diagram coming from the Ph.D. student's own problem situation is, we believe, too general to help an IR system user identify their information need. However, when we return to Sheet 3 (Figure 7) in the next series of question–answers (A5 below in added italics), the Ph.D. student switches back to his topic diagram (Figure 6), which we believe may be a better indicator of his own problem situation.

7.2.1 Ph.D. Student Goes Back to Sheet 3 (cf. Figure 7)

Q1: Is this, the one you drew here, metacognition here or is that information literacy? Sheet number three [cf. Figure 7].
A1: O.K., this is . . . Let's call it ISP.
Q2: [Kuhlthau's] Information Search Process.

Too many doors.

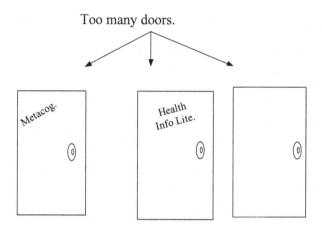

Figure 8. Subject's fourth sheet: Diagramming his/her own problem situation.

A2: Which I quit information literacy. So, this is, meta "without".

Q3: Are you associating "without" [metacognition] this broken down wall?

A3: Ya.

Q4: O.K., and the "with" meta[cognition] is the carefully constructed wall. Can you explain that a little bit further why did you do that?

A4: O.K., because this is a constructive process, building knowledge, seeking meaning, O.K., so, to seek meaning, you, it helps if you have metacognition literacy research process. Anyhow, this is a solid wall, and this is a weak wall, a weak knowledge.

Q5: Really? Are you saying that sounds like your adolescent seeking health information would have a weak wall?

A5: No, well... *That's the conceptual framework. So the question for me is in metacognition question, do people know how to use it.* If we believe they need it the constructive solid wall, if I am constructing this one, probably. O.K.?

Q6: I don't quite understand the association between ISP [Kuhlthau's ISP model] and "without-" or "with-" [cognition], because the ISP essentially would be ...

A6: I know what you are getting at. The ISP relationship there is that... the stage focus formulation ... Stage 4 [of Kuhlthau's 6 stage ISP model], which you know, that is a descriptive model in prescriptive terms in that information literacy ...

Q7: Oh, Stage 4 is information literacy.

A7: In information literacy, focus formulation, they are constructing knowledge. ISP is a theoretical model, but it has been applied to the class situation and life situation as information literacy.

Q8: So it's possible then you are talking about adolescents here, you might be talking about [Kuhlthau's] stage 1,2,3.

A8: I don't know yet.

Q9: Because they don't have this wall, they don't have the well-constructed wall

A9: Well, lets look at ... they go through the process, here's meta process. Here is where they get a *break, break, break* [she is drawing "x's" indicating breaks beside the bricks [the Ph.D. student] has just drawn on Sheet 2 (cf. Figure 6)].

Q10: Sheet 2 [cf. Figure 6]? She's drawing bricks on finding, interpreting, evaluating and using knowledge.
A10: O.K., so, if you are constructing your knowledge and if you see process, you are adding the bricks to the wall. And hopefully, maybe there is one brick missing here... Anyway.

In A9 (above, in italics) from the question–answer dialog, the Ph.D. student draws "x's" beside bricks on Sheet 2 (Figure 6) while saying "break", "break", "break". The x's and breaks are where the Ph.D.'s problem situation (Figure 6) joins the Ph.D.'s intended subjects' (adolescents seeking health information) problem situation—the gap in the left-hand side brick wall in Figure 7.

In summary, we point out that the problem situation of the Ph.D. student is expressed in the two diagrams derived from his topic terms (Figures 5 and 6), but the topic term diagrams are not metaphors. The metaphor diagram the Ph.D. student chose to draw is for his intended subjects' problem situation (Figure 7). The Ph.D. student, however, at the end of the interview (Question A9), extended the brick metaphor into his own problem situation when he added bricks and then drew x's beside the bricks on the topic term diagram (Figure 6).

The object of getting the subject to think of their problem situation in terms of a metaphor is to facilitate the user's self-identification of their information need—in other words, to promote cognition. Unfortunately, the bit of cognition we could see occurring during the interview with the Case Study 2 Ph.D. student was when the Ph.D. student almost attributed the elimination of the gap in the intended subjects' problem situation (Figure 7) to the focusing Stage 4 of Kuhlthau's ISP model. However, the Ph.D. student clearly stepped back from this in the interview (cf. A8 from our question–answer dialog). The authors thought it would be worthwhile to continue exploring metaphor instantiation with a Ph.D. student who was farther along in the Ph.D. process, by refining further the distinction between the problem situation of the Ph.D. student himself and the problem situation of the Ph.D.'s intended study subjects.

7.3 Case Study 3: Third Year Ph.D. Student

The third case study focused on the problem situation of a third year information science Ph.D. student at McGill University's Graduate School of Library and Information Studies. The interview was conducted on November 30, 2004. At the time of the interview, the student was in the final stages of creating a research proposal for his Ph.D. thesis. The purpose of the third case study was to further explore and extend our experience with using metaphor instantiation as a methodology for facilitating user identification of their information need. In the third case study, there were two primary concerns:

- to further develop the most appropriate problem situation focus for IR and
- to begin developing a methodology for applying metaphor instantiation in IR design, with a view to the later testing of its efficacy for facilitating information need identification against a control group.

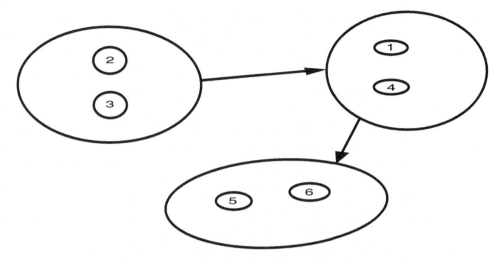

Figure 9. Third year Ph.D. Student's diagram.

The third Ph.D. student wrote down his Ph.D. thesis topic as: How do perceptions of value of IT system affect perceptions and practices of information sharing in the supply chain?

He then listed the concept terms derived from this topic statement:

- value-added information system,
- information sharing,
- supply chain, and
- inter-organizational information systems.

In a departure from the methodology in Case Studies 1 and 2, for the purposes of focusing in on the student's problem situation, here we asked the student to list four research questions he wanted information sources to answer. This four question device has proven to be an effective technique for getting at the information need attribute of the subject's problem situation in another of our research projects (Cole et al., in press-a, b; Leide et al., 2003). We give here only the Ph.D. student's highest ranked research question: How do individuals in organizations perceive the value of information sharing in supply chains?

We then asked the Ph.D. student to diagram out the concept terms derived from this highest ranked research question, shown in Figure 9. The terms are listed in Figure 9's caption in square brackets; the circled numbers in the diagram refer to these same concept terms.

In Figure 10, the Ph.D. student drew a metaphor for the highest ranked research question. The metaphor consisted of a heart, to represent the attitudes of the people in his study group toward information sharing in a supply chain, a brain to represent motivations of the people in his study group, and a hand to represent behaviors of people

[1] attitudes

[2] motivation

[3] behaviors

[4] relationship between
attitudes and behaviors

[5] relationship between
motivations and behaviors

[6] relationship between
attitudes and motivations

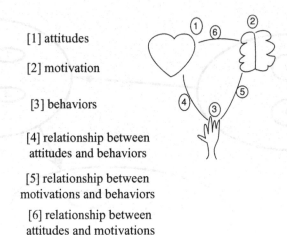

Figure 10. Metaphor for highest ranked research question.

in the study group. The other numbers (4–6) represent the relationships between the
heart, brain, and hand.

We then asked the Ph.D. student to list the terms he would use to query an IR system
from the metaphor diagram shown in Figure 10 (Sheet 6). The dialog is reproduced here:

Q: So Sheet 6, you are looking at this one now: it's the heart, the brain, and the hand.
A: Uh-huh.
Q: Could you please list the terms you would use for this for queries to an IR system?
Can you list your terms here?
A: Terms for these terms?
Q: Terms for this and this. The terms you would use to query an IR system. Could
you list vertically?
A: O.K. Both for the metaphor and for terms?
Q: For the metaphor. Start with the metaphor.
A: O.K. [Ph.D. student is listing the terms]
Q: So this is Sheet 6:
   • attitudes towards information,
   • motivation of information sharing,
   • belief in information sharing,
   • relationship between attitudes, motivations, beliefs, or beliefs in information
     sharing.

The listing of terms he would use to query an IR system are almost the same as the
labels he used to label parts of the metaphor diagram in Figure 10. We return to this observation in the Discussion (below). To investigate the difference between the problem situation of the people the Ph.D. student intended to study, shown in Figure 10, and the Ph.D.
student's own research problem, we next asked the Ph.D. student to draw a metaphor for his

own research problem. Interestingly, the Ph.D. student focused on his topic statement (A5 in the dialog in added italics). We reproduce this part of the question–answer dialog here:

Q1: Can you describe your research problem situation as a metaphor? The problems that you are going to answer for your research maybe helps you to understand this part of the interview. Your research problem situation. What kind of problem you have to answer?
A1: As a metaphor?
Q2: As a metaphor, that you can draw.
A2: O.K. The question is not for the first one?
Q3: This question is?
A3: Not for the first question? I mean the question [questioner's name] asked me is not for this? *For the whole topic?*
Q4: Maybe, ya.
A4: You mean I have to draw something?
Q5: Can you draw it as a metaphor?
A5: O.K. [Ph.D. student is drawing].
Q6: O.K., this is on Sheet 5. Could you please explain your metaphor?
A6: O.K. This represents individuals in organization. The circle represents organizations of contextual factors on organizational environment.

... [the rest of this description is as the Ph.D. student drew the metaphor, shown in Figure 11.]

The metaphor for his own problem situation is reproduced in Figure 11. The Ph.D. student then explained the metaphor, particularly the two circles with the two stick figures inside them:

Q: O.K. Now can you in words explain your metaphor to us?
A: O.K. I want to know how individuals in different organizations in supply chain communicate between ...
Q: Communicate between them? Between each other?
A: Ya, between individuals. But two individuals located in different organizations.
Q: O.K. So is this [the top circle] a different organization?
A: Yes.

We wanted the Ph.D. student now to derive query terms from his own problem situation metaphor, as if he were querying an IR system. (We asked him to give numbers to each term, continuing from the six terms listed for the metaphor from Figure 10, thus encouraging him to consider combining together the metaphor for his problem situation and the metaphor for his intended subjects' problem situation.) He wrote down:

[7] inter-organizational communication,
[8] cross-boundary communication,
[9] environmental scanning,
[10] individual in organization,
[11] information sharing in supply chain, and
[12] intra-organizational communication.

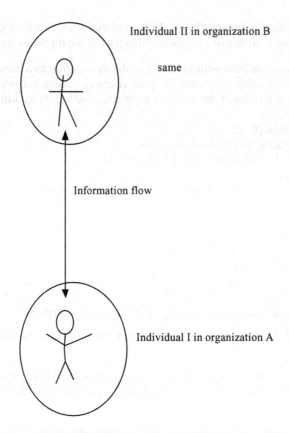

same

Individual II in organization B

Information flow

Individual I in organization A

Figure 11. Ph.D. student's drawing of the metaphor for his own problem situation.

We notice immediately that the list of terms derived from the Ph.D.'s metaphor of his own problem situation is focused on behaviors of his intended study group: their various communication behaviors, scanning behavior, and information sharing behavior. We return to this observation in the Discussion. At the end of the interview, we asked the Ph.D. student to select which of the seven sheets he preferred as a query to an IR system, as follows:

Q: O.K., this is Sheet 7 that you just completed. when we put the sheets in order, O.K., and I want to ask you, just let the preferred sheet for querying an IR system, and you must tell me why you prefer it.
A: Uh-huh.
Q: O.K.? So, we have [pointing to 7 sheets done during the interview]: 1, 2, 3, 4, 5, 6, 7.
A: I'd like to use this. No. 6
Q: O.K., now can you please tell me why you prefer this?
A: O.K. Because it will be more specific than the others? And . . .

Q: More specific than?
A: Than others?
Q: Than the others?
A: And second, it, at the same time, it is comprehensive, I mean, comprises all necessary components I need.
Q: So it's more specific and it's more comprehensive.
A: Yes. I think so.

As he had chosen Sheet 6, we also particularly asked him to compare Sheet 6 with Sheet 1, which contained his original topic terms:

Q: Could you now look at the first sheet that you wrote with the topic statement and terms and can you put more reasons why you prefer Sheet 6 to Sheet 1? Why is it better than Sheet 1? (Ph.D. is writing reasons ...)
Q: Now, you added another reason?
A: Yes.
Q: What is that reason?
A: Because Sheet 1 seems will elicit too much, I mean, too many results and it will be time consuming for me to find proper results, proper literature.

8. DISCUSSION

The metaphor instantiation we discuss in this chapter is part of an ongoing effort to create IR systems that will facilitate user identification of their information need when they are in an exploration phase of researching a project and decide to interact with the representation of the IR system's document organization scheme to aid in this exploration. Metaphor instantiation has the potential to provide an information searcher using an IR system with an ad hoc category structure in the early part of domain learning and exploration. The purpose of the three case studies just described was to begin to flesh out a methodology for enabling metaphor instantiation and the creation of an ad hoc category structure for the domain novice user. We purposely included extensive dialogue from the transcripts of the three case studies to indicate difficulties with methodology development. However, the three case studies reported here allowed us to make some progress toward our objective, primarily in identifying and dealing with problems we have to solve.

The first problem is the general problem of creating a methodology for testing hypotheses for metaphor instantiation in naturalistic settings—that is, with real users engaged in real information problems. Between the Professor Morton case study in November–December 2002, and the second and third cases studies 2 years later, our research team had made some progress in identifying methodologies for testing information need identification devices in a naturalistic setting (cf. Cole et al., in press-a, b; Leide et al., 2003), which we applied to Case Studies 2 and 3.

The Professor Morton case study taught us something about an appropriate metaphor, allowing us to move on from the Poor Angeline tag, which was not a metaphor, to the concrete "peg in a hole" metaphor, which had a structure capable of structuring-out

Professor Morton's problem situation. Also, the metaphor diagram for Professor Morton was drawn for him, which we realized created a conundrum for Professor Morton, forcing him to evaluate the pertinence of a diagram done by someone else to represent what he was thinking. In the second and third case studies, we (i) focused in on creating concrete metaphors and (ii) we had the subjects draw their own metaphor diagrams. As can be seen in the dialogue transcripts, this was not an easy task.

We made further progress in developing a methodology during the second and third case studies. After the second case study, we realized that it was essential, after each cognitive activity we had the subject do, to ask the subject to derive and list-out query terms for accessing information from an IR system. This created a series of benchmarks for the subject to evaluate the efficacy of one metaphor activity in the interview schedule over another. Specifically, the establishment of a "benchmark" for the methodology means that we now have the beginnings of methodology to test which problem situation is best for eliciting metaphor instantiation.

A second methodology problem occurred during the second case study where the Ph.D. student, when asked to draw the metaphor based on the Ph.D.'s own problem situation, seemed to naturally think in terms of the people he intended to study in the future. We had to deliberately re-ask this student to focus in on his own problem situation, but got only an overly general metaphor representation of three doors he had to select from to go through (Figure 8). (It is possible that for this first year Ph.D. student it was too early in the research process for the problem situation question to have any metaphorical resonance.)

However, it became evident during the second case study, when the Ph.D. student transferred bricks from the metaphor diagram of the problem situation of his intended study group to his topic diagram, that the problem situation can be defined in a third way, in terms of the topic statement (note that the third case study also equated problem situation with topic statement). This created three possible sources of metaphors:

- from the user's own problem situation;
- from the user's own topic, which is a part of the user's own problem situation; or
- from the perceived problem situation of the group the Ph.D. student intends to study.

By the third case study, but before we conducted the interview, we knew we had three possible problem situation scenarios to look at. We also wanted to study which of the three problem situation-derived metaphor diagrams would be the most efficacious for facilitating user information need identification. The presence of three possible problem situations indicated to us that we would have to refine the methodology to include evaluation measures (i.e., a preference measure), which we instigated in the third case study—that is by getting the subject to (i) list-out query terms from all activities and diagrams during the interview intervention and at the end of the intervention and (ii) indicate which he/she preferred as query terms to access information from an IR system.

In order to get the subject's own problem situation, in the third case study we used a technique from our larger research project to get at the essence of the informational aspect of the Ph.D. student's problem situation. We asked the Ph.D. student to list-out four research questions he wanted answered by some information source, to rank order the four, then to focus in on the top ranked research question. However, as in the second case study, the third case study Ph.D. student also focused in on his/her intended study group's problem situation.

When we specifically asked the third case study student to draw a metaphor diagram for his own problem situation, the student asked if we meant his original topic statement; then the student produced a completely different listing of terms. The topic statement focus seemed to create the right question format for getting at the subject's own problem situation, producing terms that centered on the Ph.D. student's expectations of information behaviors of the members of the intended study group—various communication behaviors, as well as scanning behavior and information sharing behavior (Sheet 5)—while the query terms derived from the problem situation of the intended study group consisted of their attitudes, motivations, and beliefs (Sheet 6).

However, there was a discrepancy between the Case Study 3 student's labeling of the heart–brain–hand metaphor diagram and the listing of query terms derived from the heart–brain–hand metaphor, which is instructive. As with the Ph.D. student in Case Study 2, who joined together his own problem situation and the problem situation of the intended study group when he added bricks and x's to his topic diagram (Figure 6), Case Study 3 also joined together his own problem situation and the problem situation of the intended study group, which we only noticed due to the discrepancy.

Logically, the student's labels for the heart–brain–hand metaphor diagram (Figure 10) and the query terms to an IR system (Sheet 6) should have been exactly the same, but they were not. The student substituted "belief" for "behaviors" in his listing of query terms to an IR system (Sheet 6). We then realized that the label "behaviors" on the metaphor diagram brought the Ph.D. student's own problem situation—the query terms derived from the stick man metaphor diagram (Figure 11)—into the student's intended study group's problem situation.

Finally, we asked for the Ph.D. student's preference for accessing information from information sources, and the preference was for Sheet 6: the attributes or properties of the intended study group's problem situation. There is some question whether the Ph.D. student was making the correct evaluation—we suspect that for this Ph.D. student a combination of the three problem situations is preferable, as shown in Figure 12—but by continually

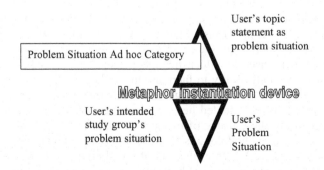

Figure 12. Model of a cognitive framework for human information organizing behavior.

getting the subject to produce query terms after each activity, we now have a methodology to test such an evaluation. A Cognitive Framework Model for HIOB is shown in Figure 12.

In this model, the diamond, first indicated in this chapter in Figure 1 as an IR system interface mechanism—a transducer—linking human memory organization and document organization schemes, is in the center of the model—which we label the "Problem Situation Ad hoc Category". The variously defined problem situations observed in the three case studies reported here surround the Problem Situation Ad hoc Category. Inside the diamond is some future metaphor instantiation device or mechanism serving as a user topic/problem situation category formation aide.

9. CONCLUSION

In this chapter, we have articulated a cognitive framework for HIOB. We feel that the HIOB sub-section of HIB leads to interesting hypotheses which may, in the long run, create information accessing environments that are closer to how people actually interact with, organize and store information in memory. LIS must do this, we believe, because the traditional purviews of LIS—information, information need, information seeking, information organization, and information access—are vitally important to human creativity and ease of living in our environment. This includes both the physical environment in which we live and the socially constructed environments we devise to exist in groups.

The specific focus of this chapter was a sub-section of HIOB which we call metaphor instantiation or metaphorical reasoning while the individual is searching an IR system's database, interacting with the IR system's representation of its document organization scheme, and organizing the found information in memory. Such schemes include subject directory schemes, thesauri, and classification schemes. With the implementation of HIOB facilitating devices based on metaphor instantiation, the role of these document organization schemes to facilitate learning, topic exploration, and information need identification, will be greatly enhanced.

Above all the chapter highlights a new direction for research into HIOB, by creating a basis for the development of a methodology that has some potential to get at the essential nature of the human acquisition of unfamiliar information via metaphor instantiation, to develop and test hypotheses concerning metaphor instantiation in HIOB, and to apply findings from these studies to the design of user-centered IR devices and systems. In this chapter, we focused on metaphor instantiation as a method of creating ad hoc categories for facilitating the acquisition of data and information related to a new and unfamiliar subject area for the user. In effect, metaphor instantiation, makes the assumption that humans have an innate ability to facilitate the ad hoc categorization of unfamiliar information stimulus by borrowing a category structure from somewhere else in memory.

With the methodology presented here, we have set out the beginnings of how researchers can ascertain the efficacy of metaphor instantiation as an information need structuring device. The methodology is to create alternative metaphor producing situations, then use the subject's own evaluation of the alternatives to test which problem situation-derived metaphor diagram is best able to elicit needed information from an information database. In our case studies of a noted historian and two Ph.D. history students, the alternatives were based on three different derivations of definitions of the their problem situations:

- from the user's own problem situation;
- from the user's own topic, which is a part of the user's own problem situation; or
- from the perceived problem situation of the group the subject has studied or intends to study.

For other types of information users, perhaps these three different definitions of problem situation can also serve as a methodology for creating a metaphor set. But this remains a question we have only begun to answer. In our own research program, future research will consist of both (i) small-scale, qualitative studies in naturalistic settings, with a variety of university-based user groups, followed by (ii) large-scale quantitative research studies testing various metaphor instantiation hypotheses, scenarios, and IR system design schemes.

10. ACKNOWLEDGMENTS

The authors wish to acknowledge the financial support of the Social Science and Humanities Research Council of Canada (SSHRC), File No. 410-2002-1394. The authors also wish to thank Yang Lin, the project research assistant, for his valuable assistance in the preparation of transcripts and the case study diagrams.

References

Anderson, J. R. (1985). *Cognitive Psychology and Its Implications*. New York: W. H. Freeman.

Barsalou, L. W. (1983). Ad hoc categories. *Memory and Cognition*, 11(3), 211–227.

Barsalou, L. W. (1992). *Cognitive Psychology: An Overview for Cognitive Scientists*. Hillsdale, NJ: Lawrence Erlbaum Associates.

Bartlett, F. C. (1932). *Remembering*. Cambridge, UK: Cambridge University Press.

Belkin, N. J. (1978). Information concepts for information science. *Journal of Documentation*, 34(1), 55–85.

Belkin, N. J. (1980). Anomalous states of knowledge as a basis for information retrieval. *The Canadian Journal of Information Science*, 5, 133–134.

Belkin, N. J., Oddy, R. N., & Brooks, H. M. (1982). ASK for information retrieval: Part I. Background and theory. *Journal of Documentation*, 38(2), 61–71.

Bower, G. H., & Clapper, J. P. (1989). Experimental methods in cognitive science. In M. I. Posner (Ed.), *Foundations of Cognitive Science*, 245–300. Cambridge, MA: MIT Press.

Brookes, B. C. (1980). The foundations of information science. Part I. Philosophical aspects. *Journal of Information Science*, 2, 125–133.

Bruner, J. S., Goodnow, J. J., & Austin, G. A. (1956). *A Study of Thinking*. New York: Science Editions.

Bush, V. (1945). As we may think. *Atlantic Monthly*, 176(1), 101–108.

Caroll, J. M., Mack, R. L., & Kellog, W. A. (1988). Interface metaphors and user inter-face design. In H. Martin (Ed.), *Handbook of Human–Computer Interaction*, 67–85. Amsterdam: North Holland.

Case, D. O. (2002). *Looking for Information: A Survey of Research on Information Seeking, Needs, and Behavior*. Amsterdam: Academic Press.

Cole, C. (2000). Interaction with an enabling information retrieval system: Modeling the user's decoding and encoding operations. *Journal of the American Society for Information Science*, 51(5), 417–426.

Cole, C., Leide, J. E., Beheshti, J., Large, A., & Brooks, M. (in press-a). Investigating the ASK hypothesis in a real-life problem situation: A study of history and psychology undergraduates seeking information for a course essay. *Journal of the American Society for Information Science and Technology*.

Cole, C., Leide, J. E., Large, A., Beheshti, J., & Brooks, M. (in press-b). Putting it together online: Information need identification for the domain novice user. *Journal of the American Society for Information Science and Technology*.

Custers, E. J. F. M., Regehr, G., & Norman, G. R. (1996). Mental representations of medical diagnostic knowledge: A review. *Academic Medicine*, 71(10), S55–S61.

Cutter, C. A. (1876/1904). *Rules for a Dictionary Catalog*, 3rd Ed. Washington: Government Printing Office.

de Mey, M. (1982). *The Cognitive Paradigm: Cognitive Science, A Newly Explored Approach to the Study of Cognition Applied in an Analysis of Science and Scientific Knowledge*. Dordrecht, Holland: D. Reidel.

Dervin, B., & Nilan, M. (1986). Information needs and uses. *Annual Review of Information Science and Technology*, 21, 3–33.

Foskett, A. C. (1996). *The Subject Approach to Information*. London: Library Association.

Gentner, D., Bowdle, B., Wolff, P., & Boronat, C. (2001). Metaphor is Like Analogy. In D. Gentner, K. J. Holyoak, & B. N. Kokinov (Eds.), *The Analogical Mind: Perspectives from Cognitive Science*, 199–253. Cambridge, MA: Bradford Book.

Gentner, D., & Markman, A. B. (1997). Structure mapping in analogy and summary. *American Psychologist*, 52(1), 45–56.

Glucksberg, S., & McGlone, M. S. (1999). When love is not a journey: What metaphors mean. *Journal of Pragmatics*, 31, 1541–1558.

Graesser, A. C. (1981). *Prose Comprehension Beyond the Word*. New York: Springer-Verlag.

Ingwersen, P. (1982). Search procedures in the library—Analyzed from the cognitive point of view. *Journal of Documentation*, 38(3), 165–191.

Ingwersen, P. (1996). Cognitive perspective of information retrieval interaction: Elements of a cognitive IR theory. *Journal of Documentation*, 52(11), 3–50.

Jacob, E. K. (2004). Classification and categorization: A difference that makes a difference. *Library Trends*, 52(3), 515–540.

Kintsch, W., & van Dijk, T. A. (1978). Toward a model of text comprehension and production. *Psychological Review*, 85, 363–394.

Kuhlthau, C. C. (1993). *Seeking Meaning: A Process Approach to Library and Information Services*. Norwood, NJ: Ablex Publishing.

Lakoff, G. (1987). *Women, Fire, and Dangerous Things*. Chicago, IL: University of Chicago Press.

Lancaster, F. W. (1998). *Indexing and Abstracting in Theory and Practice*, 2nd Ed. Champaign, IL: University of Illinois Graduate School of Library and Information Science.

Leide, J. E., Large, A., Beheshti, J., Brooks, M., & Cole, C. (2003). Visualization schemes for domain novices exploring a topic space: The navigation classification scheme. *Information Processing and Management*, 39(6), 923–940.

Markman, A. B., & Moreau, C. P. (2001). Analogy and analogical comparison in choice. In D. Gentner, K. J. Holyoak, & B. N. Kokinov (Eds.), *The Analogical Mind: Perspectives from Cognitive Science*, 363–399. Cambridge, MA: Bradford Book.

McIlwaine, I. C. (1997). The universal decimal classification: Some factors concerning its origins, development, and influence. *Journal of the American Society for Information Science*, 48(4), 331–339.

Menzel, C. R. (1997). Primates' knowledge of their natural habitat: As indicated in foraging. In A. Whiten & R. W. Bryne (Eds.), *Machiavellian Intelligence II: Extensions and Evaluations*, 207–239. Cambridge, UK: Cambridge University Press.

Mills, J. (2004). Faceted classification and logical division in information retrieval. *Library Trends*, 52(3), 541–570.

Minsky, M. (1975). A framework for representing knowledge. In P. H. Winston (Ed.), *The Psychology of Computer Vision*, 211–277. New York: McGraw-Hill.

Mithen, S. (1996). *The Prehistory of the Mind: The Cognitive Origins of Art, Religions and Science*. London: Thames and Hudson.

Mithen, S. (1998). *Creativity in Human Evolution and Prehistory*. London: Routledge.

Morton, D. (2004). *Fight or Pay: Soldiers' Families in the Great War*. Vancouver: UBC Press.

Neill, S. D. (1987). The Dilemma of the Subjective in Information Organization and Retrieval. *Journal of Documentation*, 43(3), 193–211.

Novak, J. D. (1998). *Learning, Creating, and Using Knowledge. Concept Maps (R) as Facilitative Tools in Schools and Corporations*. Mahweh, NJ: Lawrence Erlbaum.

Oddy, R. N. (2004). *Personal Communication*.

Palmer, S. E. (1975). The effects of contextual scenes on the identification of objects. *Memory and Cognition*, 3, 519–526.

Popper, K. R. (1975). *Objective Knowledge: An Evolutionary Approach*. Oxford: Clarendon Press.

Ramscar, M., & Pain, H. (1996). Can a real distinction be made between cognitive theories of analogy and categorization? *Proceedings of the Eighteenth Annual Conference of the Cognitive Science Society*, July 12–15, University of California, San Diego, 346–351. Mahwah, NJ: Erlbaum.

Russell, B. (1961). In R. E. Egner & L. E. Denonn (Eds.), *The Basic Writings of Bertrand Russell*. New York, NY: Simon and Schuster.

Saracevic, T., & Kantor, P. (1997). Studying the value of library and information services. I. Establishing a theoretical framework. *Journal of the American Society for Information Science*, 48(6), 527–542.

Schacter, D. L., Cooper, L. A., & Delaney, S. M. (1990). Implicit memory for unfamiliar objects depends on access to structural descriptions. *Journal of Experimental Psychology: General*, 119(1), 5–24.

Schank, R. C., & Abelson, R. P. (1977). *Scripts, Plans, Goals, and Understanding: An Inquiry into Human Knowledge Structures*. Hillsdale, NJ: Erlbaum.

Shannon, C. (1949). The mathematical theory of communication. In C. Shannon & W. Weaver (Eds.), *The Mathematical Theory of Communication*. Urbana, IL: University of Illinois Press.

Spink, A., & Cole, C. (in press). Human information behavior: Integrating diverse approaches and information use. *Journal of the American Society for Information Science and Technology*.

Spink, A., & Currier, J. (in press). Towards an evolutionary perspective on human information behavior: An exploratory study. *Journal of Documentation*.

Spink, A., Park, M., & Cole, C. (2005). Multitasking and coordinating framework for human information behavior. In A. Spink & C. Cole (Eds.), *New Directions in Human Information Behavior*. Dordrecht: Kluwer.

Svenonius, E. (2004). The epistemological foundations of knowledge representations. *Library Trends*, 52(3), 571–587.

Wilson, T. D. (2000). Human information behaviour. *Informing Science*, 3(2), 49–56.

Wisniewski, E. J. (1997). Conceptual combination: Possibilities and esthetics. In T. B. Ward, S. M. Smith, & J. Vaid (Eds.), *Creative Thought: An Investigation of Conceptual Structures and Processes*, 51–81. Washington: American Psychological Association.

Chapter 11

The Digital Information Consumer

David Nicholas, Paul Huntington, Peter Williams, and Tom Dobrowolski
School of Library, Archive and Information Studies
City University London, UK

1. INTRODUCTION

There have been huge changes in human information behavior (HIB) as a result of more than 40 years of continuous digital information service rollouts. Changes have accelerated in the last 5 years as a result of the extended reach of these services to the general public and to life-dependent services. In this chapter, we discuss a new dimension to HIB that results from all this change; and we are also arguing for new methods in studying the information behavior of the digital information user.

As a result of 6 years of evaluating the rollout of digital information and advisory services in the newspaper (Nicholas & Huntington, 2000), health (Nicholas, Huntington, & Williams, 2004), and publishing fields (Nicholas et al., 2005). These studies employed deep log analysis methods. We examined, via their digital fingerprints, the digital information behavior of millions of people. We have worked with very large and heterogeneous populations; not just academics and professionals, but also the general public—included amongst them children, the elderly, infirm, and socially deprived.

In this chapter, we present the results of our evaluation of information behavior in large-scale digital environments done primarily by employing evidence-based methods (logs) to map the behavior. Essentially, what we discovered is that information behavior in digital environments on the Web and digital interactive television of touch screen information kiosks, irrespective of the field or industry, have both much in common. This is because both are largely shaped by the same things—the digital interface and its unique position in today's frenetic world.

A "big bang" has occurred in the information field wherein information and ways to access it are increasing on an exponential basis. However, most research within the LIS field still deals with a world that has long gone, employing concepts and methodologies that grew out of—and were applicable to—that world. The purpose of this chapter is to demonstrate the new human information traits that have established themselves as a result of that bang.

Our work is situated within the broader context of HIB (Spink & Cole, in press) and also Web research (Spink & Jansen, 2004). With reference to the theme of this book, what we are portraying in this chapter is much more than information-seeking behavior. According to Spink and Cole (in press), information seeking is purposive. But what we

A. Spink and C. Cole (eds), New Directions in Human Information Behavior, 203–228.
© 2006 *Springer.*

see in our logs is a form of behavior more common in the media and entertainment worlds than in the world of university libraries. In our logs, we see people searching for fun or entertainment, because they are bored, or to obtain stimulation or simply just wish to feel in touch or connected.

1.1 Change: Seismic Shifts and Change Agents

We focus on understanding the information behavior of the users of today's digital information services and how different this information behavior is from the hard copy and OPAC users upon which much of our HIB theories and concepts systems were built. In order to do this, we first need to consider the seismic changes that have occurred in the last 10 years or so in the information environment. If there is any meaning left in that overworked term, paradigm shift, it has occurred with regard to HIB in a big way.

1.2 From Control to No Control

People used to do most of their searching in controlled, supervised, and mediated environments—typically through catalogs, bibliographies, and secondary services, in libraries. But no longer is it a case of searching static, archival systems in public or work places, but mobile systems, real-time systems, interactive systems in the home or in the office. Patently, this is a big change. Searchers are now on their own and have a high degree of freedom as to what they do (or do not do). Of course, we would naturally expect them to behave differently now than they did previously, and they do. However, in many ways the differences in the ways people now search as compared to previously, are not only different, but are completely unforeseen, as this chapter will show.

1.3 From Bibliographic Services to Full-Text, Visual, and Life-Critical Services

Digital HIB is no longer simply a case of using OPACS to find references, as it now involves factors like the Web, the Internet, downloadable music, and even interactive television to check out on an ailment with a broadband nurse (Nicholas, Huntington, & Williams, 2003). Searching is now more comprehensive, interesting, rewarding, and most importantly, seemingly less demanding. More often now, searching is undertaken on systems that owe more to the media world than they do to the information retrieval world, although the information retrieval world continues to live on in rejuvenated popular forms in the likes of Google.

What is often easily overlooked is the fact that, the once archival and document-based Internet now contains what we term "life-dependent" or "fundamental to living" services, the kind that were previously only ever provided orally and in a mediated form by professionals in health, education, and housing. These services are being tossed into the information abyss that is the Internet; not quite willy-nilly but really without thought about how problematical it is to find and use them, and what happens when they are juxtaposed with recreational (i.e., sport, holiday, and hobby) services. We should not necessarily expect that these new services, with different content and their different intended outcomes will be searched in the same way as traditional, textual, set-in-concrete services. And they are not.

1.4 From Niche to Universal Systems

We have moved from searching single, subject-specific services like Whitakers Almanac in hard copy, and ERIC on CD-ROM, to encyclopedic, multichannel services, like the Web or DiTV, where many other services catch the eye, compete for our attention, and provide us with a choice and a means of comparison. We need to understand more fully what occurs as a result of such services being juxtaposed with entertainment, leisure, and business services. Logically there must be an impact on information behavior and the evidence shows that it has become far more horizontal—that is, instead of going for depth, users are now happy to spread their search out, and to grab what they can from a wide variety of sources and services.

1.5 From a Few Searchers to Everyone

Toward the middle of the 1980s the number of end-users went through the roof, from hundreds to thousands and then on to millions in the 1990s and tens of millions in the new millennium. It is not just the numbers of people using the systems that have changed so dramatically, important though this is economically; the types of people using the systems have changed too. There are millions of people searching today who bring with them no previous experience of information systems at all—the children, the elderly, those without higher education, and the unemployed.

Traditionally, because these people were regarded as non-users, we know virtually nothing at all about their information behavior. Also, of course, there is no reason at all that we should expect to behave in the same way as that HIB research favorite, the information science student. For example, at a recent conference on information seeking in a health context, the authors were approached by a member of the audience, a health information worker, who said he did not recognize the portraits being drawn of health information seekers and, of course, the reason for this was that the types of people who used his service were not representative of those people who use the Web.

1.6 From End-User to Consumer

There was some initial hostility toward the first "end-user" recruits in the late 1970s/early 1980s and the consequent disparaging of their search styles and HIB had much to do with a professional insecurity that arose from the idea that someone could and would actually want to search an information system themselves. However, all of this was relevant only to bibliographic systems, which are largely devised for information professionals, academics, and scientists. These were niche information players, using niche and targeted systems; all that has now changed. No one disparages them anymore.

However, people still talk about them in that most unconsumer of all terms, the end-user, but since there are too many of them, and since they have considerable clout, we should really begin calling them consumers. These consumers have an array of choices and information is simply one of the things in the digital shop window that can be obtained by them, giving them a chance to exercise their economic power.

1.7 From Corner Shop to Mega Store/Shopping Mall

There are now a bewildering number of choices with regards to digital information, while previously there was very little, if any. The Web is really all about choice and the excitement of making choices within information seeking, and therefore, the information behaviors must surely reflect that. The problem has moved from having to put up with something that was not quite perfect or relevant, to having to choose from an Aladdin's cave of shifting information sources. Just think of how you might behave in a small corner shop, where you have to ask for the goods behind the counter, as opposed to a store where you have a personal shopping trolley and were allowed to browse and pick out anything you liked from the miles of shelves?

Of course your behavior would be markedly different in the two situations, but would it be the same kind of difference in behavior if the goods are information services/products instead, and if we are given a chance to browse and pick out the information we need as opposed going through a mediator like a librarian? Our data suggest that it is so, and that our behaviors in the two situations are not that different.

Given the seismic shifts chronicled above and the fact that our knowledge of the information user has too often been based on one-off, small, parochial, and biased studies of unrepresentative user groups (typically academics) we would *expect* the new digital information consumers to act and react very differently from those landmark Dialog, Nexis, DataStar, and Reuters end-users, who were mainly professionals. We now have copious (log) data available to us that tell us how different people approach the information, but we as a profession have not been good at really utilizing these logs and, as a consequence, we suspect that some people are working with old models of behavior and promulgating the wrong messages (and systems, of course).

The main purpose of this chapter is then to describe the key characteristics of the information behavior of the "new" digital information consumer so as to inform information intermediaries, producers, search engine designers, and especially those charged with running information and digital literacy programs, which sorely need the data to inform the design of their programs.

Our chapter has two purposes:

1. To move toward evidenced-based investigations of actual user behavior and away from theoretical constructs of need etc. which have, arguably, either not really helped our understanding of the user, or have not been recognized by policy makers as having done so.
2. To demonstrate our methodology, which we call deep log analysis, that enables us to portray and evaluate HIB in a digital context in real-time.

2. METHODS

Methods are the key to obtaining the kinds of insights into HIB that we are looking for, hence the need to describe them in some detail. Instead of asking people about their information behavior, a methodology prone to exaggeration, dishonesty, and lapses of memory, we examine the evidence provided in usage (transaction) logs, of how people have *actually* behaved. We refer to our brand of enhanced transactional log techniques as "deep log analysis". The techniques were born as a result of the frustrations experienced in seeing the huge opportunities provided by logs but finding that proprietary log softwares could not provide the robust big picture information analyses that policy makers required.

All digital information platforms have a facility by which computer transaction logs are generated, and which provide an automatic and real-time record of use by everyone who uses them. They represent the digital information footprints of the users. By analyzing and magnifying them you can track and map their information behavior, and, when enhanced by user demographic data, they can tell us something about the kinds of people who use the services. Qualitative, follow-up work, and desk research can answer our why questions, inform the outcomes and, also tell us something about the non-users.

The attraction of logs is that they provide abundant and fairly robust evidence of use. Spink and Jansen (2004) have also used Web search logs extensively during their Web search studies. Using log analysis, it is possible to monitor the use of a system by millions of people from around the country or the world. Logs record use by everyone who happens to engage with the system—there is no need to take a sample.

The great advantage of logs is not just their size and reach, although the dividends here are indeed a rich and unparalleled one. Most importantly, logs are a direct and immediately available record of what people have done: not what they say they might, or would, do; not what they were prompted to say, not what they thought they did. The data are unfiltered and speak for themselves and provide a reality check that both represents the users and complements important contextual data obtained by engaging with real users and exploring their experiences and concerns.

Finally, log data provide for real-time and continuous analysis, something which provides a fantastic opportunity to create a digital laboratory for the monitoring of changes in HIB.

A detailed explanation of how raw log data—something at the very heart of deep log analysis—are analyzed can be found in a number of articles published by the authors (Nicholas & Huntington, 2000, 2003; Nicholas, Huntington, & Williams, 2002). However, in general, many users will visit a Website and leave without viewing content. Users on the Internet are by and large difficult to track, because users are generally identified by an Internet Protocol (IP) number. However, there is not a complete or good mapping of IP number to user. IP numbers are allocated to computers rather than to individual users and there may well be a number of people using the same computer. Hence, IP number usage will not accurately represent user numbers.

Furthermore, some Internet providers allocate a temporary or floating IP address and hence we cannot be sure that a returning IP address identifies the same user. And, lastly, users may connect to the Internet via a proxy IP number in which case a number of organizations or computers will access the Internet using the same IP number. Pages are counted by looking at the complete download of a page from the server to the users' or clients' computer. However, the server will not necessarily count all pages viewed by the user. This occurs because the client's computer will cache recently viewed Internet pages to the hard drive and subsequent views to these pages will be accessed from the hard disk rather than requested from the server.

Where log analysis has been employed by researchers, they have tended to use the processed data obtained from proprietary software like Web trends rather than the raw logs. In such circumstances, the analyses are inevitably constrained—the software is really produced for a marketing purpose, and the researchers at one remove are blinded by the digital dust storm kicked up by such vast quantities of data. This means that they do not always understand what the log data mean, do not always get the data they need, and do not understand what the limitations of the data are. As a consequence, huge opportunities are missed for evaluating information behavior.

Thus, instead of helping we answer the big policy questions that are confronting us all about the nature and role of HIB in the digital environment, the sheer enormity of the data proves too overwhelming to analyze.

Raw logs also offer more relevant analysis. Proprietary software, by definition, gives a set report that will not examine specific questions, but raw log analysis can hone in for an in-depth analysis. Log lines are directly imported into SPSS and the data are analyzed and manipulated in a variety of ways. Whereas raw log analysis raises more questions than it often answers, proprietary software restricts analysis to descriptive single variable statistics. Raw log analysis offers the opportunities for a multivariate analysis. Furthermore, raw log analyses give a better report structure. Proprietary software tends to deliver unreadable non-user-friendly reports that give endless pages of unrelated and often meaningless data.

Deep log analysis (including the qualitative component) provides numerous metrics by which we can portray HIB. As we shall show in this chapter, deep log analysis can provide a powerful information profile of the digital consumer. In this regard, we look at the number of items viewed in a session (Website penetration), frequency of visits (repeat behavior), and the number of Websites visited, among others.

These three metrics offer extremely good platforms for characterizing and comparing the information behavior of sub-groups of users. We need to do this because generalizations based upon millions of users, while sounding impressive, can prove very misleading indeed, camouflaging possibly big differences between individual user groups. For instance, we have characterized researchers and academics by: occupation, subject category of journal used, place of work, type of subscriber (big deal, non-subscriber etc.), geographical location of user, type of university (old and new), referrer link used, and use/non-use of Athens authentication (Nicholas et al., 2005).

3. INFORMATION BEHAVIORS OF THE DIGITAL CONSUMER

For the purposes of this chapter, we will be referring to a number of individual research studies that we have conducted in the consumer health (Nicholas, Huntington, & Williams, 2004; Nicholas et al., 2003b) and scholarly journal fields (Nicholas, Huntington, & Watkinson, 2002; Nicholas et al., 2003a). In both cases, the "sample" populations can be numbered in the hundreds of thousands and the number of individual HIB events in the millions. Using a number of log and qualitative metrics, we have profiled the digital information consumer and produced the kind of data that policy makers require to take decisions about the success or effectiveness of digital information services.

However, it should be noted that what we report here is a work in progress, and is cutting-edge work for which we do not yet have the full picture or all the answers. However, we do have enough data to begin to sketch out the outlines of information behavior in the new digital information environment that we all find ourselves in. What we have done is bring together important data scattered across our different studies and pieced it together to create a coherent picture of HIB in a digital environment. What you will find here is not a review of our previous studies but a mining of the data in these studies to provide a data panorama and juxtaposition not previously seen before.

Four characteristics for which we have most evidence are presented in some detail (brief information of the studies from which the evidence is taken is given in parentheses; more details and publications can be found on the CIBER Website http://www.ucl.ac.uk/ciber):

- *Depth of Searching Behavior*—typically shallow.
  - ○ Source Study 1. Nicholas et al. (2003–2004).*The Virtual Scholar Research Programme—Use and Impact of Digital Libraries in Academe.* Study of the usage logs of hundreds of thousands of academics and scholars using two digital libraries—Synergy and Emerald Insight. Funded by Blackwell/Emerald/Elsevier, 2003–2004;
  - ○ Source Study 2. Nicholas et al. (2000–2004). *The Web, the Kiosk, Digital TV, and the Changing and Evolving Face of Consumer Health Information Provision: A National Impact Study.* Study of the usage logs of hundreds of thousands of health information users, the majority of them British, of touch screen kiosks, digital interactive television services, and two health-related Websites—Surgery Door and NHS Direct. Funded by Department of Health, 2000–2004.
- *Repeat Behavior*—not very loyal (Sources: Studies 1 and 2 as above).
- *Range of Searching Behavior*—wide and "promiscuous" (Sources: Study 2).
- *Changes in Behavior*—volatile (Sources: Study 1).

In addition, we briefly discuss a number of characteristics for which we have some evidence but not sufficient enough to portray them completely. For example, we discuss:

- *"Trusting" behavior*, wherein users are generally untrusting, except in the case of search engines (Sources: Study 2); and
- *Retrieval behavior* (Sources Study 3).
  - ○ Source Study 3: Nicholas et al. (2004–2005). *Users of the BBC Website*: study of search logs of health users of BBC's Website. Funded by the Department of Health, 2004–2005.

Type of User/Session	Number of Items Viewed	Emerald (January–December 2002)	Blackwell (February 2004)
Bouncer/checker	1–3	70	67
Moderately engaged	4–10	20	26
Engaged	11–20	6	5
Seriously engaged	Over 21	4	2
Total		100	100

Table 1. Digital Journal User Classification by Number of Items Viewed in a Session

3.1 Information Behavior Characteristic 1—Depth of Searching

Digital information consumers are generally characterized by their shallow searching. On its own, this might suggest an unsuccessful, uninformed, or lazy form of behavior. However, when taken with some of the other characteristics yet to be described, shallow search behavior probably suggests a horizontal, checking, comparing sort of behavior that is a result of fast and easy access to information, as well as a shortage of time and a huge digital choice. Website penetration is the metric we use to determine this and it represents the number of items viewed during a search session. It provides an indication of how involved or engaged people get with Websites or digital services. The metric typically shows that visits are characteristically brief, to-the-point, and possibly, cursory.

Research conducted in the health field (Nicholas, Huntington, & Williams, 2004) alerted us first to the fact that many Web users did not dwell long, they examined just a few items/pages before they left, perhaps satisfied, or if not, gave up altogether and searched for information elsewhere. In many cases, only a home page or introductory page was visited and in these cases no substantial content was consumed, although knowledge of a kind had been gained (even if all that is that this Website has nothing to offer) To reflect the uncertain purposes and outcomes, we call these people "bouncers" or "checkers".

Let us look at this metric in the light of usage of a digital library of scholarly journals or of publishers' platforms. Table 1 classifies users according to their level of penetration and shows that well over two-thirds of Blackwell Synergy[1] and Emerald Insight[2] users viewed between one and three items[3] or pages and that in the case of Emerald 42% of users viewed just one item.

The similar figure for the Blackwell dataset suggests that the metric is quite stable. Given the vast size of most Websites, the fact that just one page is typically used has big implications and repercussions for Web managers. How deeply a person penetrates or investigates a Website is clearly an interesting metric, showing variously, interest, satisfaction, and "busyness".

---

[1] http://www.blackwell-synergy.com
[2] http://www.emeraldinsight.com
[3] An item could be an abstract, a table of contents, or full-text document (the latter generally can only be viewed if the user is a subscriber or is willing to pay by credit card for the item.

Depth of searching might also tell us something about searching style, digital visibility (how prominent a page or Website is), and the structure, the architecture, and the nature of the Website. We can postulate reasons for this distribution. Users might access the Website just to see what is there but return later to pick up their material. Alternatively, users (students more likely) may be given the exact Internet citation of an item in a bibliography or link to an A&I service like *Pubmed*, and thus go directly to view the item without investigating other pages.

A further possibility relates to the nature of the Internet itself. In many cases, people use a Web search engine to find the Website and these engines return a number of clickable links that the user will cycle through, clicking on the first link, viewing maybe a page or two to see what's there and then go on to the next link, especially if their search has not been satisfied or only partially satisfied, hence the term "checkers". The question to which we particularly needed an answer was whether there was anything about a digital journal library and its academic users, in Website penetration terms, which made it any different from other consumer Websites?

For example, in an essentially academic digital library you might expect a higher level of penetration as a result of: (a) the bibliographic and full-text mix which gives a natural movement as a result of moving from one item to another; (b) the massive choice of data on offer (hundreds of full-text journals); (c) the investigative/research nature of some information behavior; and (d) the presence of an embedded search engine and other retrieval aids.

However, our work with health consumers shows this does not make much difference: the respective figures for a health consumer Website, Surgery Door[4], were: 74% (1–3); 20% (4–10); 4% (11–20); and 2% (21+). What we appear to be witnessing here is classic Web consumer searching (shopping) behavior that results from massive choice.

The number of views made in a session provides an idea of the degree of penetration of a Website, but, the metric says little about the quality or substance of content retrieved. For example, a session featuring one to three views suggests limited or "checking" use; however, this would be truer if these pages were what we might term menu pages (issue lists and table of contents) rather than article (or abstract) views, which might suggest a more targeted approach to searching. Clearly, *what* the user is viewing in a session impacts the Web Website penetration metric.

Thus, in the case of Blackwell Synergy users, a breakdown of sessions according to their use of menu pages and combination of menu pages shows that just over a quarter (27%) of sessions featured views of both the table of contents and the issue lists, 3% viewed a table of contents but not the issue lists, 20% viewed the issue lists but not the table of contents, and a surprising 50% of sessions had no issue lists or table of contents being viewed. This latter user group either landed directly on the page (via *Pubmed*, for instance) or used the search engine/option to find what they wanted, or accessed it through a menu page cached on their hard drives. We suspect that they used the search engine and went direct to the full-text. So it appears that we have an almost even split between "checkers" or "browsers" and the users who are more specific and hone down on to a particular piece of information.

[4]http://www.searcherydoor.co.uk

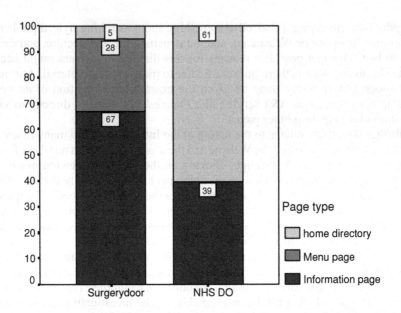

Figure 1. Distribution of pages viewed in a single session by users of online health Websites.

A study of two consumer health Websites, Surgery Door, and NHS Direct Online[5] (Nicholas et al., 2002), throws further light on the nature of their use, and in particular, how productive it was for the user. Figure 1 provides evidence of the depth and productivity in user's visits to two health information Websites by showing how many of the pages viewed were actually information pages.

Figure 1 shows the distribution of pages viewed by single session one-page users only. In order to determine how users arrived at an information or content page, we classified the pages into three types: an information page, a menu page, and the home directory. If the user accessed either a menu or home directory page then the user has not accessed an information page and has left without accessing any significant information from the Website, other than negative information (i.e., it was not relevant or useful to them, compared poorly with others etc). These users can be thought of as the "bouncers"—they have bounced in and out of the Website without having accessed an information page. There are marked and interesting differences between the Websites within Surgery Door showing a high level of targeted information seeking.

Turning our attention more closely to these "bouncers", 61% of NHS Direct single session one-page users (accounting for 8.5% of all session accesses) and 33% of Surgery Door users (13.9% of all session accesses) viewed the opening menu/home directory screen and left without accessing any further pages. These users did not access an information page and have as it were voted with their feet and have left without delving into the Website further.

[5]http://www.nhsdirect.nhs.uk

The explanation for this big difference between the two Websites most likely lies in the "digital visibility" of each service, something that powers and directs information-seeking behavior. Digital visibility says something about the positioning of the service within the electronic environment (Nicholas et al., 2002). For the Web, this is partly defined by the Websites' "visibility" on the directories of search engines like Yahoo and Google and the Websites' positioning on the list of Websites returned by them in response to a user's search query.

The NHS positioning on the results list within search engines seems to have been poor at the time of the research. This was determined by looking at referrer log information. Some 9 of the top 20 search terms[6] used incorporated NHS in the search expression. This seems to indicate that the most popular way of linking to the NHS Direct Online Website via a search engine was by typing NHS somewhere in the search expression. Most importantly, users did not just accidentally "discover" the NHS Website because they typed in their medical condition/problem into a search engine, but purposively sought information from it because they knew there was an NHS Website.

Searchers who did not include NHS in their search expression were unlikely to be offered the NHS Website within the first two or three pages of "hits" returned by a search engine. Thus, fewer users arrived at the NHS Website via a search engine since this was further down in the results list returned by a search engine. People typically use the list returned by a search engine to bounce from Website to Website; hence NHS Direct Online attracted less bouncer hits compared to their commercial competitors Surgery Door. Furthermore, when users arrived (including those that entered NHS in their search term) they were more likely to arrive at a home directory page rather than a content page.

One implication of this kind of bouncing/flicking information behavior then is that the home page or the individual content page landed upon by the user on their first linking to the Website plays a very important role in whether or not that user decides to proceed further into the Website and view more pages within the Website or not. Once again, this relates to the digital visibility of the Website. In a previous study which evaluated the logs of the NHS Direct health channel on Kingston Interactive Television (Nicholas et al., 2002), it became clear that the channel was losing viewers over the 4-month period in which it was shown.

Furthermore, the decline was not a gradual one but was characterized by a series of big and abrupt drops in its viewer ship which coincided with a number of changes to its positioning within the KIT service. With each change, the NHS service became more and more removed from the KIT home page and consequently less visible. It is also notable that the major impact was on new customers, for new users were not coming through because of the increasing difficulty of finding the service. However, those people who had already found the service and had accessed it previously, continued to do so despite its decreasing visibility of the KIT service, and also made more extensive use of the channel when they arrived to use the NHS service.

Considering this evidence, it appears that the positioning of services within an electronic environment, whether it is pages on the Web, digital TV channels, or on stand-alone computer terminals, is a vital factor in its eventual usage. Content may still be king, but

---

[6]The top 20 accounted for 60% of all terms used to find the main server Website.

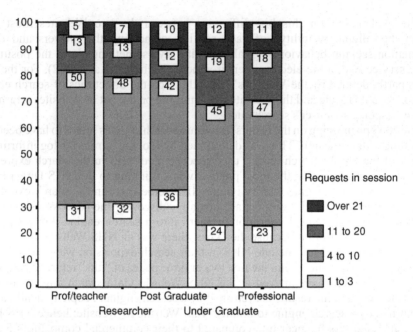

Figure 2. Number of views in a session by digital journal users by occupation/academic status (subscribers).

if that content cannot be accessed easily, its quality, relevance, and presentation are as good as wasted.

The real value of this kind of analysis is in typing users and determining user subgroups; finding who the shallowly penetrating or deeply penetrating users are or under what circumstances people search deeply or shallowly. For example, in our investigation of Blackwell Synergy, where it was possible to map usage logs to a database containing the demographic characteristics of its subscribers, we ran the Website penetration metric against the occupation/academic status of users, and found some interesting and unexpected results.

Postgraduates turned out to penetrate the Website least, with well over one-third of them viewing three items or less in a session (Figure 2).

Undergraduates, perhaps contrary to expectation, penetrated the Website deepest, with 31% viewing 11 or more items in a session. These were (by definition) registered users and the fact that the bouncer/checker proportions were about half that of the total population of users probably reflects the commitment and loyalty shown by people who had bothered to register.

3.2 Information Behavior Characteristic 2—Repeat Behavior

Digital consumers appear to exhibit an unpredictable form of behavior in which there appears to be little user loyalty or repeat visits. Although there is not sufficient evidence

Number of Visits	Emerald (January–December 2002) (%)	Blackwell (February–March 2003) (%)
1	69	63
2–5	24	28
6–15	5	6
Over 15	2	3
Total	100.0	100

Table 2. Digital Journal Users Grouped by Number of Visits
During Survey Period

to know for certain, this appears to be a very different form of behavior than what one might have supposed to have existed in a non- or partly digital world. The reason, of course, has more than a little to do with the amount of choice that is available, the fact that the choices on offer change and their changing digital visibility.

The number of times someone returns to a Website is evidently a key metric, and tells us something about Website loyalty and satisfaction. Coming back to a Website constitutes a conscious and directed use. The industry calls it "Website stickiness", and everyone wants their Website to be "sticky". However, we have found that not only do people use little of a Website's contents; they do not come back very often either. We can ascribe this to a form of behavior we term "information promiscuity" and this is another manifestation of massive digital choice, something we shall return to.

In theory, the frequency at which people return to a Website is related to the nature and purpose of the Website—a newspaper's Website, for instance, might obtain more return visits because of the rapid turnover of information. It is not clear what would constitute a natural frequency for a digital scholarly journal Website, or a health Website for that matter—we have never had any robust data to determine this. However, in the case of academics, one would expect that they would naturally develop a repeat behavior in order to fulfill their current awareness needs. Or so one would have thought, but we have to be careful because the digital consumer is full of surprises.

Table 2 (column 2), for example, shows the number of times Emerald users returned to the Website during 2002. A large majority of people (69%) visited the Website only once during the 12-month period, and just under a quarter of the users visited the Website between two and five times, while only about 5% of users visited the Website between 6 and 15 times and just 1.5% of users visited over 15 times. Given the fact that in some cases, the user is a multiuser the numbers of returning individuals is probably an overestimation.

Interestingly, the Blackwell data (Column 3), despite being collected over a much shorter period (2 months), shows higher levels of return visits, although even here just less than two-thirds of users did not re-visit within the surveyed period.

The higher levels of return users to the Blackwell Website might well have something to do with the fact that medical and scientific users have more pressing current awareness

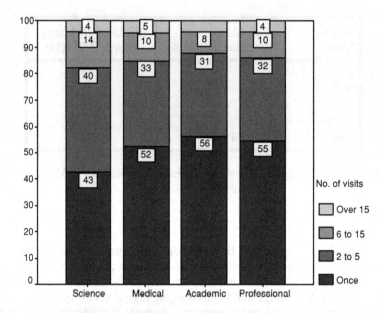

Figure 3. Number of visits by digital journal users (February–March 2003) by subject category of article viewed.

needs. This is borne out by an analysis of return visits by subject category of article viewed (Figure 3).

Science journal users were much more likely to return, and 57% did so compared to the 44% of those viewing academic social science and humanities journals. If we move now to users of our health Website case study, the Surgery Door Website (Table 3), we see that the picture is very much the same as Blackwell's, despite the very different emphasis of the Website and the different composition of the user group.

These data led us to believe that this kind of behavior is just another standard digital consumer trait that results from: (a) choice, (b) the fact that users are at the mercy of the

Number of Visits Within the Year	Surgery Door (%)
1	67
2–5	33
6–15	0
Over 15	0
Total	100

Table 3. Repeat Use of
Consumer Health Websites

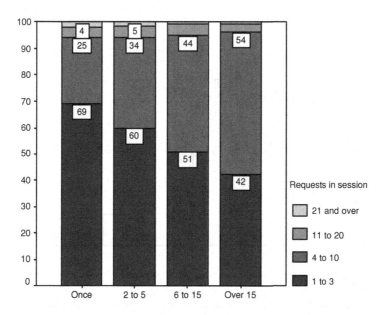

Figure 4. Blackwell Synergy users: Number of times the Website was visited within
2 months and the mean page views per session.

retrieval lottery created by search engines, (c) they have no memory of where they have been before, and (d) the Website churn rate of the search engine. It comes as no surprise to learn that those people who do not return to a Website tend to be those who do not penetrate a Website very deeply. Figure 4[7] gives the number of times the Website was visited and the mean page views per session for users of Synergy over a 2-month period.

Those using the Website more frequently made a higher number of page requests in a session. Over two-thirds of users visiting the Website just once viewed between one and three items; however, this was also true for 42% of those visiting over 15 times. The two metrics together—returnees and Website penetration—provide a powerful indicator of expertise, commitment, and probably satisfaction with the Website.

3.3 Information Behavior Characteristic 3—Visit to Multiple Websites

Digital information consumers search a variety of Websites to find what they want and while this is a perfectly normal, straightforward, and understandable information trait, there are further implications for this information promiscuity. As illustrated by an NHS Direct Online user who told us: "I practice yoga so I will often check out various

[7]Chi = 17,482; df = 9; p = 0.000.

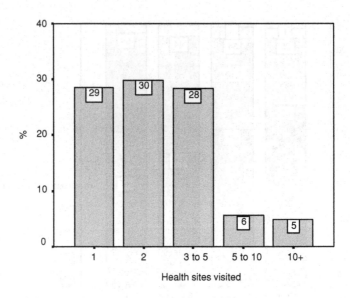

Figure 5. Number of health Websites visited by users of Surgery Door—Online
health-related Website.

Websites for possible solutions to problems", users shop around, and there are many
more of such users.

The most important reason why people adopt a "flicking" or "bouncing" behavior
is because they have a choice—the wealth of alternative digital sources enables them to
do so. Data suggest that people visit many Websites but actually "use" only a few. In
addition, users are more aware of their new found powers of searching for information
and soon come to realize that they are empowered to cross traditional boundaries, whether
they are geographic boundaries, as in offshore gambling, or knowledge boundaries, as
in health issues.

Figure 5 provides illustrative data on the number of Websites people visit, in this
particular case, health Websites.

The logs do not generally furnish these types of data; instead, we have to use data
from an online questionnaire hosted on Websites like Surgery Door. In this case, the
vast majority of people (71%) said they regularly visited two or more Websites, 29%
regularly visited three to five Websites, and 11% regularly visited five or more. Clearly,
those who used just one Website were very much in the minority. Besides, this is likely
an underestimation of the number of Websites visited by the users, as they were unlikely
to remember all Websites which they did not find useful or had visited long ago and have
not since returned.

Figure 6 provides the reasons why people searching for health information visit a
number of Websites.

As expected, the majority of the respondents (92%) who visited more than one Website
said that they did so in order to compare information from more than one Website. The
greater the number of Websites visited the greater the likelihood of a positive health

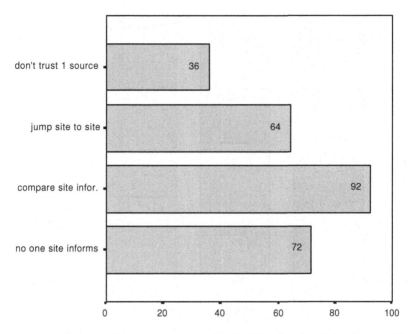

Figure 6. Reasons by users of Surgery Door—Online health-related Website, for searching more than one Website.

outcome. This provides support for an information model, which postulates that Websites should not present information in the same way, detail, or with the same design.

Users benefit from collecting information from a number of Websites partly because they find the information easier to understand or to digest on some Websites than on others, and also because the process of jumping from Website to Website gives them a chance to compare and contrast information. This also says something about how users become knowledgeable. Furthermore, 72% of respondents said that no one Website would inform, while 64% confirmed that they just jumped from Website to Website. Elsewhere, we have termed this form of information behavior "bouncing", and it appears to be the preferred, even pleasurable way of browsing for many. Finally, 35% of respondents said that they visited more than one Website because they did not trust information from just a single source.

It also appears that the younger the person, the more promiscuous the information browsing behavior they exhibited (Figure 7).

Almost half (46%) of all people under 35 years said they regularly visited more than three health Websites, whereas the same figure for the 55 years and over was a little over half of that (24%).

To shed further light on the above data, people were asked how they located health information Websites. They were asked whether they used a search engine, re-visited a Website, clicked on a health link, or clicked on a banner advertisement (Figure 8).

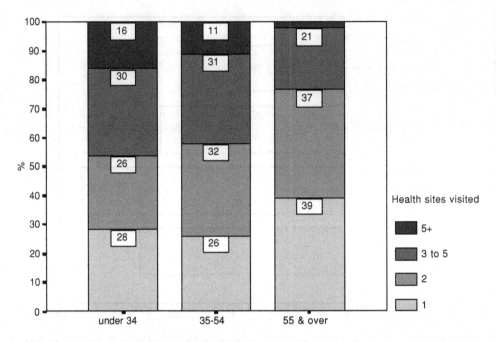

Figure 7. Age of consumers of online health-related Websites by number of health Websites visited = reported by users of the Surgery Door Website.

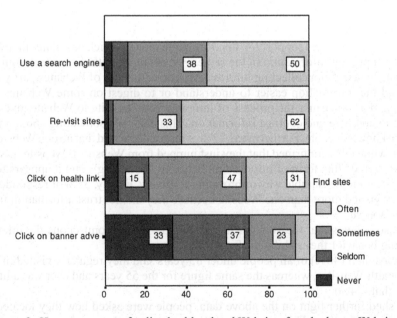

Figure 8. How consumers of online health-related Websites found relevant Websites (%)—reported by the users of the Surgery Door Website.

It turned out that people used a range of methods, with clicking on banner advertisements being the least favored. Most users located health information by re-visiting Websites that they had previously visited: 62% of respondents often did this while 33% said that they sometimes did this. This does not quite come through in the log data, and needs reconciling, it could be of course, and that people say one thing but do another. Using a search engine was also popular and 88% said that they had often or sometimes done this. People appear to like using both methods—regularly returning to favored Websites but comparing information with additional sources found by using a search engine.

A surprisingly high percentage of health consumers said that they had clicked on health links: 31% said that they had often done this while 47% said that they sometimes did. Respondents, it seems, do value and will use the health links and references placed at the bottom of the page by health Websites. Clicking on a health banner advert was found to be the least popular way of finding health information. Only 7% said that they had often done this while 23% said that they sometimes had. The majority of respondents, 37%, said that they seldom clicked on a health banner advert while 33% said that they never did.

3.4 Information Behavior Characteristic 4—Volatility

The digital information consumer's "bouncing", "checking", and "promiscuous" form of behavior creates enormous volatility and unpredictability and creates a seemingly frenetic information environment. The volatility caused by large numbers of people "flocking"—going from Website to Website in their attempt to find and verify information and find the best "bargains"—can be demonstrated by the research of the use of the Emerald Insight Website by scholars, which provides us three pieces of important information.

Firstly, it provides us with an idea of the huge numbers of people who are floating around looking for information, who often dwarf resident populations of subscribers. During the month of June 2002, 154,536 people used the Emerald Insight service, a testament to how popular digital libraries truly are with the digital consumer. Of these, an astonishing 63% were non-subscribers, including trialists (people who tried out the service for a month), who accounted for 7% of all users (Figure 9).

Plainly this is a consumer-friendly Website in anyone's terms, and has little in common with its predecessors like Dialog and DataStar. It also suggests that there are plenty of casual users seeking journal articles, certainly in the social sciences anyway; of course, most never seem to come back.

Secondly, we have evidence of the stability of the population of virtual scholars is over time, and it certainly appears not to be as stable as one might have supposed. Table 4 compares full-text downloads from Emerald's library of around 150 journals for two 6-month periods between August 2001 and January 2002 and August 2002 to January 2003 for 91 UK universities.

One can see that there is a huge seesawing in use from 1 year to another; the majority of increases/decreases are of the order of 25% and over, although on the whole there is a 17% increase in use. One in nine universities saw increases in downloads by more than a 100%. Of course, we have no way of knowing whether this actually went on in the

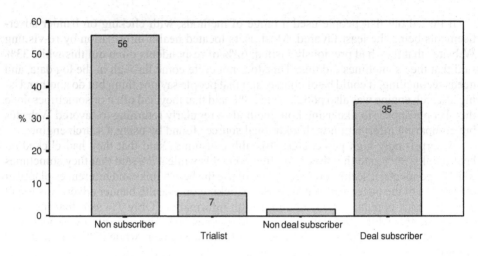

Figure 9. Emerald insight users by type of user (%).

world of hard copy journals where use went largely unrecorded. However, there is more than enough evidence produced elsewhere in this chapter to suggest that it is in fact a function of choice, relying on search engines to find information (and not memory) and the promiscuous behavior that results from it.

Thirdly, we have users who are easily swayed in their choices by seemingly attractive "offers", even in the case of the "staid" scholar. For example, on the Emerald Website,

Movement	Percentage Change
Increase	
More than 100%	11
+ 75–99%	2
+ 50–74%	3
+ 25–49%	16
+ 1–24%	29
Decrease	
− 1–24%	24
− 25 – 49%	10
− 50 – 74%	3
− 75 – 99%	1
Average	17

Table 4. Information Behavior Volatility:
Comparison of Full-Text Downloads from
the Emerald Insight Website Over Two
6-Month Time Periods (August 2001/January
2002 and August 2002/January 2003)

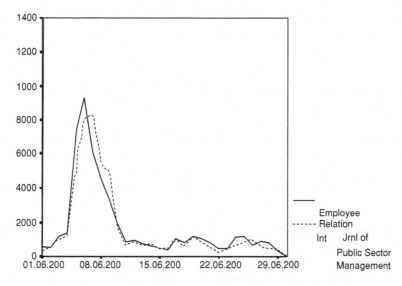

Figure 10. Emerald insight: Impact of free-download week on usage of employee relations and *International Journal of Public Sector Management*.

every week, two journals are offered for which downloads are free in that particular week. Figure 10 shows what happens as a result, with use jumping suddenly by a factor of 10, only to drop down again to pre-"sale" levels.

Clearly, it is not just the fact that the journals are "free" that fuels their use but also has something to do with the enhanced digital visibility of these particular journals at the time. An analysis of download times before and after free week suggests that a husbanding or squirreling behavior is being observed. What transpired was that download times in free week were much faster, suggesting people were simply storing for a later day, rather than "reading" at the time.

3.5 Information Characteristic 5—Trusting

Another characteristic, for which we are still obtaining log evidence to describe it fully, is "trusting", or more accurately, untrusting behavior. The multiplicity of access points to information—TV, newspapers, consumer magazines, learned journals, radio, Internet, PDAs, Online services—confuses the consumer and leads to a breakdown in trust and to information dissonance or noise. In comparison with print media, all electronic media (including analog broadcasts) are difficult to navigate and to reference.

For in essence, they are two-dimensional, whereas print is three-dimensional in that the shape of the whole experience can be successfully deduced from the physical form. For example, even the briefest knowledge of a print newspaper (which is not usually indexed at primary use level) leads the consumer to an understanding of what they will find and where in a relatively standard formula. Digital formats and the Web in particular, have a tendency to break down this easy familiarity and leave the consumer floating in a sea of uncertainty. The consumer responds by putting aside considerations of trust and loyalty.

Of course, there is also the problem of "authority" that rises out of a relatively new and fast-changing environment with new players coming in all the time. In the digital environment, it is difficult to determine ownership because there are so many parties associated with the production of a digital information service. For example, consider the touch screen health information kiosk, produced by the Surgery Door consumer health Website, incorporating some information from NHS Direct Online and located in a Safeway[8] store. To the person shopping in the supermarket that sees the kiosk and decides to use it, who would they attribute its qualities to: Safeway, Surgery Door—a company of which they have probably never heard, or to the NHS, should they be alert enough to spot its logo? There is no easy answer of course, but one suspects they might attribute it to Safeway, on account of its stronger brand name, or because its a place with which they are more familiar with than with a health center. This kind of confusion over the "authority" of information has big implications for libraries, as they are increasingly becoming e-journal and e-book "portals" for publishers.

At one time, consumers trusted the information provider, namely information professionals. In the flattened world of the Internet, where all things are seemingly equal, this appears less important than ever, and hence the diminishing role of information professionals in the search process. There is a sense that consumers are more brand conscious, but less brand loyal. This applies to information just as much as to any commodity sold in the market. Information specialists have largely accepted that information has become a commodity (but without an expressed value attached to it) but do not often accept the consequences of this.

Our health studies have clearly shown that the general public displays a healthy dose of skepticism when it comes to the quality of information on health Websites (Nicholas, Huntington, & Williams, 2003). They are far from the gullible and innocent people that information and health professionals would have us believe. Fewer than half the respondents said that they only believe "some" or none of the information found, though they were talking about Websites carrying supposedly scientific or medical information, while 45% said that they had actually found misleading information.

With so much information available to them, health consumers inevitably take advantage of this choice by shopping around and cross-checking the data they find, and the more they shopped around the more their quality concerns were realized. Respondents who visited five or more Websites were about five or four times more likely to find information they thought was misleading compared to respondents who just visited one Website. This is a considerable difference.

It is not just information professionals who are concerned with the source of the content; consumers saw this as an important issue too. Thus, the main reason that respondents gave for questioning the reliability of a Website was that the source was felt to be unqualified (88%). Other reasons for questioning the reliability of information on a Website (in order of importance) was that the information had contradicted other information found on the net (87%), and that the Website had not referenced its sources

---

[8]British supermarket chain.

(81%). In the latter case, puzzlingly, only 49% of respondents said that they checked the source. Older respondents and respondents viewing more health Websites were more likely to do this.

3.6 Information Behavior Characteristic 6—Retrieval

The digital consumer is faced frontally with the problem of retrieval. It is an inescapable process of digital information consumption. For all but experienced researchers (a minority of users), this is the first time they have faced the dilemmas of precision vs. recall, of noise, and of deciding on the validity of sources. Information providers have to be aware of this and solve these problems in the same way as in the past when they have provided contents pages, indexes, and TV guides. The role of content is becoming inescapably linked, in the user's mind, with its ease or difficulty of retrieval, and this is often something quite outside the control of the original publisher. Content providers therefore should be moving beyond questions of "how accurate is this?" or "how readable" to "how visible is it?"

Of course, the Web is essentially a library of unorganized and unqualified information. Users generally sift through this information to find what they want using electronic agents (search engines). Among consumers there is almost a total delegation of trust to the search engine, which is invested in almost magical powers of retrieval. So powerful is the magic (and memory) that few people even ask how the search is conducted, what is being searched (and, more importantly, what is not), or even note down where they went. Of course, people bookmark, but there is anecdotal evidence to suggest that many find it easier to simply re-search than to pull down a list of pre-saved Websites. Arguably, this would not be too serious a problem if all people were doing was searching for references or e-shopping, but when it comes to health-related issues these are important considerations.

Typically, the user enters a search term (most often the first word that comes into their head associated with the topic) and is provided in return with a (long) list of links to documents that the agent recognizes as matching their search query. In the health and publishing fields, the documents that are being used as a result of using search agents. We have obtained this information from server transactional log files. We are only just beginning to discover how successful users' search terms are in yielding relevant documents. In order to determine the search success of very large digital information consumers, we have developed two success or outcome metrics related to the search process: the lapse of time following the entry of a search term and the number of different searches made by the user on the same topic.

Repeated searches may indicate the fact that a user has not found all that they wanted the first time around while a lapse of time following a search might indicate either reading or surfing of links on the part of the searcher. The key findings to date are: the number of queries used in a search session was 1.9; people used 2.1 words to describe their search query; and those using more than one word in their search term were about three and half times more likely to repeat their searches than those using a single word. It is still early in our research but it points to fragile searching, with possible ramifications for the rollout of life-dependent services to the general public.

4. DISCUSSION

We have identified what we believe to be fundamental changes in information behavior as a result of both the moving of increasingly large and varying kinds of information into the digital environment, resulting in a juxtaposition of this information in that environment. These changes have led to new forms of behavior and we have identified and labeled these forms of behavior, most notably "bouncing" and "promiscuity". We have also identified a key behavioral "driver", digital visibility. We have highlighted research methods that provide the big picture data required for investigation of HIB.

Today's information consumer in information behavior terms tends to be a "flicker" or a "bouncer". Just as people use the remote to channel hop, so do they use the Web to information hop or bounce their way across the digital information terrain that is the Internet. We need to be careful as to how we interpret this. In this one is reminded of the father, who, upon watching his young daughter use the remote to surf from one television channel to another, is irritated, and asks his daughter why she cannot make up her mind as to which channel she wants to watch. To which she answers that she is not attempting to make up her mind but is actually watching all the channels. Most of us are "surfers". We can surf only when we have a lot of choices. Digital consumers are also far less loyal and predictable than the users who once inhabited the libraries of the 1980s and 1990s. This is as true of academics as it is true of digital information consumers anywhere. If nothing else, the digital consumer is also unpredictable and volatile.

Let us now try and explain the kind of information behavior that we have mapped. As we have already suggested, what we are seeing is probably what happens when people are presented with massive and increasing choice, wherein they have to make decisions by themselves. The traditional library-driven user of the not-so-distant past relied on the library for their choice, and limited though it was, it had the stamp of quality or authority. The assumption was that if it was in the library it was good and, anyway, the choice was largely already made for the user because an intermediary conducted the search. On the other hand, today, most people search for themselves and search from non-library or non-evaluated information environments, most obviously seen in the health field.

As a consequence, they are forced to make the kind of evaluations once made by informed librarians, and with so much choice and with new products joining the stream constantly, they have to make an increasing number of evaluations all the time. They do this largely with the help of a search engine, on the basis of long experience with searching the Web, and the practice in making constant comparisons through a process of trial and error. The phrase "we are all librarians now" is said to reflect the situation we are in, or does it? Perhaps, it would be more accurate to say that none of us are librarians now—we have lost the need to index, to store, and to catalog. Even using an Internet "Favorites" file is too much for many people, who prefer to simply search and search again, even when they are looking for material on the same subject. As another of our interviewee respondents said *"you never know what will be out there next time!"*

There is a sense also that what we are observing in our logs is people playing with information enjoying the interaction with the data (Nicholas & Dobrowolski, 2000). Google gives people not only information but also the pleasure of information seeking. There is powerful evidence from our investigations that HIB has become far more horizontal, that is, instead of going for depth, users are now happy to spread their search out, and to grab what they can from a wide variety of sources and services.

Information professionals viewing such behavior should not be misled into believing that all of what we witness from logs and questionnaires is a dumbed down form of information searching and retrieval; that people cannot make up their minds and they have short attention spans and memories, and that as a consequence they are obtaining just a thin veneer of information. This is of course true for some but for others it is just a different form of behavior and the advantage of it is the amount of exposure they get to information sources and on the numerous occasions when they have to determine what they want. There is nothing better than juxtaposition to do this. The single authoritative source, which is always returned to and deeply mined, seems to be a thing of the past. Loyalty also might be a thing of the past.

As a consequence, not only do we need to challenge our assumptions about the information behavior of the user–consumer, but we also need to ask where digital information, and especially the World Wide Web, is taking them, for after all, many spend a lot of time on the Internet. Consumers are being fast-forwarded to a data-driven world, in which the only thing that changes is the amount of information made available to them and the platforms on which this information is disseminated. Loads of links, endless links, thousands of postings characterize this journey, an endless information journey with seemingly no destination. Consumers do not even remember where they went on their journey or if they will retain any of the information, nor how they can get return to it. Intuitively we all know this has happened, for after all, we are digital consumers ourselves, but until relatively recently we have not had the data to confirm it.

5. CONCLUSION

Our findings in this respect raise a concern over knowledge building. The real problem is that the (false) sense of engagement and action associated with online searching/surfing makes the consumer feel that something is being achieved, while this may not always be the case. People tend to want fast knowledge and not just fast access to information.

Our chapter plainly addresses the wider issue of information behavior and provides data which provide full justification for the employment of the term human information-seeking behavior, not just because we have captured a wide range of users on a number of different platforms, but most importantly because we have examined a wide range of consumer activities. In recognition of this we have also introduced our own term, *the digital information consumer*, and studying this digital information consumer is an important and much needed new direction in HIB studies.

References

Nicholas, D., & Dobrowolski, T. (2000). The information player: A new concept for the internet user. In A. Scammell (Ed.), *Handbook of Special Librarianship and Information Work*. Aslib: London.

Nicholas, D., & Huntington, P. (2000). Evaluating the use of newspaper website logs. *The International Journal on Media Management*, 12(3), 7–15.

Nicholas, D., & Huntington, P. (2003). Micro-mining and segmented log file analysis: A method for enriching the data yield from internet log files. *Journal of Information Science*, 29(5), 391–404.

Nicholas, D., Huntington, P., Hamid, R., Jamali, M., & Watkinson, A. (2005). The users of digital scholarly journals and their information seeking behavior: What usage data and deep log analysis can disclose. *Journal of the American Society for Information Science and Technology*.

Nicholas, D., Huntington, P., Rowlands, I., Russell, B., & Cousins, J. (2003a). Opening the digital box: What deep log analysis can tell us about our digital journal users. *Charleston 2003 Conference Proceedings*, Charleston, SC.

Nicholas, D., Huntington, P., & Watkinson, A. (2002). Digital journals, big deals and online searching behavior: A pilot study. *Aslib Proceedings*, 55(1/2), 84–109.

Nicholas, D., Huntington, P., & Williams, P. (2002). Evaluating metrics for comparing the use of websites: Case study two consumer health websites. *Journal of Information Science*, 28(1), 63–75.

Nicholas, D., Huntington, P., & Williams, P. (2003). Perceptions of the authority of health information: Case study digital interactive television and the internet. *Health information and Libraries Journal*, 20, 215–224.

Nicholas, D., Huntington, P., & Williams, P. (2004). *Digital Consumer Health Information and Advisory Services in the UK: A User Evaluation and Sourcebook*. London: City University/DoH (available http://www.ucl.ac.uk/ciber).

Nicholas, D., Huntington, P., Williams, P., & Dobrowolski, T. (2000–2004). *The Web, the Kiosk, Digital TV and the Changing and Evolving Face of Consumer Health Information Provision: A National Impact Study.* Funded by Department of Health.

Nicholas, D., Huntington, P., Williams, P., & Dobrowolski, T. (2003–2004).*The Virtual Scholar Research Programme—Use and Impact of Digital Libraries in Academe.* Research Study Funded by Blackwell/Emerald/Elsevier.

Nicholas, D., Huntington, P., Williams, P., & Dobrowolski, T. (2004–2005). *Users of the BBC Website*. Funded by the Department of Health.

Nicholas, D., Huntington, P., Williams, P., & Gunter, B. (2002). Digital visibility: Menu prominence and its impact on use of the NHS direct information channel on kingston interactive television. *Aslib Proceedings*, 54(4), 213–221.

Nicholas, D., Huntington, P., Williams, P., & Gunter, B. (2003b). Broadband nursing: An appraisal of pilot interactive consumer health services: Case study in-vision. *Journal of Documentation*, 59(3), 341–358.

Spink, A., & Cole, C. (in press). Human information behavior: Integrating diverse approaches and information use. *Journal of the American Society for Information Science and Technology*.

Spink, A., & Jansen, B. J. (2004). *Web Search: Public Searching of the Web*. Dordrecht: Kluwer.

Williams, P., Huntington, P., & Nicholas, D. (2003). Health information on the internet: A qualitative study of NHS direct online users. *Aslib Proceedings*, 55(5/6), 304–312.

SECTION 5

Integrating Framework and Further Research

Chapter 12

Integrations and Further Research

Amanda Spink
University of Pittsburgh

Charles Cole
McGill University

1. INTRODUCTION

Human information behavior (HIB) is a basic human condition within the framework of the social sciences. The human information condition is also a mosaic of information behaviors. Placing yourself in a location where information is exchanged is an information behavior, and the way the location is arranged, in itself organizes information transfer, is another information behavior (Fisher & Naumer; Chapter 6). A government written book setting-out procedures regulates information behavior directing the conversation between a midwife and an expectant mother (McKenzie, 2005; Chapter 5). In the Upper Paleolithic Era 10,000–70,000 years ago, drawing the movement of herds of animals on cave walls to organize what you have seen is an information behavior, producing strategies for the hunt (Spink & Currier, 2005; Chapter 2).

Likewise, organizing information on the condition of roads on a map is an information behavior which determined Napoleon's military strategy (Spink & Currier, 2005; Chapter 2). Myths, religion, etc., important components of the oral tradition of the aboriginal communities of Australia, giving significance to certain trees where ancestral spears were placed, and to the deposits of red ochre where their ancestors bled helps present-day communities remember enormous quantities of geographic information—another information behavior (Madden, Palimi, & Bryson, 2005; Chapter 3). The complex information mosaic continues to build. How do we integrate the mosaic of HIB into a framework or model that will help people to understand their own information behaviors?

2. INTEGRATED HIB FRAMEWORK

This section provides an initial integrated framework for HIB based on the new directions discussed in the various chapters in this book. The chapters have been grouped into three sections: (1) the evolutionary and social framework approaches, (2) the spatial and collaborative framework approaches, and (3) the multitasking, non-linear, organizing, and digital framework approaches. We begin the process of conceptualizing these diverse

A. Spink and C. Cole (eds), New Directions in Human Information Behavior, 231–237.
© 2006 *Springer.*

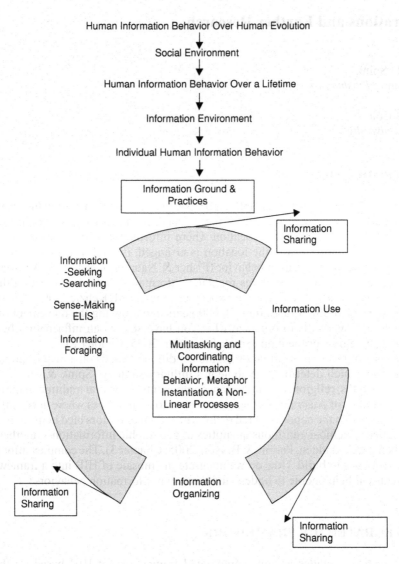

Figure 1. Integrated HIB framework.

framework approaches and the various aspects or elements of these approaches, within an integrated HIB framework and model.

Figure 1 provides an initial integrating framework of the various approaches discussed in each chapter of this book.

Figure 1 builds upon the model developed by Spink, Park, and Cole (2005) in Chapter 8 of this book—*Multitasking and Co-ordinating Framework for Human Information Behavior*. The constitutive elements of the Figure 1 are divided into two parts. The top part places HIB in the broad frame of human development, including HIB over the course of human evolution, and the social environment of people given our biological and psychological makeup. The model extends further to include HIB over a human lifetime, which takes place inside some information environment. The top part of the model ends in the individual's HIB, and the spatial information ground and practices he or she comes into contact with during that lifetime.

The bottom part of the framework, on the left-hand side of Figure 1, summarizes the attributes of the diverse approaches to HIB, including the *problem solving/seeking, ELIS/sense-making*, and *information foraging* approaches. Each diverse approach highlights different processes of HIB (Spink & Cole, in press). These include multitasking and co-ordinating processes, the metaphor instantiation process, and other non-linear processes, including information sharing, organizing, and information use.

The *problem solving/seeking* approach has traditionally focused more on examining what cognitive/social issues initiate an information seeking process within an individual (Spink & Cole, in press). For the problem solving/information seeking approach, information seeking is purposive. The goal state is the resolution of the problem or cognitive state.

The e*veryday life information seeking/sense-making* approach has focused more on understanding how humans make sense of the discontinuity of human existence during an HIB process. ELIS is a combination of non-purposive and purposive information behavior (Spink & Cole, in press). The goal state in ELIS is mastery of life, the small moment when we say to ourselves "I know what I am doing".

The *information foraging* approach views HIB from an evolutionary perspective for the total foraging environment, but empirical research thus far has focused on foraging during human–computer interaction (Spink & Cole, in press). (The foraging approach offers a potentially exciting new direction in HIB research, providing a nexus between HIB and a diverse group of social science theories and models.) For the information foraging approach, information searching is based on hard-wired strategies and tactics, and input and output involve the same unchanging, hard-wired knowledge. The start state involves patches, clues, and internal and external decision states. The process is an interaction between the person and their environment that includes the concepts of cues and diet enrichment. The goal state is a stable state, which maximizes gains of valuable information per unit cost.

The preliminary associations in Figure 1 provide an initial attempt to conceptualize the various information dimensions/behaviors, approaches, and processes within an integrated framework. Problem solving/information seeking has been the dominant information behavior approach for LIS. It has served LIS well, allowing us to examine, theorize, and otherwise explain highly deliberate information seeking among mostly educated user groups. However, problem solving and the information seeking perspective attached to problem solving is one perspective among many, one that emphasizes a specific aspect of information behavior. The integration of the principles and issues that have arisen from recent advances in evolutionary psychology and ELIS widens the current LIS information behavior paradigm beyond traditional information seeking, to the point where we can place the HIBs of information seeking and searching, ELIS, information foraging, organizing and use, as well as information sharing, information grounds, and social practices, into juxtaposition with each other. We propose that certain processes, such as multitasking/coordinating, metaphor instantiation, which suggests sudden shifts of data from one human intelligence module to another to facilitate human pick-up and processing of unfamiliar environment stimuli, as well as other non-linear processes, are part of all these approaches and HIBs.

An integrated HIB framework also enhances the development of a pre-historical HIB framework, one that operates as a constant throughout the history of human–information interaction. The most important implication of the integration of the evolutionary perspective, however, is the elevation in status of information need from a secondary to a fundamental human need, due to the primacy evolutionary psychology gives to information foraging for human adaptation and survival. Humans may exhibit characteristics that include at times seeking and at other times foraging or sense-making. Our approach is not to discount any approach, but to attempt an initial integration and give new direction to a more holistic HIB framework.

3. FURTHER RESEARCH

The chapters in this book have identified areas of further research for HIB scholars.

3.1 Evolutionary HIB Framework

HIB is the study of the human information condition within a social science framework. The goal is a greater understanding of the human information condition. Therefore, the development of an evolutionary framework, in line with general moves within the broader social sciences, is essential and already underway. The chapters by Spink and Cole, and Madden, Palimi, and Bryson highlight the emerging area of evolutionary HIB as a crucial area of further research. Recent papers by Spink and Cole (2002), and Spink and Currier (2005, in press) also provide an initial framework and chronology of HIB studies from an evolutionary perspective.

The research field of HIB needs to recast the framework of our understanding of the human information condition. Further, theoretical and empirical studies are needed and are crucial to more fully develop the evolutionary understanding of HIB. Key to this development will be an explication of how human evolutionary theories apply to the development of HIB over the millennia. Such research, using the concept of information as a methodology, will cast light on how people interact with their environment, including their social environment, in order to adapt and survive.

3.2 HIB Over a Lifetime

Currently, we lack models that plot the evolving patterns of HIB development over a human lifetime from birth to death. How are HIBs learned? Or are they genetically determined? The old nature versus nurture argument applies. HIB studies have not been longitudinal to the degree that we can observe the process. We have many studies of adults and an increasing number about children, but the data are disparate and unclear. As a social science, HIB research needs to recast its framework toward more longitudinal and lifetime modeling studies. This also requires a more holistic view of HIB, including a more fully developed mosaic of information behaviors. Such studies would have to not just track the evolution of processes delineated by the human information seeking/sense-making/foraging approaches, but also include the evolution of human information organizing and use process development. This is an area of great research potential, the results of which will also help people understand more about their own information behavior.

3.3 Social Aspects of HIB

To recast the field of HIB—enriching it in a social sciences framework—for research examining contemporary behaviors means a greater understanding of the social dimensions of HIB. Much of the HIB research has been based in a cognitive level (e.g., Cole & Leide, 2005; Chapter 10 in this volume), which has left relatively underdeveloped a more organizational and social HIB theoretical level. Two chapters have highlighted the importance of developing a greater understanding of the social aspects of HIB. In their chapter, Hargittai and Hinnant highlight the need to further develop an understanding of the social aspects of HIB. Talja and Hansen (2005) also point to the importance of information sharing, collaboration, and a social approach as a fundamental aspect of HIB. Further research is needed that explores the organizational and social HIB framework, but also juxtaposes the relationship between the levels (i.e., how one level affects another).

3.4 Spatial Aspects of HIB

The study of contemporary information behavior is increasingly taking into account the spatial dimension of HIB. By spatial is meant that humans move through physical dimensions and processes during their information behavior. The cognitive and physical dimensions are related and need to be further explored. Various chapters have highlighted the importance of the spatial aspects of HIB. The chapters on concepts of information ground by Fisher and Naumer and information practices by McKenzie are key to this development.

3.5 Non-linear, Multitasking, and Co-ordinating Aspects of HIB

In this book, chapters by Spink, Park, and Cole, and also by Foster highlight new non-linear HIB research directions. The major focus of HIB research, particularly within an LIS perspective, has been at the cognitive level. Approaches have been drawn from psychology and other social sciences to develop the problem solving/information seeking, sense-making/ELIS, and information foraging approaches. Within these approaches, a new cognitive level of HIB understanding can be reached through the development of non-linear and multitasking process perspectives. This level of HIB understanding has been missing until recently but is now being developed. The key to future research from this perspective is the further explication of HIB as an overall theory that involves processes common to all approaches and information behaviors, such as the switches and changes processes co-ordinating the HIB of multitasking. How much these processes are universal across humans in the mosaic of HIB is a research question for review.

3.6 Human Information Organizing Behavior

In Chapter 10, Cole and Leide begin the exploration of human information organizing behavior (HIOB). The evolutionary psychology notion that humans can see one thing as something else has contributed to our ability to adapt to our environment and survive can be used to explain day-to-day human adaptive behavior. The cognitive architecture of human intelligence may be modular, building in a metaphorical perspective to the way humans react to the world through information inputs. Metaphor instantiation, involving the shifting of data and memory organization structures (e.g., category structures) from one intelligence module to another to facilitate the pick-up and processing of unfamiliar environmental information stimuli, is but one part of HIOB. Issues that need to be further explored will involve modeling and extending our understanding of HIOB, and examining how HIOB operates in conjunction with other aspects of HIB. In this regard, the link between HIOB and the co-ordinating and switching processes involved in multitasking is an area of immediate interest.

3.7 Digital/Information Retrieval Approach

In Chapter 11, Nicholas, Huntington, Williams, and Dobrowolski explore the nature of the digital consumer. Further research is needed to more fully develop our understanding of human interaction with technology during HIB processes. Information retrieval interaction and HIB are intertwined. These issues are being addressed in the forthcoming book by Spink and Cole (2005)—*New Directions in Cognitive Information Retrieval*—published by Springer.

3.8 Integrated HIB Framework

A major area for further research is the development of a more integrated framework for understanding HIB. Presently, HIB research is fractured and devoid of holistic approaches. Chapter 12 of this book and a forthcoming paper by Spink and Cole (in press), and Spink and Currier (2005, in press) are working toward a more holistic and integrated framework, including aspects of information seeking/sense-making/foraging, organizing and use.

4. CONCLUSION

This book provides a new framework for understanding the human information condition within the human condition. HIB is a social science that is continuing to adapt its framework with the evolving human information condition. There is a need to further develop a more overarching understanding of HIB within an interdisciplinary environment. This book contributes to the process of widening the HIB perspective so that it includes various diverse approaches within the broader framework of social science theories and models. In line with evolutionary psychology, we place information at the center of human adaptation. This is a worthy start.

References

Cole, C., & Leide, J. E. (2005). Human information organizing behavior: A cognitive framework for human information behavior. In A. Spink & C. Cole (Eds.), *New Directions in Human Information Behavior*. Springer.

Fisher, K., & Naumer, C. M. Information ground. In A. Spink & C. Cole (Eds.), *New Directions in Human Information Behavior*. Springer.

Foster, A. (2005). Non-linear information seeking models. In A. Spink & C. Cole (Eds.), *New Directions in Human Information Behavior*. Springer.

Hargittai, E., & Hinnant, A. (2005). Toward a social framework for information seeking. In A. Spink & C. Cole (Eds.), *New Directions in Human Information Behavior*. Springer.

Madden, A., Bryson, J., & Palimi, J. (2005). Information seeking in pre-textual societies. In A. Spink & C. Cole (Eds.), *New Directions in Human Information Behavior*. Springer.

McKenzie, P. (2005). Information practices. In A. Spink & C. Cole (Eds.), *New Directions in Human Information Behavior*. Springer.

Nicholas, D., Huntington, P., Williams, P., & Dobrowolski, T. (2005). Digital information consumer. In A. Spink & C. Cole (Eds.), *New Directions in Human Information Behavior*. Springer.

Spink, A., & Cole, C. (in press). Human information behavior: Integrating diverse approaches and information use. Journal of the American Society for Information Science and Technology.

Spink, A., & Cole, C. (2001). Everyday life information seeking research. *Library and Information Science Research*, 23(4), 301–304.

Spink, A., & Cole, C. (2002). Towards an evolutionary understanding of everyday life information seeking. In *HBES 2002: Proceedings of the International Conference on Human Behavior and Evolution*, June 19–23, Rutgers University, New Brunswick, NJ.

Spink, A., & Cole, C. (2004). A human information behavior framework to the philosophy of information. *Library Trends*, 52(3), 373–380.

Spink, A., & Cole, C. (2005). *New Directions in Cognitive Information Retrieval*. Springer.

Spink, A., & Currier, J. (2005). Emerging evolutionary approach to human information behavior. In A. Spink & C. Cole (Eds.), *New Directions in Human Information Behavior*. Springer.

Spink, A., & Currier, J. (in press). Towards an evolutionary perspective on human information behavior: An exploratory study. *Journal of Documentation*.

Spink, A., Park, M., & Cole, C. (2005). Multitasking and coordinating framework for human information behavior. In A. Spink & C. Cole (Eds.), *New Directions in Human Information Behavior*. Springer.

Talja, S., & Hansen, P. (2005). Information sharing. In A. Spink & C. Cole (Eds.), *New Directions in Human Information Behavior*. Springer.

New Directions in Human Information Behavior

BIOGRAPHIES OF AUTHORS

Jared Bryson

Jared Bryson is currently undertaking graduate research at Brunel University's Centre for Intelligence and Security Studies. Before transitioning into the field of strategic intelligence, he spent more than a decade working in the heritage sector as an archeologist and museum educator. After taking a bachelor's degree in archeology from the University of Virginia's Department of Anthropology, he worked as a professional archeologist, excavating sites along the eastern seaboard of the United States for clients such as the National Park Service and the National Trust for Historic Preservation. He has excavated in Turkey on the upper Euphrates River exploring the emergence of urbanism in the region, as well as in Jordan examining the transition from Christian to Islamic society. He received a Master of Arts in museum education from the College of William and Mary and subsequently worked as a community archeologist and curator of education for the city of Alexandria, Virginia. This experience allowed him to join a research team at the Centre for the Public Library and Information in Society (CPLIS) in the University of Sheffield's Department of Information Studies. While there he produced several reports of national significance, which evaluated the social impact of museums, archives, and libraries throughout the United Kingdom.

Charles Cole

Charles Cole is a Research Associate at the Graduate School of Library and In- formation Studies, McGill University, Montreal, and an information design consultant (Colemining, Inc.). At McGill, he is currently participating in a three-year Social Sci- ence and Humanities Research Council (SSHRC) funded project. The project objective is to design Information Retrieval (IR) system interface devices for undergraduate social science students researching their course essays when they have just selected their es- say topic and are exploring the topic using an IR system. Findings have been published in the *Journal of the American Society for Information Science and Technology* (two forthcoming in 2005). The objective of the research is to produce a prototype interface for undergraduate history students researching their essay, in an exploring phase of their research; the interface will facilitate the students' interaction with representations of document organization schemes, enabling them to form effective queries to IR systems.

Charles Cole holds a B.A. (History–Geography) and M.L.I.S from McGill University, a Ph.D. from the University of Sheffield, and held a two-year SSHRC funded post-doctoral fellowship at Concordia University's Department of Communications. He has published over 30 refereed articles in such journals as the *Journal of the American Society for Information Science and Technology*, *Information Processing and Management*, *Library*

Trends, Library Quarterly, and *Library and Information Science Research.* Charles has co-edited (with Amanda Spink) two special topic journal issues: one on everyday life information seeking (IS) for *Library and Information Science Research,* and one on IS for the *Journal of the American Society for Information Science and Technology.*

James Currier

James "Kip" Currier is engaged full time preparing his doctoral dissertation proposal and working as a Teaching Assistant in the Department of Library and Information Science (DLIS) at the University of Pittsburgh, School of Information Sciences (SIS). His broad area of research concentration is Human Information Behavior (HIB). More specifically, James is looking holistically at the HIBs of several famous persons from past eras. In addition to co-authoring the emerging evolutionary perspective for HIB chapter in this book with Dr. Amanda Spink, James has co-written with Spink before in producing *Toward an Emerging Evolutionary Perspective of Human Information Behavior* (in press—*Journal of Documentation*). His other areas of research interest include information needs/behaviors of underserved populations, access to information, and information-related ethnographic studies.

James Currier holds a B.A. in Japanese (1985) from the University of Pittsburgh; a Juris Doctor (1988) from the University of Pittsburgh School of Law; and a Master of Library and Information Science (1996) from the University of Pittsburgh, School of Information Sciences. He has previously worked in public interest law and public library service/administration in California, New Mexico, Ohio, and Pennsylvania. James Currier is a native of Western Pennsylvania and resides in suburban Pittsburgh.

Tom Dobrowolski

Tom Dobrowolski was originally trained as a librarian at the University of Warsaw, and then spent one year at the Kent State University, Ohio. He worked for 20 years in the Warsaw University as Senior Lecturer at the Department of Library Science. At the department, Tom was responsible for postgraduate studies. He is now Senior Lecturer in the Information Science Department, while concentrating on consultancy studies for libraries and information services. Tom has published two books about the Internet in Polish and some articles in English (with David Nicholas of City University, London).

Karen Fisher

Dr. Karen E. Fisher (née Pettigrew) is an Associate Professor and Chair of the M.L.I.S Program at The Information School of the University of Washington where she teaches information behavior, qualitative research methods, community analysis, and outcome-based evaluation. Her B.A. (English and Russian, 1989) is from Memorial University of Newfoundland, and her M.L.I.S. (1991) and Ph.D. in Library and Information Science (1998) from the University of Western Ontario. Karen's research addresses information behavior in everyday contexts (IBEC). The author of over 50 articles and books, her current research is funded by the National Science Foundation and the Institute of Museum and Library Services. Karen's most recent books include: *Theories of Information Behavior* (2005; co-edited with S. Erdelez and E. F. McKechnie) and

How Libraries and Librarians Help: A Guide to Identifying User-Centered Outcomes (2005; co-authored with J. C. Durrance). Her latest research addresses why people turn to other people for everyday information. For more information about Dr. Fisher, visit ibec.ischool.washington.edu.

Allen Foster

Dr. Allen Foster took up post as Lecturer with the Department of Information Studies, University of Wales, Aberystwyth in 2002. He lectures in information literacy, information retrieval, and research methods. Allen holds three degrees awarded by the University of Sheffield, UK: B.A. (Hons.) in Social History (1994), an M.Sc. Information Management (1996), and a Ph.D. (Foster, 2003). Formal qualifications were matched by research experience gained as a Research Associate and include work on computer-mediated communication and information seeking (IS) behavior in the "Uncertainty in Information Seeking" project (Wilson et al., 1999). These provided a foundation for further research embracing a number of key areas of IS including serendipity (Foster & Ford, 2003), and an exploration of IS behavior leading to development of a new perspective (Foster, 2004). Allen's recent research interests have begun to develop the non-linear model further, and particularly work exploring the implications of the non-linear perspective as a tool for understanding human information behavior.

Foster, A. E. (2003). *Interdisciplinary Information Seeking Behaviour: A Naturalistic Inquiry*, unpublished Ph.D. Thesis, University of Sheffield, UK.
Foster, A. E., & Ford, N. J. (2003). Serendipity and Information Seeking: An Empirical Study. *Journal of Documentation, 59*(3), 321–340.
Foster, A. E. (2004). A Nonlinear Model of Information Seeking Behaviour. *Journal of the American Society for Information Science and Technology, 55*(3), 228–237.
Wilson, T. D., Ellis, D., Ford, N., & Foster, A. E. (1999). *Uncertainty in Information Seeking: Final Report to the British Library Research and Innovation Centre/Library and Information Commission on a Research Project Carried Out at the Department of Information Studies*, University of Sheffield, Grant number LIC/RE/019.

Preben Hansen

Preben Hansen is a senior researcher at the Swedish Institute of Computer Science (SICS), a non-profit research institute. The research at SICS, both theoretical and applied, is carried out in close collaboration with industry and the international research community. Preben Hansen works specifically with research questions within the area of Information Seeking (IS) and Information Retrieval (IR) from a broader perspective. This includes theoretical models of IS and IR processes as well as empirical studies of users and use of interactive information access systems as well as research on information searching in mobile and collaborative environments. He investigates situation-, context-, and task-specific factors in IS&R and engage in developing methods and techniques for analysis and evaluation in different contextual and situational environments. These factors will have impact on the different aspects of the design process. Currently, he is investigating the effects of collaborative IS and retrieval in information-intensive and mobile environments.

Preben Hansen participate in both national and international projects, for example EU-projects such as: DELOS Network of Excellence (IST-2004); CLARITY (IST 2000-25310), DUMAS (IST-2000-29452), SCHOLNET (IST-1999-20664), and DELOS-NoE (IST-1999-12262), focusing on Interactive IR, UI design, and user and usage evaluation. He also participated in Swedish project cooperating with small and large companies. Preben have also been at the program committee at large conferences such as SIGIR, ECDL, and CoLIS. Preben has also served as a reviewer for the U.S. NSF initiative (2002). Finally, he has acted as invited lecturer at both LIS Schools and at business seminars.

Eszter Hargittai

Eszter Hargittai is an Assistant Professor of Communication Studies and Sociology, and is Faculty Fellow of the Institute for Policy Research at Northwestern University. She received her Ph.D. in Sociology from Princeton University where she was a Graduate Fellow of the Fellowship of Woodrow Wilson Scholars. Her main research interests are the social and policy implications of information technologies with a particular focus on how IT may contribute to or alleviate social inequalities. Much of Eszter's work has looked at differences in people's Web-use skills and digital literacy. In particular, she studies people's information-seeking behavior and has also been following the evolution of search engines and the organization and presentation of online content. Additional research interests include the political uses of information technologies and how IT influences the types of cultural products people consume.

Amanda Hinnant

Amanda Hinnant is a doctoral student in the Media, Technology, and Society program at Northwestern University. She has a background in magazine journalism and holds a Master's degree from the Missouri School of Journalism. Her research interests include health information seeking and mass-mediated medical reporting.

Paul Huntington

Paul Huntington is a Research Fellow in the School of Library, Archive and Information Studies and is a founder member of the Internet Studies Research Group and CIBER. Previously Paul has worked as a researcher at City University, the University of North London, and the University of Hertfordshire. He has undertaken extensive research into the social, behavioral, and economic impact of the availability of digital information in areas such as health, newspapers, and educational journals. His special research interest is the analysis of Server transactional log files and has analyzed log files across a variety of platforms, including the Internet, Digital Interactive Television, mobile phones, and touch screen kiosks. Further Paul has linked additional datasets, including questionnaire date, to transactional log data. Paul has pioneered techniques for the analysis and understanding of transactional log files and has been instrumental in the development of concepts and metrics related to search and online user behavior. While at UCL and City University, he has worked on number of major research projects, including for the Department of Health, The Times Newspaper Group, The Independent, Emerald publishers, Blackwell publishers, and NHS Direct online. Paul has a degree in Economics, is studying for a Ph.D., and has a strong publishing record of over 80 published journal articles.

John E. Leide

John E. Leide is an Associate Professor in McGill University's Graduate School of Library and Information Studies. He obtained a B.S. (mathematics–humanities) from the Massachusetts Institute of Technology, an M.S. (Library Science) from the University of Wisconsin (Madison) and a Ph.D. (Library Service) from Rutgers University. At the Graduate School of Library and Information Studies, John teaches organization of information, classification and cataloging, systems thinking, and abstracting and indexing. John's current research interests are integrating classification visualization devices for undergraduate users of information retrieval (IR) systems, and bilingual thesaurus development in gerontology and geriatrics.

John Leide is currently Principal Investigator of a three-year Social Science and Humanities Research Council funded project, the objective of which is to design IR system interface devices for undergraduate social science students researching their course essays when they have just selected their essay topic and are exploring the topic using an IR system. Findings have been published in the *Journal of the American Society for Information Science and Technology* (two forthcoming in 2005). The objective of the research is to produce a prototype interface for undergraduate history students researching their essay, in an exploring phase of their research; the interface will facilitate the students' interaction with representations of document organization schemes, enabling them to form effective queries to IR systems.

Andrew Madden

Andrew Madden is currently working as a Research Associate in the Department of Information Studies at the University of Sheffield. He has just completed a project looking at various aspects of Internet use by schoolchildren. Andrew Madden has a B.Sc. in Biology and Maths, a Ph.D. in Agricultural Botany, and an M.Sc. in Information Management. After a short spell in the agrochemical industry, he began working for the U.K. government's Natural Resources Institute as a research ecologist, and published several articles in agricultural journals. In 1995, he became involved in a project based at Aberdeen University to develop software for teaching students about land use and agricultural science. As a result of this experience, he developed an interest in the use of computers in education. From 1996 to 1998, he was employed at Sheffield Hallam University to research the impact of Computer Assisted Learning on teaching within the university. He stayed in Sheffield to take the Masters in Information Studies at Sheffield University (1999), and then moved to London, where he worked for two years to set up and run a Library/Learning Center at a secondary (11–18) school in Camden. In 2001, he returned to University of Sheffield where he resumed to his research career.

Pamela McKenzie

Pamela McKenzie is an Assistant Professor in the Faculty of Information and Media Studies at The University of Western Ontario. Her major research focus is on information needs, seeking, and use. She considers information behavior to be located within local and extra-local social practices, and is interested in the ways that information behavior is collaboratively constructed by individuals in local settings. Pamela's doctoral research analyzed the ways that individuals construct their information-seeking accounts to represent various kinds of information sources as authoritative, and the ways that they use these accounts to make claims about themselves. Her major current project, funded by the Social Sciences and Humanities Research Council of Canada, and on which this chapter is based, looks broadly at midwife–client communication, information seeking (IS) and information exchange within the setting of the clinical midwifery visit. Two smaller observation studies consider the uses of public libraries as sites for information behavior: McKechnie and McKenzie's American Library Association Baber Award—funded study of story times for very young children and their caregivers, and a study of public library-hosted knitting circle whose primary author is M.L.I.S student Elena Prigoda. Through all of these projects, she seeks to develop a better understanding of the social uses of public library space, the everyday life IS of unpaid caregivers, and the workplace information behavior of the professionals who serve them.

Charles Naumer

Charles Naumer is currently a Ph.D. student in Information Science at the University of Washington's Information School and has a Masters degree in Public Policy from the Kennedy School of Government at Harvard University. His research interests are in how information and information systems are used to support decision-making of individuals in everyday contexts. Charles is especially interested in how these decision-making contexts may impact the formation of public policy and the implementation of public programs.

David Nicholas

David Nicholas is Chair of Library and Information Studies and Director of the School of Library, Archive and Information Studies, University College London. He is also Director of the research group, CIBER (Centre for Information Behaviour and the Evaluation of Research). David was previously Head, Department of Information Science, City University. His main research interests are the: impact of ICTs on strategic user groups; policy implications of digital environments; digital information consumers; digital health services; deep log analysis; and scholarly communication. David has undertaken more than two dozen funded research projects, the most recent of which are: *Maximising Library Investments in Digital Collections Through Better Data Gathering and Analyses*, Institute of Museum and Library Studies, 2005–2007; *Deep Log Analysis of Evaluation of Institute of Physics journals*, The Institute, 2005–2007; The Digital Health Consumers of the BBC website, Department of Health, 2004–2005. David has also been the author of more than 300 publications, including: *Assessing Information Needs: Tools and Techniques and Concepts for the Internet Age.* Aslib, 2000.

Joe Palimi

Joe Palimi is a Lecturer in the School of Business Administration at the University of Papua New Guinea. He is involved in the preparation of courses which, through the

University's Open Learning Colleges, are delivered throughout Papua New Guinea. Joe is currently researching the effect of financial report information on the governance of corporate entities, especially entities whose ownership and control are based on traditional egalitarian clans or tribes. Joe is a member of the Kope Tribe from the Western Highlands Province in the Central Highlands of Papua New Guinea. He has a B.A. from the University of Papua New Guinea, B.Bus from Deakin University, Australia, and an MBA from Sheffield University, U.K. He began his working life with the then "big six" Accounting Firm, Coopers & Lybrand, and qualified as a Certified Practicing Accountant in Papua New Guinea and Australia. He joined the University of Papua New Guinea after leaving the accounting profession.

Minsoo Park

Minsoo Park is a doctoral student and researcher assistant to Dr. Amanda Spink in the School of Information Sciences at the University of Pittsburgh. Minsoo holds a Master's degree in Library and Information Science from the School of Communication, Information, and Library Studies at Rutgers University. Her research interests include information retrieval (IR), human–computer interaction, user modeling, human information behavior, and individual differences and information systems. Minsoo holds a Master's degree in Library and Information Science from the School of Communication, Information, and Library Studies at Rutgers University. She has conducted studies in Web information seeking behavior, interactive IR, multitasking, and individual differences and user interfaces. MInsoo has published over 16 journal articles and conference.

Amanda Spink

Amanda Spink is Associate Professor at the School of Information Sciences at the University of Pittsburgh. She has a B.A. (Australian National University); Graduate Diploma of Librarianship (University of New South Wales); M.B.A. in Information Technology Management (Fordham University); and a Ph.D. in Information Science (Rutgers University). Amanda's research focuses on theoretical and applied studies of human information behavior (HIB) and interactive information retrieval (IR), including Web and digital libraries studies, and information science theory. The National Science Foundation, the American Library Association, Andrew R. Mellon Foundation, Amazon.com, NEC, IBM, Excite.com, AlltheWeb.com, AltaVista.com, FAST, and Lockheed Martin have sponsored her research. She currently has two large-scale research projects underway with the Web companies Vivisimo.com and InfoSpace, Inc.

Amanda has published over 220 journal articles, refereed conference papers and book chapters, with many in the *Journal of the American Society for Information Science and Technology, Information Processing and Management, Journal of Documentation, Library Trends, Interacting with Computers, IEEE Computer, International Journal of Information Management, Information Research, Online Information Review, Cyberpsychology and Behavior, Internet Research, the ASIST, IEEE ITCC, CAIS, Internet Computing, ACM SIGIR, and ISIC Conferences*. Her new book *Web Search: Public Searching of the Web,* published by Springer, is the first research monograph detailing human interaction with Web search engines. Amanda co-edited with Dr. Charles Cole (McGill University), the books *New Directions in Cognitive Information Retrieval* and *New Directions in Human Information Behavior*—Springer.

Sanna Talja

Sanna Talja is Senior Assistant Professor at the Department of Information Studies at the University of Tampere, Finland. She holds a Ph.D. in Information Science from the University of Tampere, and was awarded a docentship in 2003. Dr. Talja's work focuses on the interaction between new technologies and scholarly communities' information and collaboration practices. She is interested in theories, approaches, and empirical studies related to the use and shaping of ICTs in scholarly communities. Her teaching areas include social informatics, user-centered digital library design and evaluation, organizational learning, and knowledge management. Sanna's other research interests include epistemic issues within information science and discourse analysis. She has written and co-authored four books and contributed articles to a number of journals, including *Journal of the American Society for Information Science and Technology, Journal of Documentation, Information Processing and Management, Library and Information Science Research, Information Research,* and *The New Review of Information Behavior Research.*

Peter Williams

Peter obtained his M.Sc. in Information Science at City University in 1995, having come back to the United Kingdom from teaching English in various countries across the world. He stayed at City as a Research Fellow until his move to UCL in October 2004 when David Nicholas, the principal investigator on Peter's research projects, became Director of SLAIS, and brought the projects and staff with him. Peter has spent the last nine years investigating the use of the Internet and other ICT applications in the fields of health, and the news media. He is currently working on an ESRC (PACCIT) funded project developing ICT systems to help adolescents with severe learning disabilities, in their communication and self-advocacy skills. This project is being run jointly with UEL, UEA, and Mencap. Peter has just completed a Department of Health funded project examining the use of digital TV and satellite to PC delivery of Continuous Professional Development training for NHS staff. In addition to this education-related project, and his general interest in pedagogy, he is also interested in health information for the general public, and in the use and usability of electronic information systems. Peter is currently on the NICE new media users' panel and on the editorial board of *Aslib Proceedings.*

Index

Aboriginal, 20
Aboriginal Australians, 18, 22, 231
Aborigines, 22
abstraction, 21, 61
activities
  asynchronous, 122
  coordinated, 122
  differentiated, 122
  loosely, 122
  synchronous, 122
  tightly coupled, 122
actual online skill, 66
ad hoc categories, 8, 175, 176, 178, 195, 197, 198
ad hoc category formation, 176
Aeneas Tacticus, 24
Alexander the Great, 23–27
ancient art, 22
ancient Bradshaw-like human figures, 18
Ancient Greeks, 23
ancient humans, 20, 22
animal foraging behavior, 49
Answer Gardens, 122
apes, 6, 17
Aristotle, 26
art of tracking, 38
audiorecordings, 89
Australian prospectors, 34
autobiographies, 27
autonomy of use, 59, 60, 64, 65
  degrees of, 60

bands, 34
barbarism, 47
Barkow, J., 15, 16
Breuil, H., 17
Bronze Age, early, 43

capital-enhancing, 60, 65
  websites, 60
care providers, 73, 81, 82, 84, 86, 89
category activation or instantiation, 176, 177
cave paintings, 4, 19–22
  Upper Paleolithic Era, 22

changes in behavior, 209
chaos theory, 155
Cheuk's model, 156, 161, 162
Christianity, 42
collaborative information behavior (CIB), 7, 114,
    116–126, 129, 130
  definitional issues in, 114
  dimensions, 114, 123, 124
  embeddedness in social practices, 125
  everyday life context, 121
  in academic settings, 118
  in library context, 118
  professional settings, 119
  research, 114, 116, 117, 129
    issues and questions, 114
    theoretical grounding, 114
  studies, 117, 118, 125, 126
    social practice approach, 123
CIBER website, 209
classic information seeking models, 114
Classical Greece, 25, 27
  8th-2nd century B.C., 18, 23
  collection and transmission, 24
  information gathering in, 24
clinical care, 73
  role of documents, 73
clinical context, 76, 77
clinical images, 87
clinical midwifery
  care, 6, 73, 74
  visits, 75
    extra-local participants in, 74
clinical settings, studies of documents, 73
Cochrane database, 119
cognitive approaches, 156, 159, 162, 165
  flexible and adaptable, 159
  holistic, 159
  in LIS, 175
  multiple user, 8
  nomadic, 159
  openness, 159
cognitive archeology, 16
cognitive psychology, 16

collaborations, 6, 7, 113–116, 118, 120–123, 126,
    127, 129
  co-located, 122
  contented, 120
  direct, 122
  indirect, 122
  intergroup, 122, 123
  intragroup, 122, 123
  planned, 122
  remote, 122
  unplanned, 122
collaborative data mining, 114
collaborative information activities, 114,
    116
  document-based, 114
  human related, 114
collaborative information searching, empirical
    studies, 118
collaborative information seeking and retrieval
    (CIS&R), 114–117, 119, 123
  practices, 119
    strategic, 119
    paradigmatic, 119
    directive, 119
    social, 119
  research, 116, 117
communication, 4, 49, 51, 60, 75, 83, 85, 107,
    117, 120–122, 126, 127, 149, 160, 167,
    194, 197
  asynchronous, 122
  computer-mediated, 62, 122
  inter-generational, 38
  interpersonal, 80, 84, 108, 118
  intra-generational, 38
  personal, 119
  synchronous, 122
  tasks, 145–148
communities of practice (CoP), 127, 128
Computer Supported Cooperative Work (CSCW),
    117, 119
  studies, 117
conceptual framework, 56, 62, 66, 74, 189
consciousness, 41, 43
  post-literate, 45
  pre-literate, 45
consolidation, 156, 158, 163, 166, 180
consulting, 113, 122, 144
contested collaboration, 120
co-ordination theory, 149, 150
cross-boundary communication, 193

cultural transmission, 40
  through signs, 41
  unreliability of, 42
  writing and, 43

Darwin, C., 18, 27
data collection, 6, 16, 56, 63, 65, 75, 76, 117,
    144
databases, 113, 146, 174, 182–184
DataStar, 206, 211
decoding, 174, 176, 177, 181
defining tribal identity, through history and
    mythology, 35
desk-top videoconferencing, 114
Dewey Decimal Classification System, 141, 171
Dialog, 206, 221
diaries, 27
digital divide literature, 5, 56
digital fingerprints, 203
digital HIB, 204
digital information consumer, 8, 9, 203, 209, 210,
    217, 221, 225–227
digital interactive television, 9, 203, 209, 232
digital literacy, 64
  programs, 196
dimensions of social practices, 125
document selection, criteria, 119
Down's syndrome, 87, 88

early man, 17
Easter Island's moai rock, 20
eclecticism, 156, 157, 165
elaboration, 180
elderly, 37, 58, 96, 203, 205
  care of, 40
  role as repositories of public knowledge, 41
Everyday Life Information Seeking (ELIS), 14,
    33, 39, 50, 57, 106, 113, 122, 138, 166,
    171, 232, 233, 240
  approach, 61
  sense making, 139, 140, 233, 235
  studies, 121
Ellis' model, 114
e-mail, 48, 114, 122, 183, 184
encoding, 174, 176, 177
environmental scanning, 193
ERIC on CD-ROM, 205
European Information Seeking in Context (ISIC),
    93
everyday information on Internet, 97

everyday information seeking, 186
  principle of, 104
everyday life information behavior, individual, 60
evolution, 4, 13, 15–18, 24, 25, 27–29, 34, 57,
    162, 164, 175, 232, 233, 235
  of systems within species, 13
evolutionary biology, 13, 15, 16
evolutionary psychology, 16, 17, 140, 174, 233,
    234, 236

follow-up interview, 75, 85, 90, 121
foot clinic programs, 97–100
  in-depth qualitative studies, 100
Foster's Nonlinear Model of Information Seeking
    Behavior, 156, 159–162
  contextual interaction levels
    cognitive approaches, 156, 159
    external context, 156
    internal context, 156
  core processes
    consolidation, 156
    opening, 156
    orientation, 156
frequently asked questions (FAQ), 116, 122
Freud, S., 27
future behaviors, 17, 28

Google, 148, 183, 184, 204, 213, 226
graffiti, 14
Greece from the Dark Ages, 25
Gutenberg, J., 46

health websites, 212, 218
health care professionals, 88
Herodotus, 24–26
human information behavior (HIBs), 3, 4, 7, 13,
    17, 24, 28, 29, 33, 55, 113, 137, 138, 155,
    171, 203, 231–234
  cognitive framework, 8, 171
  collective aspects, 113
  co-ordinating aspects, 235
  co-ordinating framework, 7, 137, 149, 151
  current conceptual approaches, 14
  data analysis, 144
  data collection, 6, 56, 63, 65, 75, 76, 144
  digital, 204
  emerging evolutionary approach, 13, 28
  everyday life information seeking, 3, 14, 139,
      171, 233
  evolutionary interdisciplinary approaches, 14

exploratory case study, 143, 149
  framework, 137–140
  in-depth understanding, 59
  information foraging, 3, 14, 138, 140, 171
  information foraging level, 140
  information organizing behavior, 171
  information organizing level, 141
  information search, 171
  information searching level, 139
  information seeking, 171
  information seeking/problem-solving approach
      3
  information seeking/problem-solving level,
      138, 139
  information sense-making approach, 233, 235
  information sense-making/everyday life
      information-seeking level, 139
  information task interplay, 143, 147, 148
  information task switching, 143, 147–149
  information use, 8, 14, 21, 27, 56, 58, 120, 125,
      137, 138, 140, 171, 232, 233
  information use level, 140, 223
  information use/modular thinking level, 140
  integrated framework, 138, 140, 142, 231, 236
  multitasking aspects, 4, 149, 235
  multitasking behavior, 141, 236
    model, 143
    research, 151
    role of, 141
  multitasking framework, 137, 149
  multitasking information behavior, 142, 149
  multitasking information seeking, 162, 164
  non-information task interplay, 7, 137, 143,
      145, 150
  non-linear aspects, 235
  non-linear perspective, 8, 155, 156, 158–168
  processes, 8, 138, 142, 144, 150, 151, 156,
      158–162, 165–167, 176, 177, 233–236
  quality of measurements, 65
  research, 3, 14, 16, 28, 29, 33, 114, 117, 126,
      129, 139, 142, 150, 151, 168, 205,
      233–236
  understanding, 4, 13, 57–59, 63, 67, 160,
      234–236
    evolutionary approach, 28
    new direction, 114
  research, perspective, 29
  social aspects, 56, 235
  social aspects study, 56
  spatial aspects, 235

human information behavior, (HIBs) *(cont.)*
  study of social factors of, 66
  study participant, 144
  task frequency, 145, 146
  task switching, 7, 137, 141, 143–145, 147–150,
      161
  tasks interplay, 143, 145, 147, 148
  tasks types, 145
  theories, 4, 98, 125, 162, 164, 204, 234
  through IT, 55, 67
HIB-relevant studies, 18
human information-organizing behavior (HIOB),
      8, 141, 171–173, 175, 176, 179, 198, 236
  cognitive, 172
  cognitive, metaphor instantiation, 172
  cognitive framework, 197, 198
  metaphor in, 171
hobby-related information seeking, 122
holism, 162, 164, 165
Homer, 24
Homo sapiens, 17, 21, 174
human behavior, 13–17, 19, 21, 25, 28, 137
  evolution of, 15
human existence, 4, 13, 14, 17–19, 23, 28, 139,
      233
  chronology, 17
human information co-ordinating behavior
      (HICB), 142, 149, 150
  framework, 151
  sustaining process, 149, 150
humans, 1, 7, 8, 13–16, 19–22, 24, 28, 29, 33, 38,
      42, 51, 115, 126, 137, 139, 141, 149–151,
      173, 198, 233–236

Ice Age art, 19, 20
Industrial Age Era, 5, 18, 19, 27
informal documents
  electronic records, 74
  formal paper, 74
information behavior, 3–7, 14, 15, 21, 23–29, 55,
      57, 59, 60, 64, 73, 75, 77, 90, 93, 94, 96,
      98, 107, 108, 115, 120, 137–141, 143, 144,
      156, 160, 161, 163, 167, 168, 171, 185,
      197, 203–211, 213–214, 217, 219, 221,
      222, 225–227, 231, 233, 235 *see also*
      human information behavior
  associated with text, 35
  current models, 151
  definition, 14, 73
  ethnographic study, 73
  history of, 15

multitasking, 142, 143, 149–151, 161
  related research, 21
  research, 119, 121, 126
  studies, 162
  the digital consumer, 208
information exchange, 6, 39, 48, 75, 77, 80, 96,
      97, 101, 105, 107, 114, 120, 244
  groups, 118
information flow, 6, 24, 93, 97–99, 106, 194
information foraging, 3,14, 49, 50, 138, 140, 171,
      233–235
information gathering, 18, 19, 21, 23, 24, 118
information grounds, 6, 7, 93, 94, 96–108, 121,
      232, 233, 235
  campus, 103, 105
  church, 102, 103
  empirical findings, 93
  farm worker's medical clinic, 102
  food-oriented cloacles, 102
  garages, 102
  hair salons, 102
  Hispanic radiostation, 102
  research, 93
  school, 102
  students', 105
  theoretical basis, 93
  workplace, 101–103
Information Need Identification for Information
      Retrieval System (INIIReye System), 141,
      182
information organization, 8, 27, 141, 172–174,
      176, 177, 179, 198
information organizing, 8, 14, 21, 22, 27, 28, 137,
      138, 141, 174, 235
information practices, 73, 76, 113, 114, 116, 117,
      119, 121, 128, 129, 235
information presentation, 36
information preserving, 48
information roles, 5, 33, 37–39, 41, 45, 50
  and Internet, 48
information science, 3, 5, 16, 33, 34, 49–51, 56,
      62, 75, 137, 140, 155, 156, 160, 162, 168,
      185, 190, 205
  and writing, 49
  creation, 16
  literature, 33, 34
information searching, 7, 73, 118, 120, 122, 137,
      139, 140, 140, 145–149, 159, 171, 185,
      227–233
information seekers, 3, 6, 51, 90, 142, 150, 151,
      156, 158–161, 163–166, 168, 205

information seeking, 3, 5, 6, 8, 13, 14, 21, 22, 25,
    27, 28, 50, 55–62, 64, 65, 89, 93, 104, 106,
    113, 114, 119, 120, 122, 123, 125, 127,
    128, 137–140, 143, 145, 147, 151,
    157–167, 168, 171, 185, 186, 198, 205,
    206, 212, 226, 232, 233, 235, 236
  approach, 3, 14
  behavior, 27, 28, 49, 55, 58–63, 114–118, 122,
    138, 142, 150, 155, 157, 160–163, 165,
    171, 203, 213
  definition, 14
  models, classic, 114
  models, 126
  models, habits, 104
  models, paradigm, 181
  models, strategies, 160
  non-linear perspective, 155
  purposive, 14
  research of, 57, 113, 117, 125, 126, 143
  social framework, 55
  theories, 113, 121
  using computers, 59
information sharing, 7, 93, 96, 98, 99, 107, 108,
    113, 114, 191–194, 197, 232, 233, 235
information skill, 165–167
  training, 162, 165
information studies
  macro, 39
  micro, 39
information technologies (IT), 50, 55–60, 64–67,
    114, 116, 126, 129
information tools and systems, 27, 113
information use, 5, 14, 21, 22, 27, 35, 49, 56, 58,
    120, 125, 137–141, 171, 232, 233
information
  abundance of, 104
  accessibility of, 55, 104
  availability, 55, 224
  nature of, 104
  reliability of, 104
  systematic arrangement, 28
  unanticipated, 104
  valuable, 50, 100, 140, 233
information-seeking behavior, in-depth
    understanding, 63
initiation, 36, 39, 115, 120, 161
institutional ethnography, 73
  method, 75
  perspectives, 75
interdisciplinarity, 13, 15, 16
interdisciplinary splicing, 16

Internet, 6, 7, 47–49, 51, 55, 58, 63–66, 97, 103,
    122, 141, 172, 204, 207, 208, 211, 223,
    224, 226, 227
  and information roles, 48
inter-organizational communication, 193
inter-organizational information systems, 191
interpersonal berrypicking, 102
interpersonal communication, 77, 80, 84, 108,
    118
interpersonal exchanges, 128
interpersonal skills, 101
interpersonal transaction, 77
interwoven situational awareness, 120
intranet, 114
intra-organizational communication, 193
IR applications, 113
IR interfaces, 118
IR paradox, 113
IR problems, 118

journals, 27, 126, 210, 211, 216, 221–223

kinship hierarchies in polygamous society, 35
Knowledge management (KM), 117
Kope tribe, 5, 34
  gossip, 35
  information roles, 37
    dissemination, 37
    induction, 37
    interpretation, 37
    organization, 37
    presentation, 37
    preservation, 37
  information uses, 35
  main function of tribal information, 35
    defining tribal identity, 35
    preserving social networks, 35
    promulgation of practical skills, 35
  news, 35
  Papua New Guinea, 34
  storytelling, 35
Kuhlthau's information search process (ISP)
    model, 8, 114, 139, 160, 161, 186,
    188–190

language of art, 21
Lascaux, 20, 22
Leahy brothers, 34
Leakey, R., 13, 17, 19, 20
Leonardo Da Vinci, 26
Lewis-Williams, D., 20

library and information science (LIS), 13, 14, 16,
    55, 57, 63–65, 95, 106, 137, 141, 171–173,
    175, 198, 203, 233, 235
  cognitive school or cognitive approach, 175
  literature, 63
  researchers, 55, 64, 65
library catalogs, 113
library of place, 95
linotype, 47
local clinical settings, 89
local inscriptions, extra-local use, 83, 86
local practices of inscription, 80

manga rapa, 34, 37
medical work, 77
  clinical record, 73
Memex machine, 172
Mesopotamia, 44
  temple libraries, 46
metaphor consolidation, 180
metaphor diagram, 184, 185, 188, 190, 192,
    196–198
metaphor instantiation, 8, 172, 174, 175, 180–184,
    190, 195, 196, 198, 199, 232, 233, 236
metaphor reasoning, 180
methodological framework, 62, 66
METIS, 119
Middle Ages, 27
midwife's client charts, 77, 80, 85
midwife's professional library, 79
midwife's pre-visit planning tool, 85
midwife-client visits, communication and
    information exchange, 75
midwife-pregnant women, prenatal visits,
    documents, 79
midwife-pregnant women, transaction, 77
midwifery, 74, 75, 85, 87, 244
  care, 6, 73, 78, 81, 86
  clinics, 6, 73, 77, 89
  high-risk, 75
  model of care, 75
  practice, 75–78
mind functions, 15
Minsky's frame theory, 176, 178, 179
mnemonic rituals and rhymes, 42
multiple websites, 217
multitasking information behavior, 142, 143, 150

Nambikwara tribe, Brazil, 44
Napoleon Bonaparte, 18, 27, 231

nature of place, 94
network-connected machine, 59, 65
new digitial information consumer, 9, 206
Nexis, 206
NHS Direct Online, 209, 212, 213, 217, 224
non-linear theory, 8, 155, 156
non-linearity, 8, 156, 161, 165, 166, 168
  concept, 155, 160
  development, 156
non-linearity aspects
  holism, 162
  information skill training, 162
  methodology, 162
  timing, 162
normal, meaning of, 88
notion of place, 94, 95

online activities, 59
online public access catalogs (OPAC), 118, 127,
    184, 204
online publishing, 47
Ontario Antenatal Record, 80–83
Ontario's Health Services Restructuring
    Commission, 88
OPAC users, 204
opening, 156–158, 163, 166
operative reports, 88, 89
  narrative structure, 73
optimal foraging models, 49, 50
oral societies, 46
orientation, 43, 73, 156, 158, 163, 166
  social, 41

patient/client, social construction, 73
peer influence, 113
personal letters, 27
personal source use, 113
Phaedrus, 44
Plutarch, 23
Post-industrial Information Age, 5, 18, 19
post-literate consciousness, 45
pregnant woman, 6, 63, 75–81, 84, 86, 90
  breastfeed, 79
  urine test, 81
pre-historic art, 20
  in Africa, 20
pre-historic cave art, 15
pre-literate consciousness, 45
pre-literate cultures, 41, 42, 50
pre-literate society, 5, 33, 35, 40, 43, 44

pre-literates, 41, 44, 45
  reactions to writing, 44
prenatal care, 75, 88
prenatal clinical visits, 74, 77, 90
prenatal midwifery visits, 75, 76, 85
preserving social networks, 35
printing press, 27
  invention, J. Gutenberg, 46
problem situation, ad hoc category, 198
promulgation of practical skills, 35
  agronomy, 35
  house-building, 35
  hunting, 35
psychoanalysis, 27
psychology, 13, 16, 17, 34, 140, 172, 174,
    233–237
  researchers, 15
published documents, 47

Queens Borough Public Library, 97, 99, 100
  programs, in-depth qualitative studies, 100

radiological records, accomplishment of
    accountability, 73
range of searching behavior, 209
recreational activities, 61
religion, 20, 36, 37, 44, 231
Renaissance Era, 5, 18, 19, 26, 27
repeat behavior, 208, 209, 214, 215
reports, creation, 87
retrieval behavior, 209, 225
Reuters, 206
rock art, 18–21
  chronology, 18
rock engravings, 19, 22
routine anatomic survey, 87, 88
  definition of, 88

Schrödinger, E., 16
science journal users, 216
searching behavior, 118, 209
  depth of, 209, 210
  range of, 209
sense-making, 93, 137–140, 150, 151, 234–236
  approach, 3, 14, 140, 232, 233
  theories, 37, 38
skill, 35–37, 41, 56, 59, 60, 63–67, 97, 99, 100,
    101, 121, 162, 165–167, 188
small worlds, 6, 39, 57, 95, 96, 106, 139, 171
social act of remembering, 41, 42

social attributes, 5, 56, 57
  age, 57
  education, 57
  ethnicity, 57
  gender, 57
  in studies of information behavior, 57
  income, 57
  race, 57
social norms, 96
social practice, 6, 73, 114, 233, 244
  approach, 126
  dimensions, 125
social settings, 6, 7, 74, 93, 96, 97
social support, 56, 60, 65
  networks, 63–65
social types, 96, 98, 102
socially organized practices, 74, 75
socio-technical infrastructure, 119, 128, 129
socio-technical interaction networks (STINs),
    126
sources and channels approach, 114, 117
speech, 45
Spink's conceptualization of multitasking
    information seeking, 28, 162
steam press, 47
Stonehenge, 43
supply chain, 191, 193
Surgery Door Website, 209, 211–213, 216,
    218–220, 224
symbolism, 21
Symphysis fundus height diagram, 83

temple libraries, Mesopotamia, 46
text-based information sources, 33, 48, 116
text-based societies, 35
textual documents, 49
Thamous, Egyptian God, 44
Thcydides, 24
Theophrastus, 24–26
Theuth, Egyptian God, 44, 45
threshold questions, 15
time, 4, 8, 13, 18–20, 23–25, 27–50, 63–65, 74,
    83, 103, 106, 108, 148, 150, 159–165,
    176–179, 221
timing, 162, 164
tribal information, 35
tribal knowlegde, repositories, 37
tribal politics, 36
tribal society, 37, 39
  Papua New Guinea, 40

trusting behavior, 209, 223
Tuc d'Audobert, 20

Upper Paleolithic cultures, 15
Upper Paleolithic Era, 3, 18–20, 22, 23,
     231
  art, 21
  cave paintings, 22
  chronology for the evolution of art, 18
Upper Paleolithic human behavior, 21
Upper Paleolithic images, 17
use and user studies, 93
use behaviors, 13, 14, 22, 25, 27, 28,
     140

valuable information, 50, 100, 140, 233
value-added information system, 191
volatility, 221, 222

Washington, B. T., 18, 28
Web
  digital environments, 9, 203, 207–209,
     224
  research, 57, 203
  search, 141
    engine, 148, 211
    studies, 63, 207

Web-use skill, 59, 66
  proxy measures, 66
  men's online abilities, 66
  women's online abilities, 66
Wells, H. G., 20
Whitakers Almanac, 205
Wilson's problem-solving model, 14, 114, 163
Wopkaimin hunter-horteculturalists of New
     Guinea, 22
work, 6, 21, 56–59, 65, 66, 77, 79, 82, 84, 95, 104,
     106, 113, 114, 116–123, 125–129,
     142–146, 149, 158, 162, 165, 207–209
  practice, 113, 116, 117, 120, 125–127, 129
workplace, 7, 9, 101–103, 130, 149, 161, 204
  studies, 123, 125
world view, 96
World Wide Web, 47, *see also* Web
writing
  and information science, 49
  arts, 15
  respect for, 46
  system, 22, 44
    Mesopotamia, 44

Xenophon, 23, 24

Yahoo, 213

Information Knowledge and Science Management

1. C. W. Choo, B. Detlor and D. Turnbull: *Web Work*. Information Seeking and Knowledge Work on the World Wide Web. 2000   ISBN 0-7923-6460-0
2. C. A. Bean and R. Green (eds.): *Relationships in the Organization of Knowledge*. 2001   ISBN 0-7923-6813-4
3. R. Green, C.A. Bean and S.H. Myaeng (eds.): *The Semantics of Relationships*. An Interdisciplinary Perspective. 2002   ISBN 1-4020-0568-7
4. M. Huysman and D. de Wit: *Knowledge Sharing in Practice*. 2002
                    ISBN 1-4020-0584-9
5. B. Detlor: *Towards Knowledge Portals*. From Human Issues to Intelligent Agents. 2004   ISBN 1-4020-2053-8
6. A. Spink and B.J. Jansen: *Web Search: Public Searching of the Web*. 2004
                    ISBN 1-4020-2268-9
7. R. Szostak: *Classifying Science*. Phenomena, Data, Theories, Method, Practice. 2004
                    ISBN 1-4020-3094-0
8. A. Spink and C. Cole (eds.): *New Directions in Human Information Behavior*. 2006
                    ISBN 1-4020-3667-1
9. H. F. Moed: *Citation Analysis in Research Evaluation*. Towards a Critical, Accurate and Policy Relevant Bibliometrics. 2005   ISBN 1-4020-3713-9